Japan Decides 2014

Japan Decides 2014
The Japanese General Election

Edited by

Robert J. Pekkanen
Professor, Henry M. Jackson School of International Studies, University of Washington, USA

Steven R. Reed
Professor of Modern Government, Faculty of Policy Studies, Chuo University, Japan

and

Ethan Scheiner
Professor, Department of Political Science, University of California, Davis, USA

First published 2016 by
PALGRAVE MACMILLAN

Palgrave Macmillan in the UK is an imprint of Macmillan Publishers Limited,
registered in England, company number 785998, of Houndmills, Basingstoke,
Hampshire RG21 6XS.

Palgrave Macmillan in the US is a division of St Martin's Press LLC,
175 Fifth Avenue, New York, NY 10010.

Palgrave Macmillan is the global academic imprint of the above companies
and has companies and representatives throughout the world.

Palgrave® and Macmillan® are registered trademarks in the United States,
the United Kingdom, Europe and other countries.

ISBN 978–1–137–55199–3

This book is printed on paper suitable for recycling and made from fully
managed and sustained forest sources. Logging, pulping and manufacturing
processes are expected to conform to the environmental regulations of the
country of origin.

A catalogue record for this book is available from the British Library.

A catalog record for this book is available from the Library of Congress.

For Jack, Will, Adam, Dylan, Daniel, and Billy
– Robert
For Kunkun for playing with Jiji-Baba
– Steve
For Dick (Gaga) and Nila (Lola) Hurley
– Ethan

Contents

Part I Introduction

Part II Political Parties

Part III Campaigning, Candidates, Districts

Part IV Governance and Policy

Part V Conclusion

Figures and Tables

Figures

Tables

Acknowledgments

In December, you might have heard the editors complaining about this snap election. However, at some point in the process, we became unambiguously happy. The obvious reason for this was that we realized the book was going to be good. In fact, at least one of the editors never tires of saying that "the book is better than the election." We are very happy with the result. For that, we have to thank, above all, the contributors. We learned a huge amount from them. The primary job of chapter authors is to write fantastic chapters. They delivered. On top of that, everyone was really engaged in the project of trying to understand the meaning of this election, and almost everyone gave comments on multiple chapters in this volume. This really warms an editor's heart. Axel Klein and Daniel M. Smith went above and beyond and gave comments on practically every chapter in the book. We thank all of our authors.

Robert thanks his family for support and inspiration. He also thanks his co-authors, Masahisa Endo, Steve, Ethan, and Dan. He loved working with Steve and Ethan to make this book a reality. There is undoubtedly a little election geek in all three of us, but working together made thinking about this election a real joy. "A *little*," you ask? Robert can hear you.

Steve thanks his family, his co-authors, and especially his co-editors. The process can get rather intense, often receiving over ten emails to answer in a day. A combination of good ideas and good humor made it a stimulating and enjoyable experience.

Ethan mocks Steve for thinking that there were merely ten emails to answer on many days. Fortunately, Robert usually took care of answering them. Ethan thanks Steve and Robert for not removing him as co-editor after saying things like the above (and far worse), and for being wonderful to work with. He also thanks co-authors Dan Smith and Mike Thies. And most of all, Ethan thanks his family, especially Casey, Serena, and Melanie, for making every day a joy.

As always, Steve and Ethan thank Robert for his initial inspiration to do the series and for his spectacular ability to organize all features of the project (which he does with extraordinarily good cheer). Robert, we are truly fortunate to work with you.

Contributors

Masahisa Endo is a lecturer at the Faculty of Humanities and Economics, Kochi University, Japan. His research interests span voting behavior, electoral mobilization, party politics, and survey methodology. His work has appeared in *Japan Decides 2012: Japanese General Election* (Palgrave Macmillan, 2013) and *Kōmeitō: Politics and Religion in Japan* (2014). He holds an MA in Government from Cornell University, USA.

Alisa Gaunder is Professor of Political Science at Southwestern University in Georgetown, Texas. Her research interests include comparative political leadership, campaign finance reform, and women and politics in Japan. She is the author of *Political Reform in Japan: Leadership Looming Large* (2007) and the editor of the *Handbook of Japanese Politics* (2011).

Ken Victor Leonard Hijino is an associate professor at the Graduate School of Law, Kyoto University, Japan. He has published articles on Japanese local politics, party organizations, and decentralization in journals, including *Party Politics*, *Journal of East Asian Studies*, and *Social Science Japan Journal*. He is currently researching urban–rural cleavages and intra-party conflicts in Japan and elsewhere.

Llewelyn Hughes works at the Crawford School of Public Policy at the Australian National University (ANU). His research focuses on the international and comparative political economy of energy markets and the political economy of climate change. He is the author of *Globalizing Oil: Firms and Oil Market Governance in France, Japan, and the United States*. He has also contributed to journals, including *International Security*, *Energy Policy and the Social Sciences*, *Annual Review of Political Science*, and *Journal of East Asian Studies*. He received his PhD from the Massachusetts Institute of Technology (MIT) and holds a master's degree from the Graduate School of Law and Politics, University of Tokyo, Japan.

Fumi Ikeda received her master's degree from Oxford University, UK, in 2013 and is currently a doctoral student at Chuo University, Japan. Her dissertation topic is "Constructing a New Party: The Democratic Party of Japan."

Koji Kagotani is a lecturer at the Faculty of Economics, Osaka University of Economics, Japan. He received his PhD in Political Science from the University of California, Los Angeles (UCLA) in 2010. Before joining Osaka University of Economics, he served as Assistant Professor in Political Science at the University of Dublin, Trinity College, Ireland. His research interests broadly cover the linkage between foreign economic policymaking and alliance politics, security issues in the East Asian region, and the Japanese public's reaction to foreign threats. His recent works have been published in *International Relations of the Asia-Pacific* and *Japanese Journal of Political Science*.

Saori N. Katada is an associate professor at the School of International Relations and the Director of the Political Science and International Relations (POIR) Program at the University of Southern California (USC). She is the author of *Banking on Stability: Japan and the Cross-Pacific Dynamics of International Financial Crisis Management* (2001), which was awarded Masayoshi Ohira Memorial Book Award in 2002. She has also published six edited and co-edited books and numerous articles on the subjects of trade, financial, and monetary cooperation in East Asia as well as Japanese foreign aid. For her research on regionalism, she was recently awarded the Japan Foundation Research Grant and National Endowment for the Humanities Fellowship. She received her PhD from the University of North Carolina at Chapel Hill (Political Science) in 1994 and BA from Hitotsubashi University, Tokyo. Before joining USC, she served as a researcher at the World Bank in Washington DC and as International Program officer at the United Nations Development Programme (UNDP) in Mexico City.

Jeff Kingston is Director of Asian Studies at Temple University Japan. He is the author of *Contemporary Japan* (2012), *Japan in Transformation 1950–2010* (2010), and *Japan's Quiet Transformation* (2004) and is the editor of *Critical Issues in Contemporary Japan* (2014), *Contemporary Japanese Politics* (2012), *Natural Disaster and Nuclear Crisis in Japan* (2012), and *Tsunami* (2011). His current research is on nationalism in Asia, with a monograph *Asian Nationalism: A History Since 1945* and an edited collection *Asian Nationalisms Reconsidered* in production.

Axel Klein is a political scientist and Professor of Modern East Asian Studies at the University of Duisburg-Essen, Germany. He earned his PhD and Habilitation from the University of Bonn, Germany. From 2007 to 2011 he worked as a senior research fellow at the German Institute for Japanese Studies in Tokyo, focusing on election campaigning and demographic change. His most recent publication is an edited volume on Kōmeitō, with Steven Reed, Levi McLaughlin, and George Ehrhardt (2014).

Ellis S. Krauss was a professor at the School of International Relations and Pacific Studies, University of California San Diego, USA, and is now Emeritus. He has published eight authored or edited books and over 70 articles on postwar Japanese politics and on US–Japan relations in professional political science and Asian Studies journals. He published a co-authored book with Robert J. Pekkanen (University of Washington) about the development of, and changes in, Japan's long-time ruling party, *The Rise and Fall of Japan's LDP: Political Party Organizations as Historical Institutions* (2010), and in 2004 he co-edited *Beyond Bilateralism: U.S.-Japan Relations in the New Asia-Pacific*. He has also been a visiting professor or researcher at several universities in Japan and in Europe. In April 2015, he was honored as Distinguished Visitor by the Program on US–Japan Relations, Harvard University, USA.

Patricia L. Maclachlan received her PhD in Comparative Politics from Columbia University in 1996 and was a research associate at Harvard University's Program on US–Japan Relations from 1995 to 1996. After working for one year as a tenure-track assistant professor at the University of Calgary's Department of Political Science, she joined the University of Texas in 1997, where she is now Associate Professor of Government and Asian Studies. She also served as director of the University of Texas's Center for East Asian Studies from 2007 to 2010. Her research focuses on the politics and political economy of Japan. Her publications include *Consumer Politics in Postwar Japan: The Institutional Boundaries of Citizen Activism* (2002), *The Ambivalent Consumer: Questioning Consumption in East Asia and the West* (2006), which she co-edited with Sheldon Garon, and *The People's Post Office: The History and Politics of the Japanese Postal System, 1871–2010* (2011). She is now researching the politics of agricultural reform in contemporary Japan in collaboration with Dr Kay Shimizu (Columbia University).

Yukio Maeda is an associate professor at the Interfaculty Initiative in Information Studies, University of Tokyo, Japan, where he is a faculty member at the Center for Survey Research and Data Archives (also known as Social Science Japan Data Archive). His main research is in the field of public opinion, electoral behavior, and political communication. He has co-edited *Tochi no Joken* (2015), the volume on the DPJ government, published in Japanese in 2015.

Kenneth Mori McElwain is an associate professor at the Institute of Social Science, University of Tokyo, Japan. His research focuses on the politics of institutional design, and his current work examines the evolution and survival of national constitutions. He received his PhD in Political Science from Stanford University, and his AB in Public Policy and International Affairs from Princeton University. His work has been published in a number of journals and edited volumes, including *Social Science Japan, American Journal of Political Science, Journal of East Asian Studies*, and the *Handbook of Political Science* series. He was the co-editor of *Political Change in Japan: Electoral Behavior, Party Realignment, and the Koizumi Reforms*.

Douglas M. Miller is a PhD student at the Henry M. Jackson School of International Studies, University of Washington, USA, and a professional Japanese–English translator. His primary research interest is in the nature of Japanese civil society organizations and how they react to environmental disasters. This includes how social movements arise and decline, as well as sociolinguistic analyses of policy wording in the crisis communications done by the government. He holds a bachelor's degree in Political Science from Temple University, USA, and a master's in International Studies, specializing in Japan Studies, from the University of Washington, USA.

Gregory Noble is Professor of Politics and Public Administration at the Institute of Social Science, University of Tokyo, Japan. His many publications include the books *Collective Action in East Asia: How Ruling Parties Shape Industrial Policy* and *The Asian Financial Crisis and the Structure of Global Finance* (co-edited with John Ravenhill) and articles "Fiscal Crisis and Party Strategies," "The Decline of Particularism in Japanese Politics," and "The Chinese Auto Industry as Challenge, Opportunity and Partner."

Robert J. Pekkanen is Professor at the Henry M. Jackson School of International Studies and Adjunct Professor of Political Science and Sociology at the University of Washington. His research interests lie in electoral systems, political parties, and civil society. He has published articles in political science journals such as *The American Political Science Review, The British Journal of Political Science,* and *Comparative Political Studies,* as well Asian studies journals, including *The Journal of Asian Studies* and *The Journal of Japanese Studies*. Including his work as co-editor on *Japan Decides 2012* and *2014*, he has published seven books on American non-profit advocacy, Japanese civil society, Japanese elections, and Japanese political parties. His first book *Japan's Dual Civil Society: Members without Advocates* (2006) won the Masayoshi Ohira Prize in 2008 and an award from the Japanese Nonprofit Research Association (JANPORA) in 2007. His research has been supported by the Mellon Foundation, Social Science Research Council, and the National Science Foundation, among others.

Steven R. Reed is Professor of Modern Government at Chuo University, Japan, where all of his classes are taught in Japanese. His major areas of research are parties, elections, electoral systems, and Japanese politics. He recently co-edited *Kōmeitō: Politics and Religion in Japan*, with George Ehrhardt, Axel Klein, and Levi McLaughlin.

Ethan Scheiner is Professor of Political Science at the University of California, Davis, USA. His major areas of research include Japanese politics, elections, electoral systems, and political parties. He is the author of *Democracy Without Competition in Japan: Opposition Failure in a One-Party Dominant State* (2006) and *Electoral Systems and Political Context: How the Effects of Rules Vary Across New and Established Democracies* (2012) and co-editor of *Japan Decides 2012*. His research has appeared in the *American Political Science Review, Annual Review of Political Science, British Journal of Political Science, Comparative Political Studies, Electoral Studies, Japanese Journal of Political Science, Journal of East Asian Studies, Journal of Japanese Studies*, and *Legislative Studies Quarterly*.

Kay Shimizu is an assistant professor in the Department of Political Science and the Weatherhead East Asian Institute at Columbia University, USA. Her research focuses on comparative politics, with a focus on the fiscal and financial politics of Japan and China. Her publications include *Political Change in Japan: Electoral Behavior, Party Realignment, and the Koizumi Reforms* (co-edited with Steven R. Reed and Kenneth Mori McElwain); *Syncretism: The Politics of Economic Restructuring and System Reform in Japan* (co-edited with Kenji E. Kushida and Jean C. Oi), as well as articles in *Socio-Economic Review, Journal of East Asian Studies, Current History*, and *Social Science Japan Journal*. She received her PhD from Stanford University, USA, and has been a fellow at Harvard University's Program on US–Japan Relations at the Weatherhead Center for International Affairs. She contributes regularly to the public discourse on international relations and the political economy of Asia and has been a fellow with the Mike and Maureen Mansfield Foundation, the National Committee on US–China Relations, and the US–Japan Foundation.

Daniel M. Smith is an assistant professor in the Department of Government at Harvard University, USA, where he is also an associate faculty member at the Reischauer Institute of Japanese Studies, the Weatherhead Center for International Affairs, and the Minda de Gunzburg Center for European Studies. His previous research has been published in *Electoral Studies, Party Politics*, and *Annual Review of Political Science* and in several edited volumes on contemporary Japanese politics, including *Japan Decides 2012: The Japanese General Election* (Palgrave Macmillan 2013).

Michael F. Thies is Associate Professor of Political Science, Chair of the Interdepartmental Programs for Global Studies and International & Area Studies, and former Director of the Terasaki Center for Japanese Studies, all at UCLA. He has published numerous articles on Japanese politics and political economy and coalition governments in journals such as *American Journal of Political Science, Legislative Studies Quarterly, Electoral Studies, British Journal of Political Science, Comparative Political Studies, Journal of Theoretical Politics*, and *Journal of Japanese Studies*. He and Frances Rosenbluth (Yale University) recently published *Japan Transformed: Political Change and Economic Restructuring* (2010), a book about the dramatic shifts in Japanese politics and policy leading up to and following the bursting of the asset bubbles in the early 1990s.

Scott Wilbur is a PhD candidate in the Political Science and International Relations Program at USC. He is currently researching the politics of small and medium enterprise policy in Japan as a Fulbright scholar.

Joshua A. Williams is a PhD candidate at the Henry M. Jackson School of International Studies, University of Washington, USA. His primary research interest and dissertation focus on the connection between Japanese politics and the Internet. This includes both how Japanese politicians use the Internet for political campaigning and how Japanese citizens engage with politics online. He holds a bachelor's degree in International Relations from Boston University and a master's in International Public Affairs from the University of Wisconsin-Madison, USA.

Abbreviations

JD 2012   *Japan Decides 2012: The Japanese General Election* (we use this for parenthetical citations made in this volume to *Japan Decides 2012; see Appendix for chapter list*)

Political Parties

Daichi	Shintou Daichi
DPJ	Democratic Party of Japan (Minshutou)
JCP	Japanese Communist Party (Kyousantou)
JIP	Japan Innovation Party (Ishin no Tou)
JRP	Japan Restoration Party (Nihon Ishin no Kai)
Komeito	any one of the following Koumeitou, New Koumeitou, NK, Clean Government Party, CGP
LDP	Liberal Democratic Party (Jimintou)
PFG	Party for Future Generations
PLFP	The People's Life First Party (Kokumin no Seikatsu ga Dai-ichi)
PNP	The People's New Party (Kokumin Shintou)
SDPJ	Social Democratic Party of Japan (Shamintou); also called Social Democratic Party (SDP)
TPJ	Tomorrow Party of Japan (Nippon Mirai no Tou, literally The Future of Japan Party)
	The Sunrise Party of Japan (Tachiagare Nippon)
	The Sunrise Party (Taiyou no Tou)
	The Tax Cut Party (Genzei Nippon)
Unity	Unity Party
YP	Your Party (Minna no Tou)

Other abbreviations

Asahi	Asahi Shinbun
HC	House of Councillors
HR	House of Representatives
JT	Japan Times

Mainichi	Mainichi Shinbun
MP	Member of the Diet, or Diet Member (also "DM")
Nikkei	Nihon Keizai Shinbun
Nougyou	Nihon Nougyou Shinbun
Sankei	Sankei Shinbun
TPP	Trans-Pacific Partnership
Yomiuri	Yomiuri Shinbun

Note that in-text references to newspapers take the form of (*Asahi*, December 16, 2014). References are to the Tokyo morning edition unless otherwise specified. References to the papers' websites take the form of (*Asahi*, December 16, 2014, web).

Part I
Introduction

1

Introduction: Take a Second Look at the 2014 Election, It's Worth It

Robert J. Pekkanen, Steven R. Reed, and Ethan Scheiner

At first glance, the December 14, 2014, Japanese General Election was as dull and meaningless as any in Japanese history. From the moment the election was called, there was no doubt that the ruling Liberal Democratic Party (LDP), along with its coalition partner Komeito, would easily win the poll. The campaign itself scarcely raised significant policy discussion or debate. Voter turnout reached an all-time low (52.7%) for Japanese House of Representatives (HR) elections. And the overall final results looked awfully similar to the 2012 General Election, in which the ruling coalition won roughly two-thirds of all seats.

However, viewing events through this lens misses just how significant the election really was and shabbily ignores the masterful political maneuvering of Prime Minister Shinzo Abe, the man behind Japan's political curtain. Abe's snap dissolution of the lower house caught nearly everyone by surprise, giving his LDP opponents no opportunity to challenge his leadership of the ruling party and denying opposition parties the time they needed to even try to defeat the LDP.[1] And following the LDP's trouncing of the opposition, Abe used the results of the election to claim a mandate to pass his entire policy agenda.

In this volume, the second in the *Japan Decides* series, a wide array of leading scholars of Japanese politics tell the story of the 2014 "bait-and-switch" election, as we call it in the Conclusion. This deeper analysis of the election pays dividends, as a second look shows that the 2014 poll arguably numbers among the most important Japanese elections in recent memory. At the time of the election, many observers complained about the lack of intrigue surrounding the race, but, as our volume indicates, in reality many of the truly significant events surrounding the 2014 election were unlikely to appear in standard discussions of electoral campaigns and results. Our contributors shed light on important, deeper features of the election, such as a badly weakened opposition that is gradually reconsolidating, political parties whose organizations and strategies are evolving within the Japanese party system, and an LDP that is finding ways to benefit from its unique advantages. Probably most important, this book shows a prime minister who brilliantly flatfooted his opponents inside and outside of the LDP by calling a snap election, found ways to avoid discussing potentially controversial issues throughout the campaign, massively consolidated his political position, and then used the election results as justification to begin implementing his policy preferences.

In short, *Japan Decides 2014* discusses the latest General Election from a number of different vantage points to allow readers to take both a wide lens view of the race and drill down deeply into the key details of areas that were especially significant.[2] To help create a volume that coheres – as well as more fully weigh plausible interpretations of the election – there was considerable interaction and discussion among the authors in the planning and writing process, which then carried over into the chapters themselves. At its core, then, *Japan Decides 2014* tells the story of how actions (and strategic inaction) by Abe queued up the LDP to succeed so dramatically in the race and make possible the enactment of significant policy in a number of different issue areas. At the same time, the volume also provides detail on other features of the race – as well as Japan's political system more generally – that will continue to affect Japanese politics irrespective of the success of Abe's political and policy agenda.

Summary of chapters

Just as was the case with *Japan Decides 2012*, the 2014 volume divides the contributions into four different parts.

Part I: Introduction

Part I provides the key background to the election. There was much less drama between 2012 and 2014 than there was between 2009 and 2012, but the events were significant for the future of Japanese politics. In Chapter 2, Robert J. Pekkanen, Steven R. Reed, and Daniel M. Smith provide an overview of events between the 2012 and 2014 elections, highlighting the continued confusion among the opposition parties and Prime Minister's Abe's proactive leadership. In Chapter 3, Ethan

Scheiner, Daniel M. Smith, and Michael F. Thies analyze the election outcome. The bottom line looks similar to 2014: a divided and uninspiring opposition hands the LDP another landslide victory amid another drop in turnout and without much change in the LDP vote. The reasons behind this result are, however, quite different. In 2012, an increase in voter abstention and a divided opposition, both born out of disaffection with the then-ruling DPJ, spoiled a series of opportunities for non-LDP candidates to win. In contrast, in 2014, there were far fewer coordination difficulties among the opposition parties, but the declining number of opposition candidates also promoted a further decline in voter turnout.

Part II: Political parties

Part II introduces the political parties that competed in the election. Again, the 2014 election cannot match the drama of the 2012 election, but the parties and party system have evolved in important ways and each party presented a significantly different profile from its previous incarnation. In Chapter 4, Masahisa Endo and Robert J. Pekkanen analyze changes in the LDP between the two elections, studying party organization and policy, but focusing on the areas that gave a leg up on its challengers when Abe called for the 2014 snap dissolution. In Chapter 5, Fumi Ikeda and Steven R. Reed analyze the DPJ's efforts to rebuild after its devastating defeat in 2012. They find that the party was active but focused first on mending fences internally and reforming itself. As a result, the general public was unaware of the party's efforts when Abe called the snap election. In Chapter 6, Robert J. Pekkanen and Steven R. Reed analyze the splits and reorganization of the "Third Force" parties. The splits were caused less by policy disagreements than conflict over strategy: whether to merge with other opposition parties to form an alternative to the LDP, or instead to remain independent; and, whether or not to cooperate with other parties, including the LDP, on a case-by-case basis. Those parties that opted for cooperation with the LDP virtually disappeared, leaving a single significant Third Force Party, the Japan Innovation Party (JIP). In Chapter 7, Axel Klein analyzes the LDP's long-time coalition partner, the Komeito, which faced many challenges dealing with Abe's policy agenda but managed to score a major victory in getting the LDP to agree to reduce the consumption tax on necessities. Electorally, Komeito is, like its coalition partner, winning seats without gaining votes because of declines in turnout.

Part III: Campaigns, candidates, and districts

Part III analyzes the campaign, focusing in turn on the popularity of the Abe administration, the role of leaders in the campaign, candidate selection, the largely unchanging position of women (or lack of women) in Japanese electoral politics, and the birth of Internet campaigning in Japan. In Chapter 8, Yukio Maeda analyzes Prime Minister Abe's popularity, which was lifted up by hope (*kitai*) for Abenomics, even though most voters did not feel any improvement in the economy. In Chapter 9, Kenneth Mori McElwain analyzes campaign visits by party leaders, finding that Abe targeted marginal districts, non-incumbents, and districts with more independent voters. McElwain finds that these visits did seem to increase the number of independents who voted for the LDP. In Chapter 10, Daniel M. Smith analyzes candidate selection. In 2014, the number of candidates, as well as turnover in office, dropped dramatically. He argues that the snap election disadvantaged the opposition parties – who had great difficulty in finding candidates, while the LDP had a healthy stock of incumbents – even as the reduced number of candidates led to both greater de facto opposition and coordination. And, as we argue in the Conclusion, the lack of candidates contributed to a "no choice" election at the district level. In Chapter 11, Alisa Gaunder analyzes the extent to which female candidates contested and won seats in 2014, finding that due to the unanticipated nature of the election and the rigidity of incumbency there was scarcely any change from prior elections. In Chapter 12, Joshua A. Williams and Douglas Miller analyze a new phenomenon: Internet campaigning in Japan. They find that, despite the snap election, both candidates and parties were prepared to use online approaches to campaigning. As in many places in this book, these chapters show that a second look at the election reveals a very different picture from the initial impression.

Part IV: Governance and Policy

Part IV turns to the role that policy issues played in the election and the policy implications of the outcome. Here each author finds a disjuncture between the former and the latter. These policy chapters are also essential to enhance our understanding of the concept we advance in the Conclusion about the nature of the election – a "no choice" election in policy. In Chapter 13, Gregory W. Noble analyzes Abenomics, the issue that drew the most attention from the media and was framed as "the" issue of the election. Noble finds surprisingly a few differences among the major parties on economic policy and, indeed, a little specificity whatsoever in their policy proposals. Interestingly, although Abenomics was the main issue in the election, the election result had a few consequences for economic policy. This finding stands in pointed contrast to the other policy chapters, each of which finds that policies played a small role in the election but the election had serious implications for policy.

In Chapter 14, Patricia L. Maclachlan and Kay Shimizu examine agricultural reform, which has been blocked at every turn by the Japan Agricultural Cooperatives (JA). JA has traditionally been an important supporter of the LDP, but its electoral influence has been waning. Abe put the issue of JA reform on the back-burner during the election and the issue played little role in any party's election campaign. However, once the ballots were counted, Abe announced his plans to push ahead with reform. This "bait and switch" mandate claiming is a pattern in the election that we discuss in detail in the Conclusion. In Chapter 15, Ken Hijino analyzes the issue of regional revitalization policy and rural development, highlighting how the crisis of agriculture is more generally a crisis of rural areas. Because of policy convergence between the LDP and DPJ, the issue of regional development never developed was never really discussed by the major political actors in the election. In Chapter 16, Llewelyn Hughes considers energy and nuclear power policy, noting the absence of the issue in the election. Hughes points out that the Abe administration has committed to the unpopular policy of restarting Japan's nuclear power plants but shifted the responsibility for deciding when and whether to restart the newly established Nuclear Regulation Authority. In Chapter 17, Jeff Kingston analyzes nationalism in the election, surely one of the most interesting issues to those outside of Japan. Kingston poses what he cleverly dubs "the Abe Conundrum" – how Abe advances policies that are not popular, but stays in power. In the case of nationalism, he finds that Abe succeeds by not making it an issue. In Chapter 18, Ellis Krauss analyzes foreign policy and finds it similarly "missing in action" as an election issue despite the significant changes Abe has made and plans to make. In Chapter 19, Koji Kagotani analyzes the 2014 elections in Okinawa. Okinawa politics is dominated by the issue of US bases, therefore seldom follows national trends, and, in 2014, base opponents won every single-member district in the prefecture. In Chapter 20, Saori Katada and Scott Wilbur analyze the Trans-Pacific Partnernship (TPP) free trade agreement. The Japanese public has generally favored Japanese participation, but several of the LDP's basic support groups were adamantly opposed. Similar to the other issues discussed in this part of the volume, the Abe administration kept the topic of TPP out of the campaign, thus avoiding controversy that might have harmed the party's success in the race. The outlines of several patterns in these policy areas are probably already clear to readers. We think that this shows again the value of a "second look" at the election. And, we analyze some of these patterns in the Conclusion.

Conclusion

In Chapter 21, we conclude by discussing the ways in which this election – so seemingly free of television drama – stealthily might be the most significant in the past two decades in Japan. An election that appeared to have been about nothing could ultimately have profound policy consequences.

Notes

1. In case you are wondering, yes, your Editors were scrambling in November, too.
2. Our *Japan Decides 2012* authors wrote great chapters, but only a few reappear in this volume. As a matter of editorial policy, we decided to involve new authors in each volume of the series. In this volume, we were fortunate to have ten new authors pen chapters, and we feel this helps advance our goal for the series of developing new scholarship on Japanese elections.

2

Japanese Politics Between the 2012 and 2014 Elections

Robert J. Pekkanen, Steven R. Reed, and Daniel M. Smith

Japanese electoral politics and leadership in the past decade have been anything but stable. Both the 2009 and 2012 House of Representatives (HR) elections resulted in landslide defeats for the party in power. Between the 2005 and 2009 elections, Japan was led by four separate Liberal Democratic Party (LDP) prime ministers in as many years, including Shinzou Abe in his first short-lived administration (2006–2007). Between the 2009 and 2012 elections, there were three years with three more prime ministers, this time hailing from the Democratic Party of Japan (DPJ).

The 2014 election stands in contrast. For one thing, it did not result in a change in power – anything but, as the outcome of the 2014 election was quite similar to 2012, with the LDP–Komeito coalition winning a nearly identical supermajority over a weak and divided opposition (see Scheiner, Smith, and Thies, this volume). But perhaps more to the point, there were only two years and one administration between the 2012 and 2014 elections – with Abe again at the helm. The fundamental reasons for this difference in inter-electoral stability are that the second Abe administration did not disintegrate under pressure from either the opposition parties or within the LDP – quite the opposite. Abe proactively dissolved the Diet and called an election before any process of disintegration or credible challenge from the opposition could be mounted.

Even if the 2012 and 2014 election results seem as similar as any two Japanese elections have been, a lot happened in between the two elections. Throughout this period, the dominant politician was Prime Minister Abe (see Maeda, this volume) and the most prominent policy issue was his signature economic agenda "Abenomics" (see Noble, this volume). Yet in the almost exactly two years between the elections, Abe accomplished a number of his other political and policy goals, in both the domestic and foreign policy arenas. Specifically, he began to implement his economic agenda, led the LDP to a comfortable victory in the 2013 House of Councillors (HC) election, and orchestrated the unilateral cabinet decision to adopt new Collective Self-Defense (CSD) Guidelines to expand the role and capability of Japan's Self-Defense Forces (SDF). Outside of his control, but certainly in his favor, the venerable progressive bastion *Asahi Shinbun* came under withering fire for scandals revolving around the misreporting of facts related to historical issues, and the "Third Force" parties that might otherwise have posed a threat to his administration collapsed and merged in kaleidoscopic patterns (see Pekkanen and Reed, this volume). All of these actions and developments helped to set the stage for a successful, albeit uninspiring, reprise of the LDP's 2012 election victory in 2014.

The 2013 House of election

The LDP emerged from the December 2012 election in a great position – together with Komeito, the ruling coalition commanded a two-thirds majority capable of overriding any legislative disagreement from the HC. However, Abe was keenly aware of the governance problems that might arise should the LDP-led coalition lose control of the HC: in both the 2007 (during Abe's first administration) and 2010 HC elections (during the administration of the DPJ's Naoto Kan), the ruling coalition had lost its unified control of the Diet, resulting in the legislative obstreperousness and gridlock known as a "Twisted Diet." For this reason, the most important political issue of the first half of 2013 was the HC election. On the one hand, if the LDP lost control of the HC, its ability to govern could be seriously impaired (see Thies and Yanai, *JD*). On the other hand, if the LDP kept control of the HC, it would have clear sailing for three more years (at the time, no one expected Abe's snap election gambit).

Two issues loomed large in the run up to the July 21, 2013, HC election: Abenomics and energy. Elsewhere in this volume, Greg Noble provides the full context on Abenomics, which include the so-called three arrows of monetary easing, fiscal stimulus, and structural reform. After two "lost decades" of economic stagnation in Japan, Abe's economic policies were understandably the centerpiece of his administration and initially enjoyed popular support. The surge in the Nikkei Stock Index after the introduction of monetary easing early in Abe's term was pointed out as a sign that the policies were working. However, in June

2013, only a month before the HC election, stock prices dropped drastically and induced some doubts about the potential of Abenomics. The LDP responded by quickly citing figures on the successes of Abenomics (NHK, 2013).

Almost alone in the HC election, the LDP stood for restarting the nuclear power plants that remained idle since the 2011 triple disaster (see Hughes, this volume). Big data showed that this was becoming a problem, and Abe responded by changing the spin of his responses to questions about restarting the reactors to "safety first" and letting the experts decide when the plants were safe (NHK, 2013). After news reports of continued radioactive wastewater leaking around the Fukushima #1 plants, the DPJ and other opposition parties saw a weakness and started to exploit it. Abe's response was to visit Fukushima #1, promote the ice wall solution (which the DPJ had proposed two years earlier), and ask (with no authority) for TEPCO to deactivate the #5 and #6 reactors. The latter action constitutes leadership of a level previously reached only by Prime Minister Kan, when he ordered the shutdown of the dangerously situated Hamaoka nuclear plant in Shizuoka Prefecture using similar jawboning tactics (Kushida, 2013).

Despite the anxiety that the LDP might have felt, not to mention the worries of the general public about a return to the "Twisted Diet" years, the HC election produced a solid victory for the LDP–Komeito coalition (Table 2.1). Half of the HC's 242 seats are contested every three years, HC parliamentarians enjoy a six-year fixed term. Of the 121 seats up for election, 48 are allocated through national open-list proportional representation (D'Hondt) and 73 are allocated in districts that are coterminous with Japan's 47 prefectures. These districts vary in magnitude: 31 are single-seat districts, ten are two-seat districts, three are three-seat districts, two are four-seat districts, and there is a single five-seat district.

After the 2013 HC election, the LDP held 115 seats (48%), giving it a comfortable majority with its coalition partner Komeito's 20 seats (8%). The DPJ controlled just 59 seats (24%), while the Third Force – at this point Japan Restoration Party (JRP), Your Party (YP), and People's Life Party – held 29 (12%). The JCP had a good showing at 11 seats (5%). These figures represent a sizable gain for the LDP, largely at the expense of the DPJ. Going into the election, the LDP had 84 seats, so it raised its share of the chamber from 35% to 48%. In contrast, the DPJ fell from 36% (86 seats) to 24%. The number of seats the LDP picked up (29) is nearly the same as the number of seats the DPJ lost (27). Komeito picked up one seat, but other winners were the JCP (+5), YP (+5), and JRP (+6), while the other losers were smaller parties and independents.

Table 2.1 The 2013 House of Councillors election results

		Government			Opposition					Total
		LDP	Kom	DPJ	JRP	YP	PLP	JCP	Others	
Prefectural	Votes	22,681,192	2,724,447	8,646,372	3,846,649	4,159,961	6,18,355	5,645,937	4,749,564	53,072,477
	%	42.7%	5.1%	16.3%	7.2%	7.8%	1.2%	10.6%	8.9%	100%
		47	4	10	2	4	0	3	3	73
National	Votes	18,460,335	7,568,082	7,134,215	6,355,300	4,755,161	9,43,837	5,154,055	2,858,630	53,229,615
	%	34.7%	14.2%	13.4%	11.9%	8.9%	1.8%	9.7%	5.4%	100%
		18	7	7	6	4	0	5	1	48
Seats not up for election		50	9	42	1	10	2	3	4	121
	seats	115	20	59	9	18	2	11	8	242
	%	47.5%	8.3%	24.4%	3.7%	7.4%	0.8%	4.5%	4.1%	100%

Notes: Party abbreviations: LDP = Liberal Democratic Party; Kom = Komeito; DPJ = Democratic Party of Japan; JRP = Japan Restoration Party; YP = Your Party; PLP = People's Life Party; JCP = Japan Communist Party. Others include Social Democratic Party, Green Wind, New Party Daichi, Happiness Realization Party, and other minor parties and independents.
Source: Ministry of Internal Affairs and Communications.

The LDP 2013 HC victory can largely be attributed to the same forces that won the 2012 HR election: DPJ's unpopularity, opposition fragmentation, and low voter turnout (52.61%) (see Reed et al., *JD*). There were 31 single-seat districts (up from 29 in 2010, because Fukushima and Gifu both had their delegations reduced from 2 to 1) and the LDP won almost all of these single-seat districts. The LDP and DPJ had split the two-seat districts for a decade – perhaps the most secure seats in Japan for both Diet members – but the DPJ crumbled in 2013. The LDP won one seat in each of the ten districts, but the DPJ secured seats in only seven districts (losing one each to YP, JCP, and JRP). Of the 22 seats in the six remaining districts, the LDP won 8, Komeito 4, the DPJ 3, YP 3, JCP 2, JRP 1, and one seat was won by an independent.

The success of the JCP – winning three district seats (Tokyo, Osaka, Kyoto) and five (of 42) seats prefigured its modest success in 2014 (see Scheiner, Smith, and Thies, this volume). The party more than doubled its support from independents (*mutouhasou*) from 6% in 2010 to 13% in 2013 (July 22, 2013), and the JCP candidate in Kyoto garnered an impressive 25% (July 23, 2013, Kyoto edition).

Domestic and foreign policy developments in late 2013

Abenomics and economic policy would continue to preoccupy the public and policymakers for the remainder of 2013 after the election. There were several other noteworthy developments, however, with a particularly busy November 2013. On November 12, 2013, former Prime Minister Koizumi called for Japan to abandon nuclear power in a speech at the Japan National Press Club (see Hughes, this volume). Later in 2014, Koizumi joined forces with another former prime minister, Morihiro Hosokawa, to promote renewable energy and oppose nuclear power. In March, the pair took out a full-page advertisement in the major newspapers stating their case (see, e.g., June 25, 2014). Yet even the combination of two of Japan's most popular prime ministers was unable to make nuclear power an issue in the election. At the intersection of Abenomics and international relations, Japan decided to join the Trans-Pacific Partnership (TPP) negotiations (see Katada and Wilbur, this volume).

More solidly in the international relations arena (see Krauss, this volume) we find China's November 23 declaration of an Air Defense Identification Zone (ADIZ) that included the disputed Senkaku island chain (known as Diaoyu in China and Diaoyutai in Taiwan) in the East China Sea. All aircraft entering this ADIZ were required to identify themselves to Chinese air control, else China would send military jets to intercept and identify them. Japan, which has maintained an ADIZ that also covers the disputed island chain for several decades, immediately denounced China's ADIZ as a "profoundly dangerous" provocation and declared it would not abide by China's demands. The US followed suit in announcing it would also not submit to this requirement. A day later, the US announced that it had sent two (unarmed) B-52s through the ADIZ without notifying China.

A few days later, some daylight appeared between the US and Japan when the US Federal Aviation Administration advised US airline flights to identify themselves before entering the ADIZ. Observers in Japan worried this would contribute to China's assertion of sovereignty over the islands, but the US stated that these announcements were suggested to avoid the possibility of an unplanned incident that could spiral out of control. Japan continued to instruct its airlines to fly through the zone without any announcement to China. US Vice President Joseph Biden hurriedly visited both Japan and China in early December 2013 to try to diffuse tension and reassure Japanese leaders of the US commitment to Japan's security. On December 9, South Korea declared an expanded ADIZ of their own, overlapping with that of China and Japan, and encompassing a submerged rock called *Ieodo* that is also claimed by China (in China, it is known as Suyan Rock).

Only three days after China declared its ADIZ, a bill on state secrets passed the HR on November 26, 2013, with support from the LDP, Komeito, and YP, and passed the HC on December 6, 2013. The law designates 55 categories of state secrets and specifies penalties of up to ten years imprisonment for civil servants who leak and up to five years imprisonment (initially, and up to 30 with extensions) for journalists who instigate leaks. The absence of an independent watchdog led to fears that the law could have a chilling effect on government transparency (see Kingston, this volume). Members of the JRP walked out of the Diet before the bill passed in November. The mass media also took an oppositional stance, arguing that the public's right to know and information disclosure would be impaired by a law lacking clear procedures about what would be designated as secret.

The year 2014 dawns rosily for Abe

Despite such criticisms, Abe rang in the new year of 2014 in excellent shape politically.[1] He faced a few intra-party challenges to lead the LDP (see Endo and Pekkanen, this volume). The LDP dominated the HR and had just won the HC election, meaning that Abe could expect to govern all of 2014 and 2015 without having to face another national election. The ruling coalition parties had been able to agree on an energy policy (see Hughes, this volume), and were in general consensus over economic policies, meaning that Abe had political capital to spend.

Abe devoted some of this precious commodity to security issues, often seen as close to his heart, guided by an overall strategy of "proactive pacifism" (Pekkanen and Pekkanen, 2015). On April 1, 2014, Japan relaxed a long-standing ban on arms exports, and on July 1, 2014, the cabinet reinterpreted the right to exercise CSD under Article 9 of the Constitution. The right to CSD had previously been banned under the interpretation of the Cabinet Legislation Bureau (CLB), but the intransigent former head of the CLB had been shuffled to the Japanese Supreme Court and replaced with a more pliant Abe appointee who approved of the reinterpretation.

Abe's appointment of Katsuto Momii as NHK Chairman in 2014 also stirred controversy. Momii is a conservative who once apologized in the Diet after making remarks in defense of the "comfort women" system during World War II and was heavily criticized by the DPJ for seeming to allow his pro-government views to shape the nature of the nominally independent NHK (*Japan Times*, February 19, 2015). At the same time, the left-leaning newspaper *Asahi Shimbun* was also under fire. On August 5, Asahi retracted 16 articles published in the 1980s and 1990s that relied on interviews with Seiji Yoshida, a former soldier who admitted to falsifying parts of his memoirs dealing with military coercion of hundreds of Korean women into the "comfort women" system. Asahi mishandled the retractions and the investigation, including censuring its own columnist, Akira Ikegami, who had criticized the slow pace of the paper's investigation (Yoshida's account had been questioned by a respected historian two decades earlier).

Internationally, Abe maintained a more active travel schedule than any previous prime minister – visiting 49 countries by September 2014 (*The Diplomat*, September 11, 2014). In early November, he finally added China to the list when he attended the Asia-Pacific Economic Cooperation (APEC) summit in Beijing. There, he also met with Chinese President Xi Jinping to discuss strategies for safely managing future conflicts. This was the first time the two leaders had formally talked since 2012, and the meeting helped to diffuse some of the tension surrounding the territorial disputes. Abe has yet to visit South Korea since becoming prime minister again in 2012.

Motive and opportunity: Economic woes and opposition weakness

Two other developments set the stage for Abe's decision to call a snap election for December 14, 2014. First was the hike in the consumption tax from 5% to 8% that took effect on April 1, 2014. This was the first of two planned increases in the consumption tax; the second increase, to 10%, was scheduled to take effect in October 2015. Raising the consumption tax was intended to shore up Japan's finances in the face of an aging society with greater healthcare and pension costs but fewer Japanese in the workforce. The LDP had supported this policy, but it was the DPJ Prime Minister Yoshihiko Noda who staked his political life on pushing the policy through in 2012. The policy passed with LDP support – traded in exchange for agreement to hold an early election that turned out to return the LDP to power in December 2012 (the 2009 legislature's full term would have run through August 2013).

The tax hike took effect on April 1, predictably spurring the economy in March. It was also expected that the economy would suffer in April, but the effect was unexpectedly large – a massive contraction in the second quarter that also pushed Japan back into recession. Pocketbook issues were thus big in voters' minds during the 2014 campaign, especially with Abenomics being touted as the centerpiece of the new administration. July 2014 saw the first poll showing greater disapproval (47%) than approval (39%) of Abenomics (*Sankei*, see also Maeda, this volume). The dual downturns in economy and support were the darkest clouds on Abe's horizon. Ominous as well was the remaining tax increase – from 8% to 10% – due to take effect in 2015. These elements would factor into Abe's decision to call the snap election – perhaps we can think of this as "motive." It made sense for Abe to call for new elections before economic bad news could weaken his reputation, both among voters and within the LDP.

The second development might be called "opportunity." The two key elements are continuing DPJ weakness and opposition fragmentation. Elsewhere in this volume, Ikeda and Reed detail the causes of DPJ weakness, and Pekkanen and Reed explore the twists and turns of the Third Force. For our purposes here, we want only to make two points. First, DPJ support remained anemic under new party leader Banri Kaieda (never cresting 10% in 2014). Second, the latter half of 2014 saw gyrations among the Third Force parties that kept the opposition fragmented. The JRP split at the beginning of August over a proposed merger with the Unity Party, which itself had split from YP in spring 2014 after scandals embroiled YP founder Yoshimi Watanabe. On September 21, the rump JRP combined with the splinter Unity Party to form the Japan Innovation Party (JIP). The JIP was led by Tooru Hashimoto (of JRP) and Kenji Eda (of Unity Party, and before that YP, and before that DPJ, and before that LDP). The remaining splinter of JRP members formed the "neo-conservative" Party for Future Generations (PFG), led, ironically, by Shintarou Ishihara (then 81 years old) and Takeo Hiranuma (then 74 years old). Although it would be drubbed in the 2014 election, PFG did briefly boast the fifth largest party delegation in the Diet, with 19 members.

Redistricting to deal with malapportionment

An additional development between the 2012 and 2014 elections was the major redistricting of HR election districts. The 2014 election was the first time Japan elected 475 members to the HR. From 2000 to 2012, the number had been 480; it was 500 in 1996. Before the 2014 election, the number of single-seat districts (SMDs), and therefore the number of Diet members, was reduced from 300 to 295. This was done to address the persistent problem of malapportionment – the disparity in population across districts. After the 2009 election, the Supreme Court had declared that the disparity in district populations in the existing apportionment (in effect since 2003) was in an "unconstitutional state," since the most populated district (Chiba 4th District) had more than two times the number of voters as the least populated district (Kochi 3rd District) (see Christensen, *JD 2012*). In the confusion leading up to the 2012 election, the Noda administration and the LDP agreed to pass a minimal redistricting bill, but the new districts did not go into effect until 2013. The Supreme Court did not overturn the 2012 results.

With the new redistricting, five in the most rural prefectures were eliminated – one each in Fukui, Kochi, Saga, Tokushima, and Yamanashi prefectures. In each case, the prefecture went from three to two (Figures 2.1–2.5). Twelve other prefectures – Aomori, Iwate, Miyagi, Ibaraki, Chiba, Tokyo, Kanagawa, Wakayama, Tottori, Ehime, Nagasaki, and Kumamoto – experienced minor redistricting changes. After redistricting, the most underrepresented (Tokyo 16th District) had only 1.998 times more residents than the most overrepresented (Tottori 2nd District).

For the five prefectures that lost, some districts changed names but remained largely the same geographically. For example, the new Fukui

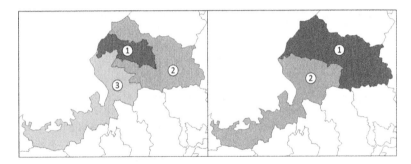

Figure 2.1   Redistricting in Fukui

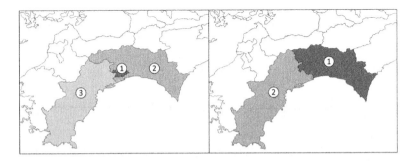

Figure 2.2   Redistricting in Kochi

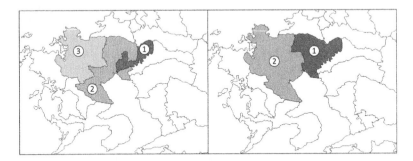

Figure 2.3   Redistricting in Saga

2nd District is mostly made up of the old Fukui 3rd District. The new Fukui 1st District combines much of the old 1st and 2nd Districts. Similarly, the new Yamanashi 1st District includes all of the old 3rd District and the western part of the old 2nd District. The new

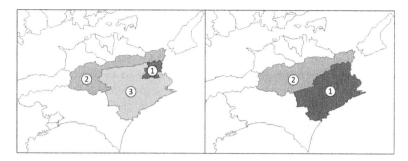

Figure 2.4   Redistricting in Tokushima

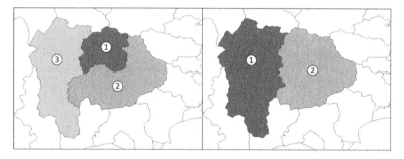

Figure 2.5   Redistricting in Yamanashi
Source: Created by the authors using ArcGIS shape files from DataforJapan.org.

Yamanashi 2nd District includes parts of the old 1st and 2nd Districts. In Tokushima Prefecture, the southern part of the 3rd District was incorporated into the 1st District, while the northern part was split between the 1st District and 2nd District. In Kochi Prefecture, most of the old 3rd District became the new 2nd District, with the new 1st District encompassing much of the old 1st and 2nd Districts. Lastly, the old Saga 3rd District was absorbed into the new Saga 2nd District, with part of its eastern territory incorporated into the new Saga 1st District.

The reduction in meant that parties, especially the LDP, had more incumbent candidates than there were districts in the prefecture. The LDP solved the problem mostly by giving senior incumbents from elimi-nated districts a safe position on the party list. For the opposition parties, which had trouble even fielding candidates in all 295, the redistricting was less of a problem (see Smith, this volume).

Abe's decision 2014: Calling the snap election

December 2014 did not seem a propitious time to call an election. The economy had dipped into recession after the introduction of the consumption tax increase. The Abe administration had also just suffered its first serious political setback when two prominent female members of the cabinet were forced to resign over violations of elections laws. That they were both female was important because one of the Abe administration's themes was "womenomics" and both were prominent symbols of that commitment (see Gaunder, this volume). Parties and candidates, not to mention voters, do not like snap elections or year-end elections. On the one hand, with two years left in his term, there seemed to be no obvious reason why Abe should call an election at this time.

On the other hand, it was an election in which the LDP–Komeito coalition could not possibly lose control of government. They had won such an overwhelming majority in 2012 that they would have had to lose 88 seats to lose their majority, and a bare majority was Abe's definition of "victory." Though the risk to the coalition may have been minimal, the risk to Abe was significant. He was putting his leadership and his policy agenda on the line. Calling a snap election was a bold and surprising move, yet another example of Abe's proactive style. First, he dissolved the Diet before the opposition parties were ready to fight an election (Ikeda and Reed, Pekkanen and Reed, both this volume). Second and equally important was the fact that opposition to Abe's policies and leadership style was building inside the LDP (Endo and Pekkanen, Maclachlan and Shimizu, both this volume). If Abenomics seemed to be failing, Abe could potentially face internal challenges to his leadership. Abe needed a renewed mandate to keep his party behind him and push through his agenda. The dissolution of the Diet was thus another example of Abe's proactive governance.

On November 18, Abe announced he would dissolve the Diet on November 21 and call a snap election for December 14. He had said only a few days before that he would decide over the weekend whether or not he would call a snap election. This was the first serious notice of a possible election, and it sent the media, not to mention opposition parties, scrambling. Although rumors frequently circulate in Tokyo about possible dissolutions, a few had seen a snap election as a realistic possibility. Abe had caught the opposition flatfooted.

In his dissolution speech, Abe said he asked for an election to give a mandate for his decision to postpone until April 2017 the hike (from 8% to 10%) in the consumption tax scheduled for October 2015. Abe framed this postponement in terms of a continuation of his Abenomics policy of stimulus, and thus he said the election was also a referendum on Abenomics. Through this framing the LDP reasonably expected to win – and whether or not people were actually voting on Abenomics (see Scheiner, Smith, and Thies Noble both this volume; Horiuchi, Smith, Yamamoto, and Fukushima, 2014) – Abe positioned himself to claim that the election results gave him a mandate for his policies (see "Conclusion" in this volume). The extended mandate also insulated Abe against the political risks of a deterioration of the economy in 2015. The election also largely inoculated Abe against the adverse political effects of the delay in the tax hike. Of course, any election poses risks to the party in power, but the results of Abe's roll of the dice made Japan's proactive prime minister seem smart as well as lucky.

Note

1. For an analysis focusing on the year 2014, see Pekkanen and Pekkanen (2015).

References

Christensen, Ray (2013). Malapportionment and the 2012 House of Representatives election. In Robert Pekkanen, Steven R. Reed and Ethan Scheiner (eds) *Japan Decides 2012: The Japanese General Election.* pp. 139–147. London: Palgrave Macmillan.

Kushida, Kenji (2013). The DPJ's political response to the Fukushima nuclear disaster. In Kenji E. Kushida and Phillip Y. Lipscy (eds) *Japan Under the DPJ: The Politics of Transition and Governance.* pp. 405–444. Stanford, CA: The Walter H. Shorenstein Asia-Pacific Research Center at Stanford University.

Horiuchi, Yusaku, Daniel M. Smith, Teppei Yamamoto, and Mayumi Fukushima (2014). Shuuin senkyo, kinkyuu kaiseki! De-ta ga akashita yuukensha no honne: yuukensha no shin no kanshin ha 'Abenomikusu' de ha nakatta. [Urgent analysis of the House of Representatives election! Data reveal the true preferences of voters: the real concern was not "Abenomics"]. *Nikkei Business Online*, December 18, 2014. URL: http://business.nikkeibp.co.jp/article/topics /20141218/275309.

NHK. (2013). Kenshou Netto Senkyo [Examining the Internet Election] broadcast on July 23.

Pekkanen, Robert J. and Saadia M. Pekkanen (2015). Japan in 2014: All about Abe. *Asian Survey* 55(1): 103–118.

Reed, Steven R., Ethan Scheiner, Daniel M. Smith, and Michael F. Thies (2013). The 2012 election results: The LDP wins big by default. In Robert Pekkanen, Steven R. Reed and Ethan Scheiner (eds) *Japan Decides 2012: The Japanese General Election.* pp. 34–46. London: Palgrave Macmillan.

Thies, Michael F. and Yuki Yanai (2013). Governance with a twist: How bicameralism affects Japanese lawmaking. In Robert Pekkanen, Steven R. Reed and Ethan Scheiner (eds) *Japan Decides 2012: The Japanese General Election.* pp. 225–244. London: Palgrave.

3

The 2014 Japanese Election Results: The Opposition Cooperates but Fails to Inspire

Ethan Scheiner, Daniel M. Smith, and Michael F. Thies

On December 14, 2014, Japanese voters turned out in record-low numbers (52.7% of eligible voters) to elect a new House of Representatives (HR). The result was an overwhelming victory by the ruling Liberal Democratic Party (LDP) and its coalition partner Komeito.

Prime Minister Shinzou Abe's decision to call a snap election in November caught nearly everyone by surprise, as his LDP–Komeito coalition government enjoyed a dominating two-thirds majority since the 2012 election and still had two years left before the constitutional end of the term. Publicly, the snap election was touted as a referendum on the administration's decision to delay a planned increase in the consumption tax and, more generally, the government's economic revitalization package known as "Abenomics" (see Noble, this volume). Famously described as a "three-arrow" package of monetary easing, fiscal stimulus, and structural reform, Abenomics had unleashed its first two arrows to mixed success and growing skepticism in the public and in the markets. Perhaps more important, the third arrow remained unlaunched, stayed by the resistance of party conservatives who quivered at the prospect of defying the powerful interest groups that had long sustained them in office. A fresh mandate would give Abe some room to maneuver around the opponents of difficult structural reforms.

But there was more to Abe's decision than the pursuit of policy goals. The LDP's popularity had been in slow-but-steady decline over the preceding months. Meanwhile, the opposition parties, whose utter failure to coordinate in single-member district (SMD) contests in 2012 contributed to the coalition's previous landslide victory (see Reed et al., *JD 2012*), were beginning to show signs of getting their act together, both as a parliamentary opposition and as a future electoral threat (Ikeda and Reed, this volume; Pekkanen and Reed, this volume). So Abe decided to act before the LDP's popularity decline could lead to any internal challenge to his leadership and before the opposition could complete its recovery in preparation for the next battle.

Abe's gamble paid off handsomely for the LDP. In the 2014 election, the ruling coalition reprised its 2012 victory, even gaining an additional seat; it won 326 total seats (291 for the LDP and 35 for Komeito) and easily renewed its two-thirds majority mandate for another four years. Any hint of a leadership challenge within the LDP was snuffed out, and Abe proclaimed a public endorsement for Abenomics and all three of its arrows (despite survey evidence that voters actually cared little for Abe's policies; see Noble, this volume, and Horiuchi et al., 2014). The Democratic Party of Japan (DPJ), whose collapse from 308 seats to only 57 was the story of the 2012 election, bounced back a little, winning 73 seats this time, and the Japan Communist Party (JCP) improved from 8 seats to 21. Meanwhile, the so-called Third Force parties – the Japan Innovation Party (JIP), Party of Future Generations (PFG), and People's Life Party (PLP) – tumbled from 81 seats to 45.

But the election was not simply a redo of the 2012 landslide victory. This time around, the main opposition parties did a much better job coordinating candidate entry in SMDs to avoid fragmenting the opposition vote. Ironically, however, this decreased candidate entry may have also contributed to lower voter turnout at the SMD level – thus further dampening the opposition's ability to challenge the ruling coalition by attracting the support of casual voters. In many districts, the main opposition parties sat out altogether, abandoning competition to the ruling coalition and the JCP. As a result, even more voters stayed home in 2014 than in 2012.

Japan's electoral system

The electoral system for the HR is a parallel "mixed-member" system that combines 295 SMD seats allocated by plurality rule and 180 proportional representation (PR) seats separately allocated in 11 regional districts that vary in magnitude (number of seats) from 6 (in the Shikoku region) to 29 (in the Kinki region). Voters cast two ballots: one for a candidate in an SMD race and another for a party in a regional PR contest. An SMD candidate may also appear on her party's list of PR candidates in the region so that she might win a seat even if she loses her SMD contest. Most often, parties place all such "dual-listed" candidates at an equal rank. Those who win their SMD races are removed from the list, and the remaining dual-listed candidates are re-ranked in order of how close they came to winning in their individual SMDs.[1]

Since Japan first used this electoral system in 1996, it has contained 300 SMDs. From the beginning, there was significant malapportionment, as urban districts contained many more eligible voters than rural districts. However, this malapportionment grew as migrational (and demographic) patterns continued to thin out rural populations and increase the number of eligible voters in urban districts. The disparity in votes per seat between the most urban and rural districts grew so large that the Supreme Court ruled in 2011 that the 2009 and thus also the 2012 elections were held in a state of unconstitutionality (although the Court did not invalidate the results or demand a new election).[2] To combat this problem, the government eliminated five rural seats and redrew district boundaries to increase the number of voters per seat in a group of rural districts, thus somewhat reducing the extent of malapportionment. As a result, the electoral system contained only 295 SMDs in 2014, in addition to the 180 PR seats (see Pekkanen, Reed, and Smith, this volume).

Such a mixed-member system can create complicated incentives for political parties hoping to gain control of the government. On the one hand, the winner-take-all nature of the SMD tier should encourage coordination within government and opposition party blocs, and the development of two-party competition at the district level (Duverger, 1954; Cox, 1997), as clearly occurred in Japan in the 2003, 2005, and 2009 elections (Scheiner, 2013). On the other hand, party leaders may have incentives to nominate candidates even in SMDs that they expect to lose, in order to show the flag and mobilize support for the party in the PR tier (Cox and Schoppa, 2002; cf. Moser and Scheiner, 2012). Moreover, it may not always be clear to party leaders whether they should expect to lose a given SMD. Indeed, when there is significant pre-electoral uncertainty over which parties or candidates are likely to be the frontrunners in the election, there may be a significant increase in candidate entry at the district level (Cox, 1997; Moser and Scheiner, 2012; Reed et al., *JD 2012*).

The results of the 2014 election: *déjà vu* all over again?

Table 3.1 shows the vote and seat totals in both the SMD and the PR tiers of the electoral system for 2012 and 2014. The LDP–Komeito coalition (henceforth simply "the Coalition") increased its SMD vote share from

Table 3.1 Seats and votes in the 2012 and 2014 HR elections

		The Coalition			The Third Force			JCP	Others	Total
		LDP	Kom	DPJ	JRP	TPJ	YP			
SMD (2012)	Candidates*	289	9	264	151	111	65	299	106	1,294
	Votes	25,643,309	8,85,881	13,598,773	6,942,353	2,992,365	2,807,244	4,700,289	2,056,350	59,626,566
	%	43.0%	1.5%	22.8%	11.6%	5.0%	4.7%	7.9%	3.5%	100%
	Seats	237	9	27	14	2	4	0	7	300
PR (2012)	Votes	16,624,457	7,116,474	9,628,653	12,262,228	3,423,915	5,245,586	3,689,159	2,189,416	60,179,888
	%	27.6%	11.8%	16.0%	20.4%	5.7%	8.7%	6.1%	3.6%	100%
	Seats	57	22	30	40	7	14	8	2	180
	Total seats	294	31	57	54	9	18	8	9	480
	Total %	61.3%	6.5%	11.9%	11.3%	1.9%	3.8%	1.7%	1.9%	100%

		The Coalition			The Third Force			JCP	Others	Total
		LDP	Kom	DPJ	JIP	PLP	PFG			
SMD (2014)	Candidates*	284	9	178	77	13	39	292	67	959
	Votes	25,461,428	7,65,390	11,916,836	4,319,646	5,14,575	9,47,396	7,040,131	1,974,315	52,939,717
	%	48.1%	1.5%	22.5%	8.2%	1.0%	1.8%	13.3%	3.7%	100%
	Seats	223	9	38	11	2	2	1	9	295
PR (2014)	Votes	17,658,916	7,314,236	9,775,991	8,382,699	1,028,721	1,414,919	6,062,962	1,696,003	53,334,447
	%	33.1%	13.7%	18.3%	15.7%	1.9%	2.7%	11.4%	3.2%	100%
	Seats	68	26	35	30	0	0	20	1	180
	Total seats	291	35	73	41	2	2	21	10	475
	Total %	61.3%	7.4%	15.4%	8.6%	0.4%	0.4%	4.4%	2.1%	100%

Notes: *Number of SMD candidates includes only officially endorsed candidates. Party abbreviations: LDP = Liberal Democratic Party; Kom = Komeito; DPJ = Democratic Party of Japan; JRP/JIP = Japan Restoration/Innovation Party; YP = Your Party; PFG: Party of Future Generations; JCP = Japan Communist Party; PLP: People's Life Party. Others include: Social Democratic Party of Japan (SDPJ), Happiness Realization Party, other minor parties, and independents.

Source: The authors, based on *Yomiuri* candidate data.

44.5% in 2012 to 49.6%, but it won 14 fewer SMD seats. The drop in SMD seats for the Coalition was fully compensated by the 15 additional seats it won in the PR tier. Overall, although the LDP won three fewer seats than it did in 2012, its coalition partner Komeito gained four seats, for a net Coalition gain of one seat from 325 to 326 (even as the number of seats contested dropped from 480 in 2012 to 475 in 2014). In contrast, the DPJ won roughly the same share of SMD votes in both elections, but it won 11 more district seats in 2014. The DPJ also improved its performance in the PR tier, gaining a larger share of the vote and five seats more than in 2012.

The most substantial shift in votes was away from the Third Force parties, who contested many fewer SMDs than in 2012. In 2012, the Third Force included the Japan Renovation Party (JRP), Tomorrow Party of Japan (TPJ), and Your Party (YP). These parties dissolved, split, or reorganized into the JIP, PLP, and PFG in advance of the 2014 election (see Pekkanen and Reed, this volume for details). Compared to 2012, the Third Force parties as a group ran 198 fewer candidates (dropping from 327 to 129) in 2014, and the combined vote total of the Third Force declined by more than 10 million votes in SMD races.

The decline in turnout in 2014 – and, as we show later, the drop in the number of SMD candidacies for the DPJ – meant that most parties actually received fewer SMD votes in 2014 than in 2012. The LDP's raw SMD vote total dropped by roughly 200,000 votes; Komeito's dropped by about 100,000; and the DPJ lost roughly 1.5 million SMD votes between 2012 and 2014. The only major party to gain votes in the SMD tier of the election was the JCP, which increased its share of the SMD vote from 8% to 13% – and its raw total by more than 2 million votes – but still won only a single SMD seat. In the PR tier, the Coalition, the DPJ, and the JCP all benefited from shifts away from the Third Force parties, even though the combined gains (3.75 million votes) were small compared to the overall decline in voter turnout (6.85 million votes).

Improved coordination among the opposition parties

In 2014, despite the surprise of the election, opposition parties showed significant improvement in coordinating nominations in SMDs. After the 2012 election, we argued that the LDP's landslide was not due to a vote swing in its favor (Reed et al., *JD 2012*). Rather, dissatisfaction with the 2009–2012 DPJ government had induced multiple defections and the establishment of new parties. In turn, this fragmented party system spoiled potential DPJ pluralities in numerous districts and handed

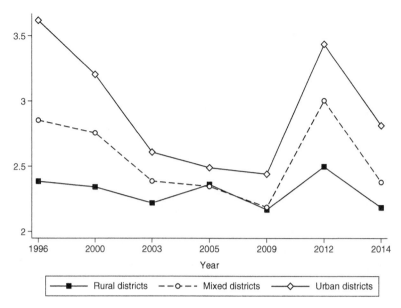

Figure 3.1 Average effective number of candidates in SMDs

Notes: Our measure of population density is based on the percentage of citizens living in census-defined densely inhabited districts within the SMD at the time of the last census in 2010. We thank Ko Maeda for providing this measure. Prior to 2014, each category had 100 districts. In 2014, there were 95 rural districts.

Source: Calculated by the authors based on *Yomiuri* candidate data.

cheap wins to the LDP. Figure 3.1 shows the average effective number of candidates per SMD for the seven elections held under the current electoral system, divided into three groups based on population density.[3] After a steady decline, the effective number of candidates per SMD spiked in 2012, as the anti-LDP camp splintered. The 2014 results show a strong correction, as the effective number of parties largely returned to pre-2009 levels.

The odd inverse relationship – in which the DPJ won approximately 1.5 million fewer SMD votes in 2014 than in 2012, but won 11 more SMD seats – was the result of improved coordination among opposition parties in 2014.[4] The DPJ contested 264 SMD races in 2012 but only 178 in 2014, as it withdrew from many districts that it had lost badly in 2012 (thus losing votes, but not seats). So the DPJ (and opposition parties, more generally) won fewer SMD votes in large part because they won fewer "wasted" votes in hopeless constituencies. Many of these would-be wasted (or protest) votes instead went to the JCP, which was the only option for voters who opposed the Coalition in 28 SMDs. The

Table 3.2 SMD-level competition within the "Big Opposition"

Raw number of candidates from DPJ or Third Force	Number of SMDs	
	2012	2014
0	13	48
1	76	191
2	130	52
3	69	4
4	12	0
	300	295

Note: Includes only officially nominated candidates from the DPJ, TPJ/PLP, JRP/JIP, YP, and PFG. Affiliated independents are not included.
Source: Calculated by the authors based on *Yomiuri* candidate data.

smaller number of Third Force candidacies meant that there was usually less of a divided vote in the face of LDP opposition (see Pekkanen and Reed, this volume), and therefore cleared the way for more DPJ wins in the districts that it did contest.

Table 3.2 indicates the significant improvement in opposition coordination between the 2012 and 2014 elections. The table shows the number of SMDs in which the DPJ and the Third Force parties (together, the "Big Opposition") fielded no candidate, a single candidate, or more than one candidate in 2012 and 2014. In 2012, parties from the Big Opposition competed against each other in 211 of 300 SMDs. In only 76 districts in 2012 did the Big Opposition field a single candidate – the optimal number to challenge the Coalition in a "Duvergerian" two-candidate contest. In contrast, in 2014 the Big Opposition improved its coordination dramatically, fielding exactly one candidate in 191 of the 295 SMDs. In 2014, the Big Opposition in the aggregate endorsed more than one candidate in only 56 districts, a sharp drop from 2012 in the number of coordination failures.

In the districts where more than one opposition candidate did run, might better coordination have deprived Coalition candidates of victories? How we answer this question depends on how we treat the JCP. The JCP has a long history of noncooperation with other opposition parties. Under the multi-member, single nontransferable vote (SNTV) electoral system in use from 1947 to 1993, the JCP would ritualistically nominate a candidate in every district, no matter what the chances of victory and despite the high financial cost in doing so (Harada and Smith, 2014). The party has since ceased that strategy, but it still eschews coordination with other parties. So should we count as coordination failures the districts in which the Big Opposition fielded a single candidate, but in which a JCP or other fringe candidate was a spoiler? Or should we treat these JCP and fringe votes as inevitable (and unavailable to the rest of the opposition) and only count as coordination failures those districts in which multiple Big Opposition candidates together outpolled the Coalition candidate, but the latter won the seat?

Table 3.3 indicates that, although coordination failure by the Big Opposition led to a large number of "undeserved" victories by the LDP in 2012, the problem was far less evident in 2014. The table displays the calculations for three different coordination scenarios in both 2012 and 2014 (with the heroic assumptions that voters wouldn't cross the government/opposition line or alter their turnout decisions were the field of candidates to change). Our calculations suggest that, in 2012, the failure

Table 3.3   Actual and hypothetical LDP–Komeito coalition SMD winners in 2012 and 2014, by coordination scenario

	2012		2014	
Actual number of SMDs won	246 of 300		232 of 295	
Coalition seat bonus due to …	*Bonus*	*Seat total without bonus*	*Bonus*	*Seat total without bonus*
(Scenario 1) … *DPJ + Third Force coordination failure*	112	134	21	211
(Scenario 2) … *non-JCP/independent/minor party opposition coordination failure*	114	132	25	207
(Scenario 3) … *full opposition coordination failure*	146	100	92	140

Note: We reported different numbers in our previous analysis of the 2012 election (Reed et al., *JD 2012*). This discrepancy is due to a calculation error that caused us to *underestimate* the costs to the opposition of poor coordination. The numbers for the LDP–Komeito coalition do not include LDP-affiliated conservative independent candidates; those candidates are included in Scenario 3. Scenario 1 includes only officially nominated candidates from the DPJ, JRP/JIP, TPJ/PLP, YP, and PFG. Scenario 2 includes the SDPJ, small parties such as New Party Daichi, People's New Party, and Japan New Party, as well as opposition party-affiliated independents, but not JCP, non-affiliated independents, LDP-affiliated independents, or fringe party candidates (e.g., Happiness Realization Party). Scenario 3 includes all non-LDP–Komeito candidates.
Source: Calculated by the authors based on *Yomiuri* election results data.

of the Big Opposition – that is, the DPJ and the Third Force parties (Scenario 1 in Table 3.3) – to coordinate on a single candidate might have handed the Coalition as many as 112 "bonus" SMD seats and, thus, may have been responsible for the Coalition's majority in the HR. In contrast, Big Opposition coordination failure in 2014 resulted in the LDP gaining at most 21 seats it would not have won against a unified opposition. In short, it does not appear that coordination failures in 2014 cost the Big Opposition control of the HR.

In Scenario 2, we examine whether including the SMD votes of the Social Democratic Party of Japan (SDPJ) and other small (but not fringe) parties, as well as those of party-affiliated independents, to the vote total of the Big Opposition might have cost the LDP additional seats. This more expanded cooperation would have added very little to the opposition's total seat haul. However, as we see in Scenario 3, JCP candidates acted as "spoilers" in many districts in both elections, but especially in 2014. That is, coordination between the Big Opposition parties and the JCP (along with other fringe candidates and independents) in 2014 could have clawed back from the governing parties an additional 67 seats: a combined Big Opposition (and non-fringe party) vote might have cost the Coalition 25 seats, but a combined opposition vote that included the JCP might have cost the Coalition as many as 92 seats. In contrast, the inability of the Big Opposition (and other small parties) to coordinate votes with the JCP in 2012 gained the Coalition only an additional 32 seats (i.e., a coordinated Big Opposition plus smaller parties force might have taken 114 seats away from the Coalition's actual total, whereas including the vote of the JCP and other minor fringe candidates could have cost the Coalition as many as 146 seats).[5]

Interestingly, even the Big Opposition's decision not to challenge the Coalition at all in a number of districts in 2014 may be illustrative of the opposition's improved strategic decision making as a group. That is, as Table 3.2 indicates, in 2014 there were 48 districts in which the Big Opposition did not enter the field at all. Were these opportunities that the opposition missed to take seats from the LDP? We think not. In seven of those 48 SMDs, the winner was a strong independent candidate competing against the LDP, a "Duvergerian" two-candidate equilibrium, but with one of the two candidates coming from outside the principal opposition group. A similar pattern involving small parties held in two other districts as well: in Okinawa 2nd District, the incumbent and winner was a candidate from the SDPJ; in Tochigi 3rd District, the Big Opposition refrained from challenging former YP leader Yoshimi Watanabe, who ran as an independent but ended up losing his race against an LDP challenger. In each of these cases, any Big Opposition entrant might have become a spoiler, splitting the anti-government vote and handing the seat to the LDP. In the 39 remaining SMDs that lacked Big Opposition candidates, the average vote share of the LDP or Komeito candidate in 2012 had been 64%. It would seem that those additional Big Opposition absences, then, were reasonably calculated to avoid wasting resources in government strongholds (see Smith, this volume).

Decreased turnout in SMDs with fewer options

Perhaps the most striking feature of the 2014 election was the continued decline in voter turnout. Based on our analysis, it appears that voter abstention in 2014 had very different roots from the lack of turnout in 2012. Whereas the decline in voter turnout in 2012 was very much a function of voters' disenchantment with the DPJ, additional abstentions in 2014 appeared to be a consequence of the supply of Big Opposition candidates failing to meet voter demand.

The 2014 election set the dubious record of lowest voter turnout in a postwar general election, "beating" the previous low, set in 2012 (59.3%). In our analysis of the 2012 election (Reed et al., *JD 2012*), we inferred that as many as nine out of every ten voters who had cast ballots in 2009 but abstained in 2012 had voted for the DPJ in 2009. It appears, therefore, that the dramatic decline in turnout in 2012 was a big part of the reason that the DPJ fared so poorly in that year's election. We interpreted that finding as evidence that millions of 2009 DPJ supporters had become disillusioned with the party but opted to stay at home in 2012 rather than vote for the LDP or choose from among a bewildering array of new and untested alternatives. In addition, low turnout tends to play to the advantage of parties with more coherent organizations and greater numbers of core supporters, like the LDP and, especially, Komeito.

Was the further drop in turnout in the 2014 election a continuation of the same story? We don't think so. The overriding difference between the 2012 and 2014 political contexts was not that voters became even more disillusioned with the DPJ. Rather, it was that voters were presented with a far narrower set of alternatives if they wanted to cast a vote against the ruling Coalition.

In support of these interpretations of the differences between the turnout decline in 2012 and 2014, we present the results of two ordinary least squares regression models (Table 3.4). In the first model, the

Table 3.4 Explaining SMD-level change in turnout in 2012 and 2014

	Model 1	Model 2
	Change in turnout 2012–2009	**Change in turnout 2014–2012**
Change in turnout 2009–2005	−0.495* (0.0779)	
Change in # cands. 2012–2009	0.554* (0.140)	
Change in winner margin 2012–2009	−0.0265* (0.00811)	
Change in turnout 2012–2009		0.0112 (0.0499)
Change in # Big Opp. (no DPJ) 2014–2012		0.574* (0.195)
Change in # DPJ 2014–2012		1.894* (0.299)
Change in winner margin 2014–2012		−0.0785* (0.0150)
PopDID	0.0420* (0.00506)	−0.00131 (0.00533)
Constant	−12.85* (0.402)	−5.099* (0.817)
Observations (districts)	300	295
R-squared	0.417	0.230

Notes: Standard errors in parentheses. *p < 0.01.

dependent variable is the SMD-level change in turnout in the 2012 election (measured as the percentage of eligible voters who turned out in the district in 2012 minus the corresponding percentage in the high turnout election of 2009). In the second model, we seek to explain the district-level change in turnout in 2014 (measured as the percentage turnout in the district in 2014 minus the percentage turnout in the district in 2012).[6]

In Model 1, we find support for the view that turnout declined most among more casual voters who had been drawn into participation by the excitement surrounding the DPJ in 2009. More specifically, the negative (–0.495) and statistically significant coefficient on *Change in turnout 2009–2005* indicates that turnout declined most in 2012 in the districts in which it had increased most in 2009 relative to 2005: for each additional increase of one percentage point in turnout between 2005 and 2009, there was a drop of nearly half a percentage point in turnout in 2012. Most likely, these were districts that saw a large number of casual voters show up in 2009 – perhaps excited about the prospect of anointing a new majority party for the first time in their lifetimes – only to become disillusioned and therefore uninterested in voting in 2012 because of that party's utter failure in government.

Other points from the results of Model 1 bear mentioning as well: the positive and significant sign on the coefficient on *Change in # cands. 2012–2009* indicates that, all else equal, district-level turnout in 2012 went up over half a percentage point with each additional candidate that ran in the district relative to 2009 (the variable ranges from –3 to 3, with half of all districts gaining at least one candidate). The positive and statistically significant coefficient on *PopDID* (the percentage of residents living in densely inhabited districts within the SMD; it varies from 8% to 100%) indicates that turnout stayed higher in 2012 in high-population-density (urban) districts. Turnout is generally higher in rural districts, so this finding is somewhat surprising, and is most likely due to a particularly large number of rural DPJ voters who turned out to vote in 2009 but returned to abstaining in 2012. Finally, the negative and significant coefficient on *Change in winner margin 2012–2009* (margin is the percentage-point difference between the vote shares of the winner and runner-up) indicates that turnout decreased in districts that became less competitive, a finding that is consistent with previous studies of Japan (Cox et al., 1998) and elsewhere (for a review, see Geys, 2006).

The results of Model 2 tell a very different story. To begin with, the coefficient on *Change in turnout 2012–2009* is roughly zero, suggesting that there was no correlation between 2012–2014 district-level turnout changes and 2009–2012 changes. What did shape the change in turnout in 2014 was the number of candidates competing in the district. The positive and statistically significant coefficient on *Change in # DPJ 2014–2012* indicates that the presence of a DPJ candidate appeared to increase turnout. The variable represents the number of DPJ candidates in the district in 2014 minus the number that ran in 2012 and is thus equal to –1 (withdrawal), 0 (no withdrawal), or 1 (entry). The withdrawal of a DPJ candidate was associated with a roughly two-percentage-point drop in turnout.

The variable *Change in # Big Opposition (no DPJ) 2014–2012* indicates the number of non-DPJ Big Opposition candidates that ran in the district in 2014 minus the number that ran in 2012 (ranges from –3 to 1). The positive and significant coefficient on the variable indicates that as the number of candidates declined between 2012 and 2014, turnout dropped as well.[7] Each withdrawal of a Third Force candidate

(JIP, PLP, PFG) is associated with a drop of over half a percentage point in turnout.[8] This result may appear to stand in contrast to the comparative literature that generally finds no relationship between the number of parties and turnout (e.g., Brockington, 2004; Blais and Aarts, 2006; Grofman and Selb, 2011). However, when the withdrawal of candidates results in uncompetitive races, such as many of the LDP versus JCP variety in 2014, it should not be surprising that voters were not mobilized to show up at the polls.

In 2012, the rout of the DPJ and the decline in turnout were two sides of the same coin. Voters who had turned out to propel the DPJ to power in 2009 went back home in 2012 rather than reward the DPJ's poor performance or support anyone else. The LDP–Komeito coalition did not win that election so much as the DPJ sealed its own fate by driving so many of its supporters to abstention. In 2014, however, the Coalition landslide and the further decline in turnout were not related in the same way. Turnout declined as Big Opposition candidates withdrew, and declined the most where the Coalition was opposed only by the JCP. But, as we discussed above, some of those withdrawals were tactical decisions by the Big Opposition to coordinate better, fielding fewer candidates and therefore inducing abstentions, but winning more seats in the bargain.

Perhaps most important, in an election in which millions more voters than ever before chose to stay home, the Coalition held on to its vote base from the previous election, while the non-Communist opposition as a group lost votes, mostly because it fielded fewer candidates.

Conclusions

In one sense, the 2014 results are encouraging for opponents of the current coalition. In 2012, a doomed incumbent party competed nationally, but its vulnerability spurred a menagerie of new parties to jump in and oversaturate the anti-LDP field. Had they stayed out, the DPJ might have lost a close election rather than a blowout. Based on our counterfactual coordination scenarios (Table 3.3), full coordination between the DPJ and the Third Force parties in 2012 might even have cost the LDP–Komeito coalition its victory. In 2014, opposition coordination was much improved and much more realistic. Other than the perennial spoiler, the JCP, the opposition demonstrated a strategic acumen – aided, ironically, by a narrow time window that made it more difficult to find additional candidates to run (Smith, this volume) – that was completely absent two years earlier.

But in another sense, 2014 reveals just how high a mountain the opposition must climb. Despite a much more savvy Big Opposition candidate entry strategy, the ruling coalition easily renewed its super-majority and even gained a seat in the bargain. Certainly, there are still some gains to be made by eliminating those last instances of coordination failure. Our results also indicate that a Big Opposition candidacy in some of the districts that featured only the LDP and the JCP in the latest election might mobilize enough 2012 voters who abstained in 2014 to swing some districts. But such marginal changes will not be enough by themselves.

The problem for the opposition is that whereas the LDP and, especially, Komeito enjoy strong, reliable organizational bases (as does the JCP, of course), the DPJ does not (Ikeda and Reed, this volume) and the JIP seems confined to the region around its Osaka base (Pekkanen and Reed, this volume; Reed et al., *JD 2012*). The 2009 election showed that the LDP is not invincible. But the 2009 recipe for opposition success combined one part LDP split and the temporary de-mobilization of traditional LDP support groups, and one part temporary turnout bump, with nearly all of the casual voters plumping for the DPJ.

If Abenomics founders because its third arrow misses the mark (or is never unleashed) and the economy stagnates again, then those casual voters might be re-mobilized to throw the Coalition "bums" out. Alternatively, if Abenomics succeeds because its third arrow breaks the LDP's clientelistic compact with vested interests (see Maclachlan and Shimizu, this volume, and Noble, this volume), the LDP's organizational vote advantage might shrivel and the opposition may find itself less disadvantaged in a competition for "the unorganized vote" (see Denzau and Munger, 1986; Bawn and Thies, 2003). The DPJ would have to overcome the perception of incompetence (justified or not) that dogged its 2009–2012 stint in government – not least by choosing new leadership and developing an attractive and coherent new manifesto – but if Abenomics essentially completes the project that Junichirou Koizumi began a decade ago, the opposition may be in a good place to challenge the LDP's efforts to remake its support base (see Rosenbluth and Thies, 2010; Pempel, 1998).

Notes

1. More specifically, equally ranked candidates on a given party's list are re-ranked according to the "best-loser" ratio that is calculated by dividing the dual-listed SMD candidate's vote by the winning candidate's vote in that

district. Candidates with higher ratios (i.e., those who came closest to winning their SMD races) are re-ranked to occupy higher positions on the party list.

2. There were nearly 2.5 times as many votes per seat in the most underrepresented urban district as in the most overrepresented rural district.

3. The "effective number" (Laakso and Taagepera 1979) weights parties (or candidates) by their shares of the vote and thus discounts contestants who win few votes. The measure is calculated by taking the vote proportion won by each contestant, squaring each of those proportions, summing all of the squared values, and dividing that sum into 1. For example, a district with four contestants who each win 25% of the vote has an effective number of parties of 4. But if the contestants win 40%, 30%, 20%, and 10%, respectively, the effective number of parties is 3.33. The measure can be as small as 1 and has no maximum.

4. As Smith (this volume) explains, however, some of this "improved coordination" was unintentional, a result of the snap election catching parties unprepared to nominate candidates in many districts.

5. Just as in 2012, opposition coordination failure was most frequent in urban districts, as suggested by the much higher effective number of parties in urban districts (as illustrated in Figure 3.1).

6. Change in turnout, margin, and number of candidates for the ten districts in the five prefectures that experienced major redistricting in 2014 (see Pekkanen, Reed, and Smith, this volume) is calculated using the 2012 values of the district mostly closely overlapping with the 2014 boundaries. For example, new Fukui 2nd District (2014) is based mostly on old Fukui 3rd District (2012), so we use the values from the latter to calculate the change rather than the values of old Fukui 2nd District. Dropping these ten districts from the analysis does not affect the results.

7. It is likely that there is some endogeneity in the model here. It is likely that fewer (especially DPJ) candidates will run in districts in which there is greater voter dissatisfaction (which may be represented by greater voter abstention). Most likely, the causal arrow actually runs both ways: in some cases, the number of candidates affects voters' decisions to turn out, and in some cases large amounts of voter dissatisfaction dissuades parties from running candidates. However, we should note that by controlling for changes in turnout (between 2009 and 2012), we are to some degree already controlling for dissatisfaction in the district, and our findings with respect to the number of candidates still hold, nonetheless.

8. We should note that, unlike the 2012 model, we find no statistically significant relationship between the population density of a district and the change in turnout in 2014. However, as with Model 1, we do find that the magnitude of the drop in turnout between 2012 and 2014 was less in districts that became more competitive, all else equal.

Bibliography

Bawn, Kathleen and Michael F. Thies (2003). A comparative theory of electoral incentives: Representing the unorganized under PR, plurality, and mixed-member electoral systems. *Journal of Theoretical Politics* 15(1): 5–32.

Blais, André and Kees Aarts (2006). Electoral systems and turnout. *Acta Politica* 41(2): 180–196.

Brockington, David (2004). The paradox of proportional representation: The effect of party systems and coalitions on individuals' electoral participation. *Political Studies* 52: 469–490.

Cox, Gary W. (1997). *Making votes count: Strategic coordination in the world's electoral systems.* Cambridge: Cambridge University Press.

Cox, Gary W., Frances M. Rosenbluth, and Michael F. Thies (1998). Mobilization, social networks, and turnout: Evidence from Japan. *World Politics* 50(3): 447–474.

Cox, Karen E. and Leonard J. Schoppa (2002). Interaction effects in mixed-member electoral systems theory and evidence from Germany, Japan, and Italy. *Comparative Political Studies* 35(9): 1027–1053.

Denzau, Arthur T., and Michael C. Munger (1986). Legislators and interest groups: How unorganized interests get represented. *American Political Science Review* 80(1): 89–106.

Duverger, Maurice (1954). *Political parties.* London: Methuen.

Geys, Benny (2006). Explaining voter turnout: A review of aggregate-level research. *Electoral Studies* 25: 637–663.

Grofman, Bernard and Peter Selb (2011). Turnout and the (effective) number of parties at the national and district levels: A puzzle-solving approach. *Party Politics* 17(1): 93–117.

Harada, Masataka and Daniel M. Smith (2014). You have to pay to play: Candidate and party responses to the high cost of elections in Japan. *Electoral Studies* 36: 51–64.

Horiuchi, Yusaku, Daniel M. Smith, Teppei Yamamoto, and Mayumi Fukushima (2014). 衆院選挙、緊急解析！データが明かした有権者の本音：有権者の真の関心は「アベノミクス」ではなかった [Quick analysis of the lower house election! Data reveal the true preferences of voters: Voters real concern was not "Abenomics"]. Nikkei Business Online, 18 December 2014. URL: http://business.nikkeibp.co.jp/article/topics/20141218/275309.

Laakso, Markku and Rein Taagepera (1979). Effective number of parties: A measure with application to West Europe. *Comparative Political Studies* 12(1): 3–27.

Moser, Robert G. and Ethan Scheiner (2012). *Electoral systems and political context: How the effects of rules vary across new and established democracies.* New York: Cambridge University Press.

Pempel, T. J. (1998). *Regime shift: Comparative dynamics of the Japanese political economy.* Ithaca: Cornell University Press.

Reed, Steven R., Ethan Scheiner, Daniel M. Smith, and Michael F. Thies (2013). The 2012 Election results: The LDP wins big by default. In Robert Pekkanen, Steven R. Reed and Ethan Scheiner (eds) *Japan Decides 2012: The Japanese General Election.* pp. 34–47. London and New York: Palgrave.

Rosenbluth, Frances McCall and Michael F. Thies. (2010). *Japan transformed: Political change and economic restructuring.* Princeton, NJ: Princeton University Press.

Scheiner, Ethan. (2013). The Electoral system and Japan's partial transformation: Party system consolidation without policy realignment. In Kenji E. Kushida and Phillip Y. Lipscy (eds) *Japan under the DPJ: The Politics of Transition and Governance*. pp. 73–102. Stanford: Walter H. Shorenstein Asia-Pacific Research Center.

Part II
Political Parties

4
The LDP: Return to Dominance?
Or a Golden Age Built on Sand?

Masahisa Endo and Robert J. Pekkanen

The LDP resurgence: Uncommon again?

The results of the 2014 election cemented both Prime Minister Shinzo Abe's hold on power and the Liberal Democratic Party's (LDP) position as the dominant political party operating in Japan – and by a huge margin.[1] It made for the third LDP victory at the polls in three years, bookending the 2013 House of Councillors (HC) election with two House of Representatives (HR) wins in 2012 and 2014. Now, the LDP is in the best position it has been in the past two decades (the only possible contender being 2005–2007, after Prime Minister Jun'ichro Koizumi's stunning 2005 HR win and before a first-term Abe led the LDP to defeat in the 2007 HC election). The party enjoys a huge majority in the HR, controls the HC (with Komeito), and is relatively untroubled by factional strife or leadership rivalry, or indeed by internal disputes over power or policy. The weakness and division of the opposition are not necessarily going to last, and floating voters today are less reliable than the organized vote of the 1980s, but at this point the LDP looks to have cleared the field of its rivals in a manner reminiscent of the 1980s glory days of LDP hegemony.[2] A good measure of this is that we feel relatively sure that the LDP will win the *next* HR election – *whenever* that is. A lot can happen in politics in four years, but the LDP looks more likely to win the *next* election than it has in the immediate aftermath of any election since perhaps 1986. With opposition parties looking about as intimidating as the Japan Socialist Party (JSP) in the late 1970s or early 1980s, and no election required until 2018 (HR) or 2016 (HC), the LDP can concentrate on advancing its policy agenda in this Diet. To add icing to their delicious electoral cake, the LDP enjoyed a recent uptick in membership and corporate contributions after years of sapping declines. Truly, this is a second golden age for the LDP.

We make three main arguments in this chapter. First, we examine party organization, including membership, fund-raising, candidate recruitment, factions, and local branches. Second, we argue that Abe learned how to be a more politically successful prime minister, improving greatly from his first term (2006–2007) to his current run (2012–). Specifically, we point out how he improved his personnel management and his communications strategy. Our third argument is that Abe used the snap election call in order to neutralize intra-party opponents to his policies, for example tax *zoku* opposed to the delay in the hike in the consumption tax. We then conclude with some ideas about the future of the LDP.

Governing the party

A divided opposition meant that Abe had reason to believe the LDP would win the 2014 snap election. However, an equally important factor that enabled Abe to surprise everyone – and we should recognize the snap election call for the audacious act of political imagination it was – was his strength within the party. His only serious possible rival to the premiership was Ishiba, whose capitulation was signaled by his remaining in Abe's cabinet in fall 2014 (Pekkanen and Pekkanen, 2015: 4). Abe could call this snap election and lose many seats, say, 30 seats, and still feel secure from any rivals to his throne. This is also the reason Abe did not face criticism from vulnerable backbenchers before the election (or during his announced "decision" period). In other words, it was Abe's strength within the LDP and his ability to enhance this with a snap election, as much as the weakness of the opposition, that made possible the snap election – in retrospect, clearly a brilliant move by Abe.

Party membership and finances

During the 2000s, the LDP's organization suffered declines both in terms of finance and membership, and these declines were accelerated by the DPJ's capture of power in 2009 (Endo et al., *JD 2012*). However, once the LDP returned to power in December 2012, we observe that there is a reversal and LDP membership began to rise. Moreover, donations to the party also began to rebound. Nonetheless, the rate of the recovery is not so dramatic, at least in the first year, and certainly nothing like the tremendous increase in the number of LDP legislators. As Figure 4.1 shows, LDP membership in 2013 was still smaller than it was in 2011

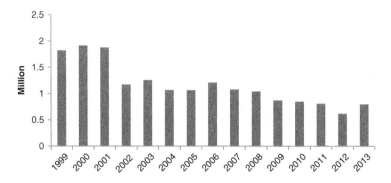

Figure 4.1 LDP membership
Source: Kanpo.

and about half of membership in the early 2000s (Figure 4.1).[3] This seems to reflect the undisputed return to power of the LDP, but on the back of tepid popular support going into the 2012 general election. Certainly, it appears to us that the LDP's return to power cannot be attributed to or said to have caused a very significant change in the downward trend of party membership.

As a strategy, the LDP still emphasizes small local meetings (*furusato taiwa*) to "listen to voices" of their ordinary supporters (and see Ikeda and Reed, this volume, for how the DPJ approaches this). More than 600 meetings were held and more than 10,000 people participated since its start under the Tanigaki leadership in 2009. After getting back to power, Abe even started to have small local meetings hosted by the government (*kurumaza furusato talk*), in which a cabinet member talks with 10–15 local people. Without further evidence, it is hard to tell how this could have affected the membership numbers. However, we can find evidence that the LDP cares about these membership numbers. Beyond the small local meeting strategy, the LDP has also considered setting a quota for recruitment of members and penalizing those Diet Members (MPs) who fell short. In 2014, Ishiba announced a goal of raising the number of LDP party members to 1.2 million in 2014. He went further and demanded DMs to collect new members in the 2014 party convention (*Asahi*, January 20, 2014). The then general council chairperson Seiko Noda even floated the idea of penalties for those MPs who fell short of achieving their quota (*Asahi*, January 16, 2014).

The LDP's return to power also appears to have affected corporate contributions. Figure 4.2 shows the trends of contributions to *Kokumin Seiji*

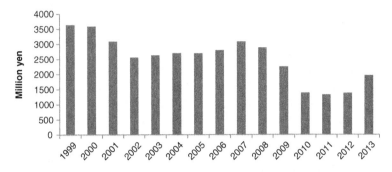

Figure 4.2   Contributions to the LDP
Source: Kanpo.

Kyokai, the LDP's political finance organization.[4] Here again, we see an uptick after the LDP returned to power in 2012. The LDP in government in 2013 received more money than the LDP in opposition (2009–2012). This shows that business leaders welcomed the LDP's comeback, or at least were rewarding a winner. However, the LDP's contributions in 2013 still fell short of where they were in 2009. Either the LDP recovery is just beginning or these variations reflect the difference between leading the country and leading the opposition.

Candidate recruitment

One of the benefits the LDP accrued from its landslide victory in the 2012 HR election was that it had many incumbents to run in the 2014 election. This was an especially important advantage given the snap nature of the election – which made candidate recruitment generally more challenging. Adding to this advantage, the LDP's task was made even easier by the smaller number of slots it had to fill with new candidates. And, in 2014, there were only 295 single-member districts (SMDs) to compete in – five fewer than 2012 (see Pekkanen, Reed, and Smith, this volume, for an explanation of the contraction). Dan Smith provides an overview of candidate recruitment across parties in this volume; so, besides the above points, we would like to relate a few interesting illustrations from selected districts (on women candidates, see also Gaunder, this volume, and Martin Murphy, *JD 2012*).

The former DPJ Minister of Finance Jun Azumi casts a long shadow over the Miyagi 5th district. In 2012, Mitsuyo Okubo ran under the LDP banner, losing in the district and winning election through the PR tier. Before the 2014 election, the local LDP branch demanded that the party not endorse Okubo and instead recruit another candidate – because Okubo did not work for the constituency during her term (*Asahi*, November 25, 2014, Miyagi edition). While Okubo did not run either in an SMD or PR, Shigeaki Katsunuma was endorsed. While Katsunuma is an incumbent DM, he is not a local from Miyagi but from Hokkaido PR district. Beyond what it says about Okubo and her relationship to her local LDP branch, this episode shows more broadly the complex relationship that PR tier DMs can have with districts, as well as how local branches can influence candidate selection (see Krauss and Pekkanen 2010 for a longer analysis of the complications of life as a "zombie").

In other districts, the LDP leadership did not even lead recruitment. Instead, they left it to the voters by having two candidates backed by different factions duke it out against each other as Liberal Democratic Independent (LDIs) in the classic single nontransferable vote (SNTV) style. In Fukuoka 1st district, two LDP incumbents ran as LDIs. Takahiro Inoue, who was endorsed as an LDP candidate in 2012 and backed by Taro Aso, was not endorsed in 2014 since Yuji Shinkai, who was elected as a PR candidate in 2012 and backed by ex-faction leader Makoto Koga, also demanded an endorsement. The LDP did not side with either of them and instead ran them head to head in 2014. This conflict ended with Inoue's win, at least in this election. On the night of the election day, after the TV programmes broadcasted their projection of his win, the LDP announced that Inoue was in fact nominated at the day before the election (*Asahi*, December 16, 2014; Smith, this volume).

Factions

As the above example perhaps makes clear, factions still persist in LDP intra-party politics. Although factional politics may not play a strong role in policymaking, factional influence can be observed in electoral politics. The Nikai faction showed particularly aggressive behavior by fielding their "guest members" as independent candidates if they could not secure official party nominations (see Smith, this volume). A good example of this behavior is the case of Kotaro Nagasaki in Yamanashi 2nd district. Nagasaki was first elected under the LDP label as an "assassin" over a postal rebel in 2005, but he has never since secured nomination from the LDP.[5] In 2012 and 2014, Nagasaki ran against and defeated the daughter-in-law of the same rebel whom Nagasaki had defeated in 2005 – even though this daughter-in-law ran with LDP endorsement! The Nikai faction houses Nagasaki as a guest member of the faction and brazenly demanded that the secretary general (SG) accept Nagasaki's accession to the LDP. Nikai cheekily even poached an incumbent from the DPJ. In 2014, in Hyogo 11th district, Tsuyoshi Yamaguchi, the former DPJ Vice-Minister of Foreign Affairs and at the time independent DM, joined the Nikai faction as a "guest member" – and Nikai demanded the LDP endorse Yamaguchi. The party conceded to the extent that it required Yamaguchi and another candidate backed by the prefectural chapter compete in the election as LDI. Yamaguchi won the election and moved up from LDI to an LDP member and DM in January 2015.

Party organization

In the LDP presidential election in 2012, Abe trailed Shigeru Ishiba in terms of popularity among party members but won the position because of the support from factions (Endo et al., *JD 2012*). Ishiba, who has not belonged to any factions since his return from the New Frontier Party, was then appointed as SG of the LDP and took some measures to weaken the influence of factions. One example is that as SG he demanded the first-term MPs to submit a report on their constituency activities. The party, and not factions, attempted to increase their role in the job training of the first-term DMs.

Factional weakening is a long-term trend dating back to Koizumi's pre-miership. In particular, under the Koizumi's landslide win in 2005, many first-term LDP DMs, called "Koizumi Children," dared to stay out of factions and attempted to have a direct connection with the party leader. Now the number of DMs who do not belong to any faction has increased and exceeds that of any single faction (*Yomiuri*, August 17, 2014). Interestingly, anti-factionist Ishiba himself organizes around 50 such DMs as a group, in his words, for the purpose of information exchange, but other factions see it as a new "Ishiba faction."

Furthermore, the SG and Party Reform Committee changed the rule of presidential election to increase the influence of local branches and non-DM party members. The rule for the 2012 presidential election, when Abe defeated Ishiba, was that if there were no candidate who won a majority among the votes of local branch (party members) and DMs in the first round, the top two vote-winners would compete in a run-off second round. In this second round, however, only DMs could cast votes – and not local branches or general party members. In the 2013 party national convention, the LDP changed its rule to give one vote for each prefectural branch in the second round (*Jiyu Minshu*, March 26, 2013). In the next year, they changed the rule again: the total number of votes of local branches was now the same as that of DMs (*Jiyu Minshu*, January 28, 2013). By these reforms, the influence of DMs relatively weakened and a potent source of factional influence in intra-party politics was dampened. If this new rule had been employed in 2012, Ishiba would have been elected as the LDP president and without a doubt won the December 2012 election and served as prime minister instead of Abe.

Emphasizing the importance of local branches is consistent with some other elements of LDP strategy discussed both above and below. It could reflect the party's recognition of weakening party organizations, which should be strengthened through making them more influential. An emphasis on reform to strengthen local branches is a policy direction the LDP shares with the DPJ (itself afflicted by weak local organizations).

Governing Japan: Abe 2 vs Abe 1

Abe had a poor tenure in 2006–2007, being fairly run out of office (to be fair, he also was hospitalized) in the wake of a tough defeat in the 2007 HC election. He had inherited an almost unbelievably favorable political situation in 2006 but did not make the most of the situation by committing mistakes in his cabinet and communications policy. To his credit, he learned from his mistakes and performed markedly better in these areas in his second term (2012–).

Ministerial selection

Factions haven't been important in Abe's selection of ministers. Here he follows in the footsteps of Jun'ichiro Koizumi. And, this has been generally well received. However, one biting criticism of Abe's first administration (2006–2007) was his "Friends of Shinzo" cabinet. Critics complained that Abe selected close associates for ministerial posts, rather than prizing ability and experience. For example, he was criticized for choosing his relatively inexperienced "friend" Yasuhisa Shiozaki for a position out of his depth. In a comparative statistical analysis of cabinet composition, Pekkanen et al. (2014) found evidence that Abe's first cabinet was indeed relatively stocked with inexperienced and inexpert ministers. Perhaps the critics were onto something. There were many resignations from Abe's cabinet. One startling example is the Ministry of Agriculture and Fisheries. Within one year, four ministers held the same post as Toshikatsu Matsuoka, Norhihiko Akagi, and Takehiko Endo, all had to resign as minister due to separate financial scandals (Matsuoka committed suicide during his term). In addition, Fumio Kyuma, Minister of Defense, also resigned due to backlash to his statement "dropping the atomic bomb on Nagasaki couldn't be helped." The weakness of Abe's cabinet was widely seen as a prime cause for his collapse (alongside the 2007 HC defeat).

However poor his initial choices in 2006, we must give Abe full credit for learning from his mistakes. In his 2012 cabinet, he again ignored demands or lists from factions, but this time he made very careful and generally praised cabinet selections. Perhaps not coincidentally, Abe then led the LDP to a victory in the 2013 HC election (see Pekkanen, Reed, and Smith, this volume). In 2014, and probably in response to a growing gender gap in support for his cabinet (see Figure 4.3), Abe made a dramatic cabinet reshuffle in 2014 – appointing five women ministers. The immediate response was an overall increase in public support of the cabinet (which is typical after reshuffles) and the reduction of the gender gap in support (which is not). In his 2014 reshuffle, Abe retained his core economic ministers, Taro Aso and Akira Amari, likely in order to provide continuity in the handling of "Abenomics." Embarrassingly, two of his women ministers had to almost immediately resign after the reshuffle due to financial scandals. Still, we must conclude that Abe has become a much more skillful personnel manager in his second term as prime minister, and this has contributed to his success.

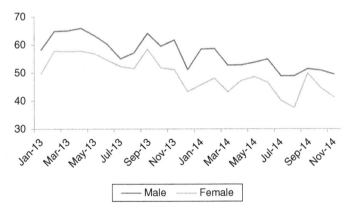

Figure 4.3   Gender gap in cabinet approval
Source: Jiji Public Opinion Polls.

Communications policy – Abenomics

Abe also greatly improved his communications policy. In 2006–2007, Abe's communications policy was marked by a few big failures – mishandling of personnel being covered above. For a politician marked on his way up as skilled at communications – and besides being young and telegenic, he had the track record of rising to prominence criticizing North Korea – Abe brutally mishandled a massive lost pension records scandal, appearing sympathetic to the bureaucrats, rather than the citizens. This contributed to the 2007 HC defeat as angry voters vented their unhappiness at the ballot box. Probably, most importantly, however, his chosen governing theme of nationalism, branded as "beautiful Japan," sank like a stone from the start with voters more concerned with pocketbook issues. But, Abe appeared out of touch.

However, as with his ministerial selections, we must give Abe full credit for learning from his mistakes. His communications policy focused on Abenomics (with a few minor wayward steps) quite consistently (for more details on his communications policy, see Pekkanen and Pekkanen, 2015). The branding of Abenomics was skillful, the messaging was consistent, and the chosen issue was probably the most advantageous to the LDP (rather than constitutional revision, for instance).

According to the results of web survey in the 2014 general election,[6] it is apparent that economic issues are more important for people than controversial collective self-defense issues (Table 4.1). Economic growth strategy and consumption tax hike are among the two most important issues, followed by monetary easing and another controversial issue of

Table 4.1 Evaluation of Abenomics policies

	The issue is important	Abe administration did a good job
Monetary easing	68.4	46.7
Flexible fiscal spending	63.2	32.7
Growth strategy	75.7	31.0
Authorizing the use of the right of collective self-defense	59.6	27.6
Resuming operations of nuclear power plants	67.1	17.1
Consumption tax hike	72.3	23.7

Source: Web survey on the general election in 2014.

nuclear power plants. On the basis of the *three arrows* of Abenomics – monetary easing, flexible fiscal spending, and growth strategy – people evaluated the Abe administration's performance highly. In particular, monetary easing is perceived as very effective; a half of voters approve the cabinet performance on it. Compared to these three aspects of economic policies, other major issues in the Diet, collective self-defense, NPP operations, and consumption tax hike have been evaluated on a lower scale. In particular, Abe's attempts to resume NPP operations are not popular.

The 2014 campaign

Snap election – why

Any story of the 2014 election probably must start with Abe's decision to call a snap election. His motive and incentives are analyzed elsewhere in this volume (Pekkanen, Reed, and Smith, this volume), but we agree that Abe made the decision when faced with an uncoordinated opposition and under economic uncertainty in the near future. Earlier, we also emphasized how Abe's strength within the party also made this gamble less risky for him. Abe's 2014 HR victory strengthened him within the party, certainly. It deterred rivals from contesting the party presidency. It also strengthened his hand against the anti-Abe group, who opposed the postponement of the hike of the consumption tax.

However, we also claim here that Abe was able to use even the credible threat of a snap election to also *enhance* his power within the party. This threat worked against the veteran politicians who are expert members in the LDP Tax Research Commission – tax *zoku*. These tax experts in the LDP used to form a very influential veto point in tax and financial policy. When Abe discussed the extension of tax hike timing to spring 2016, they openly expressed their opposition to the idea. However, when they perceived Abe to be seriously considering a snap election and when even his staff mentioned the possibilities not to endorse his intra-party opponents in the election, they gradually muted their opposition (*Yomiuri*, November 14, 2014).

Campaign

In the 2014 campaign, Abe worked to keep the focus on his "Abenomics" economic policy and did not run on his exertions to pass collective self-defense and the state secrets bill (see Noble, this volume on Abenomics; Kingston, this volume, on nationalism). The campaign slogan of the LDP was "for economic recovery, this is the only way."

In their official campaign pamphlet, the LDP showcased Abenomics and emphasized economic recovery by listing policy successes such as "an increase of one million workers" or "the highest wage hike ratio in the past fifteen years." The campaign debates were over the interpretations of these figures. Instead of shifting the focus to security issues, the opposition debated the economy but brought in different figures to counter the LDP claims and to demonstrate that the recovery was not genuine (see Ikeda and Reed, this volume; Pekkanen and Reed, this volume). Overall, this reflects a successful communication strategy characteristic of Abe's second stint as prime minister.

Major policy issues, regional inequality, and the next election

Several chapters in this book deal with the main policy issues of this election, so we do not go into detail here (Maeda; Noble; Maclachlan and Shimizu; Hijino; Hughes; Kingston; Krauss; Kagotani; and Katada and Wilbur). We will just make the point that in the unified local elections in April 2015, with more than 950 local elections held at the same time, it would be unsurprising to see the LDP focus on the regional development issue (*chiho sosei* – see Hijino, this volume, on why and how this was *not* an issue in the 2014 election). As the symbol of this LDP effort, the final legislation passed in the Diet before the dissolution in 2014 was the Local Development Issue legislation. This can be considered as a reaction to the "dark side" of Abenomics with local area revitalization. At the start of his resign, Abe's popularity was fairly even across cities and countryside. However, it started to decline among people in rural areas (Figure 4.4). The *Jiyu Minshu*, the LDP's party paper, began to focus on rural development from June 2014.

The fruits of Abenomics were felt most by Japanese living in big cities. From January 2013 to March 2014, 10–20% of those in Japan's largest cities thought that the national economy was getting better. In the smaller cities, towns, and villages, however, the story was different; there, people were less likely to perceive an economic recovery. This regional gap appeared even before the consumption tax hike. Regional inequality comes to the fore even more clearly when we examine how people saw their own household's situation. In 2013, people in large cities were more likely to feel their household was in good shape, and they were less likely to feel their situations were deteriorating. Japanese living in towns and villages, on the other hand, were more likely to feel their situation was bad, and more likely to perceive a negative trend for their households. This regional difference in perception began even before the tax hike, but it certainly continued afterward, too. After the

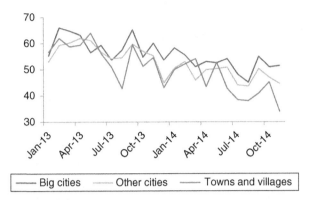

Figure 4.4   Regional gap in cabinet approval
Source: Jiji Public Opinion Poll.

tax hike, big city Japanese had no increase in perception of economic deterioration – but, again, the story was different and worse in rural areas.

Return to LDP dominance?

Returning to the question from our introduction, has the LDP begun its second hegemony in Japan? Readers might well wonder. After all, the LDP has three electoral wins in two years, including victories in both chambers and two landslide HR triumphs. The LDP is the most popular political party in the country, standing clear over an opposition field mired in disarray, self-inflicted wounds, and laughable support in the polls. Again, we think that the LDP must be considered the most favorite to win the *next* HR election – *whenever* that might be – and that is a truly remarkable statement. Membership and contributions are rising. Internal divisions are muted. Oppositional parties are fragmented. In many ways, it is a glorious time to be the LDP. However, we believe that the LDP is not as strong as the first few sentences of this paragraph might imply.

We see a few telling events in local elections. Just before and after the 2014 general elections, the LDP suffered defeats in several key gubernatorial elections, where "Abenomics" was subordinated to other issues. In Okinawa, where the gubernatorial role is decisive in the base issue, the LDP candidate was defeated in October 2014 by Takeshi Onaga, who opposed the policy of the government and LDP (see Kagotani, this volume). In January 2015, LDP leaders were shocked by the loss in Saga's gubernatorial election, where the local agricultural and fishery organization fielded their own candidate as a reaction to the JA reform attempt (see Katada and Wilbur; Maclachlan and Shimizu, this volume). Maclachlan and Shimizu (this volume) point out that the LDP may not be as "strong" as it looks by illustrating that the gap between the LDP and DPJ in the countryside narrowed between 2012 and 2014.

More importantly, perhaps, a hegemony just seems farfetched for any party these days. The LDP in 2014 may be as close as anyone gets for a while, but structural factors make it unlikely to mark a real return to LDP dominance. For one thing, the current electoral system produces greater swings, so elections can flip flop as they did in 2005, 2009, and 2012. For another, voters float more than they used to, and media and ephemeral factors matter more in election outcomes – far less reliable than the old *koenkai* system. The elections are becoming more nationalized and local factors play smaller roles (McElwain, 2012). In parallel, party leaders, instead of parties, have been more important for the past decades (Krauss and Nyblade, 2005; Jou and Endo 2015). All these factors work favorably for the Abe administration. However, the key to Abe's future is most likely the state of Japan's economy, which he proclaimed as the central issue in both 2014 and 2012 campaigns.

Notes

1. The authors thank Axel Klein, Steven R. Reed, Ethan Scheiner, and Daniel M. Smith for comments on an earlier version of this chapter.
2. Pekkanen and Pekkanen (2015: 2) assert that Abe's biggest political party headache at the outset of this administration is not the opposition but how to manage Komeito. See also Klein's chapter in this volume.
3. The data were collected from annual reports of the LDP under the Political Funds Control Act in Kanpo, the official gazette of the Japanese government.
4. The donation data were also taken from Kanpo. We included only "group" (*dantai*) donations but not donations by "individual" (*kojin*) or "political groups" (*seiji dantai*). We believe this will most accurately capture corporate donations.
5. Under SNTV, factions had incentives to run independent candidates even if the expected outcome was suboptimal for the party, and these incentives became stronger if the faction leader were challenging for the party presidency, and even stronger if the challenger entered a district with an incumbent from the challenger faction's rival faction (see Nemoto et al., 2014).
6. The web survey on the 2014 general election was conducted before the election (December 2–12, 2014) and after the election (December 18–25, 2014). The questions were asked in the first wave. The sample was drawn from Nikkei Research's pool of respondents. The composition of the target sample was

based on the proportions of regions, age, and sex among the population. The total sample size is 5093. The survey was financially supported by the JSPS Grant-in-Aid for Scientific Research (No. 25780103).

References

Endo, Masahisa, Robert Pekkanen and Steven R. Reed (2013). The LDP's path back to power. In Robert Pekkanen, Steven R. Reed and Ethan Scheiner (eds) *Japan Decides 2012: The Japanese General Election.* pp. 49–64. London: Palgrave Macmillan.

Jou, Willy, and Masahisa Endo (2015). Presidentialization of Japanese politics? Examining political leader evaluations and vote choice. *Japanese Journal of Political Science* 16(3): 357–387.

Krauss, Ellis S. and Benjamin Nyblade (2005). "Presidentialization" in Japan? The prime minister, media and elections in Japan. *British Journal of Political Science* 35(2): 357–368.

Krauss, Ellis S. and Robert J. Pekkanen (2010). *The rise and fall of Japan's LDP: Political party organizations as historical institutions.* Cornell University Press.

McElwain, Kenneth Mori (2012). The nationalization of Japanese elections. *Journal of East Asian Studies* 12: 323–350.

Martin Murphy, Sherry (2013). Women candidates and political parties in election 2012. In Robert Pekkanen, Steven R. Reed and Ethan Scheiner (eds) *Japan Decides 2012: The Japanese General Election.* pp. 49–64. London: Palgrave Macmillan.

Nemoto, Kuniaki, Ellis S. Krauss and Robert Pekkanen (2014). Over-nominating candidates, undermining the party: The collective action problem under SNTV in Japan. *Party Politics* 20(5): 740–750.

Pekkanen, Robert J. and Saadia M. Pekkanen (2015). Japan in 2014: All about Abe. *Asian Survey* 55(1): 1–16.

Pekkanen, Robert J., Benjamin Nyblade and Ellis S. Krauss (2014). The logic of ministerial selection: Electoral system and cabinet appointments in Japan. *Social Science Japan Journal* 17(1): 3–22.

5
The Democratic Party of Japan: Surviving to Fight Another Day

Fumi Ikeda and Steven R. Reed

The Democratic Party of Japan (DPJ) was founded immediately before the first election under the reformed electoral system in 1996. By its third election in 2003, the party claimed the status of the only feasible alternative to the governing Liberal Democratic Party (LDP). In 2009, its fifth election, it won power. In 2012, after three years in power, Japanese voters roundly rejected the party (Reed et al., *JD 2012*). The DPJ had simply failed to govern effectively or even consistently (Kushida and Lipscy, 2013). It was forced to share the title of "potential alternative to the LDP" with the Japan Restoration Party (JRP), which surged into a virtual tie with the DPJ (Reed, *JD 2012a*).

The rejection was severe and long-lasting. In the first polls after the 2012 election, only 11% of voters supported the DPJ as opposed to 31% for the LDP (*Asahi*, December 18, 2012). Support dropped below 10% thereafter, often falling to 4 or 5%, and was only 7% in the last poll before the 2014 election (*Asahi*, December 1, 2014). On the campaign trail DPJ candidates reported that the party's image had not improved since the 2012 defeat and many omitted the party label from their campaign pamphlets (see, e.g., *Yomiuri*, November 29, 2014).

The leadership had also been decimated. Yukio Hatoyama and Naoto Kan, the party founders and first two prime ministers, had to be disciplined for anti-party activities. After his stint as prime minister, Yukio Hatoyama had legal problems with his campaign contributions and was punished with a six-month suspension of his party membership (*Yomiuri*, July 4, 2012). He openly disagreed with party policy on several issues and began facing pressure to retire, including a movement from within his own district party branch (*Yomiuri*, November 17, 2012). He finally retired from electoral politics before the 2012 election. Kan supported an independent instead of the party nominee in the 2013 House of Councillors (HC) election in Tokyo and was punished for doing so. He remained in the party and managed to retain his seat, albeit by a narrow margin. The fact that the founding members ignored party discipline is only one of the many indications that the DPJ suffered from an extremely low level of institutionalization. The party's very survival was in doubt.

The party did not present a serious challenge to the Abe government in the 2014 election, but it did survive and even prospered relative to all other opposition parties, excepting only the JCP. The DPJ increased its seats by 11 relative to that held at the time of dissolution and by 16 relative to its performance in the 2012 election. And, as Maclachlan and Shimizu (this volume) point out, the DPJ managed to gain on the LDP in rural districts. How did they accomplish this feat? A large part of the answer lies in the failure of the Japan Renovation Party (JRP) and other "Third Force" parties (Pekkanen and Reed, this volume), but the party leadership also played an active role in preventing any further splits and rebuilding for the future.

The first step in rebuilding the DPJ was to elect a new leader. The second step was to get back in touch with its base, both its labor union supporters and its local assembly members. The party then began considering many reforms and enacted several. It also began the process of revising its policy platform and campaign themes. Finally, in August 2014, the DPJ began to move to unseat the Abe administration. Its success, in cooperation with the JIP, in forcing two ministers to resign seems to have been one reason that Abe called the snap election (Pekkanen and Reed, this volume). None of these processes, however, was complete when Abe dissolved the Diet and called the snap election.

Electing a new leader

On December 25, 2012, the DPJ chose Banri Kaieda as its next leader. Kaieda had run unsuccessfully for the Tax Party (*Zeikin-tou*) in 1986. He won his first election in Tokyo 1st district in 1993 running for the Japan New Party, joining the DPJ when it was founded in 1996. In 2011, he ran in the leadership election losing to Noda by a narrow margin. The leading candidate to replace Noda in the 2012 leadership election was Katsuya Okada, but, because he had served as deputy prime minister in the discredited Noda administration, he decided not run. Kaieda ran with the backing of those Diet members with a background in one of the socialist parties against Sumio Mabuchi, this time winning by a narrow margin (*Asahi*, December 23, 2012). Voters expressed little enthusiasm for the new leader. An Asahi Poll (December 27, 2012) asked whether respondents held hope (*kitai*) for the new leader and found that only 29% did while 61% did not.

Kaieda failed to provide strong leadership or to produce a positive image among voters. There were serious moves to replace him from within the party. Under the circumstances, however, strong leadership or a leadership election might have split the party and resulted in total disintegration. Kaieda excluded the major figures in the Noda administration from leadership positions in his administration, a move that produced much grumbling within the party (*Yomiuri*, January 17, 2013). He also moved to replace many DPJ candidates, dropping over a hundred of those who had run in 2012, causing further grumbling (*Yomiuri*, August 20, 2013). In the first wave, the party nominated only 34 non-incumbents. Despite widespread dissatisfaction in the ranks, Kaieda's ability to hold the party together during difficult times produced an "eerie stability" (*kimyou na antei*) (*Yomiuri*, November 5, 2013). None of the various moves to replace him gained momentum, yet Kaieda always seemed to be an interim figure waiting for a more dynamic leader to take over.

The Kaieda administration did, however, begin the reform process. The party established three working teams to plan the reconstruction of the party: the Party Reform Headquarters (*Tou Kaikaku Sousei Honbu*), the Committee on the Statement of Party Principles (*Tou Kouryou Iinkai*), and the Promotion of Political Reform Headquarters (*Tou Seijikaikaku Suishin Honbu*). The Party Reform Headquarters generated its first report on February 24, 2013, pointing to failures of governance that led to disunity and the weakness of local party organization as the major causes of the defeat.

Connecting with the grass roots

One of the fundamental secrets to building and sustaining a new party are links to civil society (Bolleyer, 2013). The party's most reliable support from civil society comes from the labor unions. The DPJ's major advantage over the "Third Force" parties is this link to civil society. Though the links have often been tenuous and were severely damaged by the party's failures in government, they are also a key to the party's long-term survival. The very first task under the new leadership was to visit the party's labor union supporters and do as much as possible to repair relations (*Yomiuri*, January 17, 2013).

The party also sought support from nonprofit organizations (NPOs). Sakigake (New Party Harbinger), a small party that formed one of the core components of the DPJ when it was founded in 1996, had played a central role in passing the Law for the Promotion of Specified Non-profit Activities (the NPO Law) (Pekkanen, 2006: 137–155). Hatoyama, who had belonged to Sakigake before joining the DPJ, returned to this issue after being elected prime minister under the slogan of "A New Public" (*Shin Koukyou*). After the 2012 defeat, the DPJ held meetings with NPOs at both the central and local levels, exchanging opinions and ideas and seeking support (DPJ Website, April 22, 2013; October 15 and 22, 2014).

Strengthening local party organization

A second secret to building a successful party is local party organiza-tion, and the secret to building and maintaining local party organization is winning seats in local elections. Local elections have been shown to be an effective way for small and new parties to maintain them-selves through hard times in both Western Europe (Kestel and Godmer, 2004; Bower, 2008; Cutts, 2014) and Japan (Reed, 2013b). However, it seems that each new party learns this lesson only after suffering a serious setback. The DPJ learned the lesson after the 2012 defeat and began involving local assembly members in the process of rebuilding the party.

From the end of January 2013, Kaieda, Secretary General Goushi Hosono, and acting party leader Akihiro Oohata began visiting every prefecture soliciting opinions from local DPJ members (DPJ Website, January 11, 2013). When Kaieda visited Kanagawa Prefecture in Febru-ary, the prefectural branch reported on a survey that showed that DPJ members of local assemblies were dissatisfied with the dominance of Diet members. The DPJ responded. In February, the party introduced an internet conference system linking the central and local party organiza-tions (DPJ Website, 20 February 2013). In March, it established a "Local Government Bureau" (*Chihou Kyoku*) to manage relations with local members (DPJ Website, March 4, 2013). In February, it revised the rules on the party branches by allowing local assembly members and candi-dates to establish one party branch for each municipality (DPJ Website, February 9, 2014). Until then only candidates for national elections were allowed to establish party branches.

The main reform of governance discussed was changes in the lead-ership selection process, but only one was enacted before the 2014 election. The rule had been that a primary election would be held only when the leader's term was up. If a leader resigned in the middle of his term, Diet members alone chose the new leader. The reform mandated a primary election even when a leader resigns mid-term. If Abe had not called a snap election, the DPJ might well have enacted further reforms and chosen a new leader under new rules. Indeed, the party did choose a new leader right after the election, but only one reform that had been discussed before the election was hurriedly enacted: the weight of the local party and of party members was increased. Both of these reforms were designed to strengthen the links between the central party headquarters and the party's grass roots.

Generating new policies

The Committee on the Statement of Party Principles (*Kouryou*) was established in 2011 to reexamine the statement of 1998. The 1998 statement was part of the process of merging and integrating the Liberal Party into the DPJ. The party decided that the defeat of 2012 required a similar attempt to redefine itself (DPJ Website, January 15, 2013). The final statement was published on February 24, 2013. It is only two pages long but the process and result were important steps toward building the consensus that had been so manifestly absent during the DPJ's three years in power. Local assembly members also participated in this process.

The party also published a 64-page summary of its policies on a wide variety of issues and a 15-page manifesto. The manifesto presented a well-designed attack on Abe administration's policies. The first two pages hit on collective defense and restarting nuclear power plants, Abe's most vulnerable issues. The DPJ failed, however, to forcefully articulate clear differences from the LDP on either issue. The focus of the party's campaign was, instead, Abenomics. Though this was the main issue in the election and the economy was indeed doing badly, polls indicated that more voters thought that Abenomics was succeeding than failing. The margin was 37–30% in the last Asahi public opinion poll before the election (*Asahi*, December 1, 2014). The economy was also an issue upon which Abe could debate and explain with confidence.

Finally, the DPJ was ready to go on the offensive. It employed the tactic that had helped fell the three LDP administrations that followed the Koizumi, including the first Abe cabinet, and the three DPJ administrations that followed – the alternation in power – attacking individual ministers for corruption and/or incompetence (Endo et al., *JD 2012*).

With the cooperation of the JIP, the party forced two cabinet ministers to resign (Pekkanen, Reed and Smith, this volume), but the election put this tactic on hold for the duration.

The DPJ performance out of power

The DPJ was not idle during the two years after its defeat. Indeed, given the circumstances, it is not so easy to imagine what they might have done better. The party could not withstand the stress of a leadership election or a thoroughgoing discussion of either policy or strategy. Neither was the party unified enough to face the public. Introspection and rebuilding were reasonable responses to the situation they faced.

All of the activity described above shared three characteristics. First, none of the activities was particularly creative. Indeed, the LDP was doing many of the same things (Endo and Pekkanen, this volume). Second, the activities were directed at party members and supporters, not at the general public. The only activity that generated news in the major dailies was that directed toward labor unions, and links with the unions were unlikely to generate support among the general public. The other activities were barely covered in the mass media. Third, none of these processes were complete when the election was called.

There is little reason to think that the rebuilding efforts won many votes in the 2014 election. Only 18 non-incumbent single-member district (SMD) candidates won seats in 2014, counting both incumbency and winning as either winning the SMD outright or winning a proportional representation (PR) seat. Of these 18, all had won at least once before and 17 had won at least twice previously. Only experienced DPJ candidates won and, given that many of those avoided mentioning their party label, the candidates' individual efforts seem a better explanation of their victory than the efforts of the party leadership. Indeed, there is no reason to think that the public had any idea about what the DPJ had done since its defeat. We the authors consider ourselves to be members of the attentive public but neither was aware of the DPJ's rebuilding efforts until we began research for this chapter.

The party has survived the devastating defeat of 2012, but it remains to be seen whether it is ready to continue the fight. The first real test of the effect of these party efforts and reforms was the 2015 local elections held in April. The results mirrored the results of the 2014 national election, indicating that the party's efforts have yet to have a significant effect at the local level.

References

Bolleyer, Nicole (2013). *New parties in old party systems*. Oxford: Oxford University Press.

Bower, Benjamin (2008). Local context and extreme right support in England: The British national party in the 2002 and 2003 local elections. *Electoral Studies* 27: 611–620.

Cutts, Daniel (2014). Local elections as a stepping stone: Does winning council seats boost the liberal democrats' performance in general elections? *Political Studies* 62(3): 61–380.

DPJ Website (11 January 2013). *Tou no Zennshin ni Muke Kyougi*. Discussions Toward Party Progress.

DPJ Website (15 January 2013). *To Kouryou Kentou Iinnkai Yakuinkai wo Kaisai*. Report from the Officers Meeting of the Platform Committee.

DPJ Website (20 February 2013). *Zenkoku Seisaku Tantou Kaigi wo Kaisai*. Report from a National Meeting of Policy Makers.

DPJ Website (4 March 2013). *Kyousei Shakai no tame no Kaikaku Jikkuo Chiimu*. Report on Policies to Support a Symbiotic Society from the Reform Implementation Team.

DPJ Website (22 April 2013). *Minshutou 'Atarashii Koukyou' Entaku Kaigi wo Kaisai*. The LDP Holds a Roundtable Discussion on 'A New Public'.

DPJ Website (9 February 2014). *Teiki Tou Taikai*. The Party Conference.

DPJ Website (15 October 2014). *Atarashii Koukyou: Shaikaiteki Housetu Sougou Chousa-kai Daiikkai Soukai*. A New Public: The First General Meeting of the General Social Investigation Group.

DPJ Website (22 October 2014). *Atarashii Koukyou: Shaikaiteki Housetu Sougou Chousa-kai Dainikai Soukai*. A New Public: The Second General Meeting of the General Social Investigation Group.

Kestel, Laurent and Laurent Godmer (2004). Institutional inclusion and exclusion of extreme right parties. In Eatwell and Muddle (ed.) *Western Democracies and the New Extreme Right Challenge*. pp. 133–149. London: Routledge.

Kushida, Kenji E. and Phillip Y. Lipscy (eds.) (2013). *Japan under the DPJ*. The Walter H. Shorenstein Asia-Pacific Research Center.

Pekkanen, Robert. (2006). *Japan's dual civil society: Members without advocates*. Stanford: Stanford University Press.

Reed, Steven R., Ethan Scheiner, Daniel M. Smith and Michael F. Thies (2013). The 2012 election results: The LDP wins big by default. In Robert Pekkanen, Steven R. Reed and Ethan Scheiner (eds) *Japan Decides 2012*. pp. 34–46. London: Palgrave Macmillan.

Reed, Steven R. (2013a). Challenging the two-party system: Third force parties in the 2012 election. In Robert Pekkanen., Steven R. Reed and Ethan Scheiner (eds) *Japan Decides 2012*. pp. 72–83. London: Palgrave Macmillan.

Reed, Steven R. (2013b). The survival of "third parties" in Japan's mixed-member electoral system. In Kushida, Kenji E. and Phillip Y. Lipscy (eds) *Japan under the DPJ*. pp. 103–126. Stanford, CA: The Walter H. Shorenstein Asia-Pacific Research Center.

6
From Third Force to Third Party: Duverger's Revenge?

Robert J. Pekkanen and Steven R. Reed

One of the biggest storylines of the first half of this decade in Japanese politics has been the rise of "Third Force" parties. However, the 2014 election results winnowed the Third Force down to a single party. This is a significant development and it could, as we and Ethan Scheiner suggest in the Conclusion, be the beginning of a major transition in Japanese politics (back) to mostly two major party/bloc candidate competition in the districts. Complementing chapters on the Liberal Democratic Party (LDP), Democratic Party of Japan (DPJ), and Komeito, this chapter will analyze developments in other Japanese political parties. Despite many twists and turns, we see the election results as de facto consolidation of the Third Force into a third party – one that did not exist until two months before the election.

Things were not always so clear. Only a few years ago, in 2011, "Third Force" parties seemed poised to upend Japanese politics, and the 2012 election gave some credence to the idea. Even as the 2014 election approached, there appeared to be four legitimate Third Force parties: Japan Restoration Party (JRP), Your Party (YP), People's Life Party (PLP), and Party of Future Generations (PFG). After the election, only one (the Japan Innovation Party (JIP)) remained standing. Thus, we see one of the important results of the 2014 election as the transformation from the Third Force to a third party – the JIP.

A related subplot is that the 2014 election counts among its casualties not just parties but Third Force leaders too; the election marks an end to some of the most celebrated and successful agitators or outsiders in the postwar history of Japanese political parties. It may not ever be a smart move to count out Ichirou Ozawa, but we include him, along with Shintarou Ishihara and Yoshimi Watanabe, in our list of successful outsider (or outsiderish) politicians whose influence effectively expires in 2014. Remarkably, all of these politicians had created and led Third Force parties, so their transit is symbolic of our central argument. It is definitely too early to count Tooru Hashimoto too, but the aftermath of the election could possibly add him to the list.

Third Forces arrive, split, merge, and mostly fail

The dramatic splash Tooru Hashimoto and his JRP made on the national scene in 2011 terrified established parties (see Reed, *JD 2012*). The 2012 HR election left the JRP the largest "Third Force" party and within spitting distance of becoming the official opposition, at only two seats behind the DPJ (57–55). The oldest "Third Force" party, CGP, was solidly in coalition with the winners (see Klein, *JD 2012*).

After the failure of the DPJ government, two Third Force parties, the JRP and YP, came out of the 2012 election looking like the best hope for rebuilding an opposition party capable of competing with the LDP. Both failed, split, and reorganized. The two resulting parties, PFG and JIP, fought the 2014 election. The other Third Force party, Tomorrow Party of Japan (TPJ), failed to make significant headway in the 2012 election and fell apart acrimoniously immediately after that election. The PFG fielded a rump slate of candidates in 2014, but it won only two seats.

One common thread to the failure of the Third Force parties was the failure to accomplish any significant cooperation among them or with the DPJ. There were repeated reports of one party or another seeking the cooperation of another, but nothing ever came of them. Each party was convinced that it was the wave of the future, but each party was also divided over which potential partner to choose. Indeed, the issue of which party to cooperate with was at the heart of both the JRP and YP splits.

We will begin by discussing how each of the Third Force parties failed and then turn to the story of how they split and reorganized. Finally, we will analyze the parties that ran in 2014 and how they fared with the electorate. We will discuss the parties in the chronological order in which they failed, which is the reverse of the order of finish in the 2012 election.

The failure of the TPJ: Ozawa's final failure?

The TPJ was organized less than a week before the 2012 election (Reed, *JD 2012*). Ichirou Ozawa, founding member of the Renewal Party in 1993, the New Frontier Party in 1995, and the Liberal Party in 1999, joined and then defected from the DPJ before founding the People's Life Party (PLP) in 2012. Ozawa changed the party's name to TPJ in order to recruit Yukiko Kada, governor of Shiga Prefecture, famed for her strong stance on the environment and thus seemingly a good face for the party in the wake of the triple disasters. This was a marriage of convenience that did not last long after the party's disastrous defeat in the 2012 election. Ozawa had no intention of sharing power. He immediately changed the name of the party back to PLP and began his process of rebuilding.

But, not for nothing had Ozawa earned his sobriquet "the Destroyer." Given the number of parties he had defected from, Ozawa had trouble finding any party willing to cooperate with his new venture. As the 2014 election approached, many from the PLP sought refuge in other parties, most choosing the DPJ. The party's single-member district (SMD) vote dropped from 5% to 2% and it won only two seats, losing its official status as a political party (Scheiner, Smith, and Thies, this volume). After the election, Ozawa found an unaffiliated member of the upper house willing to join his party, and the PLP regained its official status of a political party (*Yomiuri*, December 27, 2014), but for the first time since the 1980s, Ozawa is not a major player in Japanese politics.

YP fails

Yoshimi Watanabe, a defector from the LDP, founded YP right before the 2009 election. He seemed to be following a reasonable step-by-step strategy of building the party, most notably through active participation in local assembly elections. In fact, however, he was running a one-man show, which prevented the party from institutionalizing. When he was forced to resign as party leader due to legal problems, the party disintegrated (see Strausz and Pekkanen, 2014).

It slowly became clear that Watanabe was not interested in a merger with any other Third Force party. When the YP's secretary general, Kenji Eda, sought cooperation with the DPJ, Watanabe declared, "The second we link up with the DPJ is the moment we separate ourselves from the will of the people" (*Yomiuri*, January 7, 2013). The primary criticism seemed to be the DPJ's link with organized labor. While Watanabe criticized any move toward cooperation with the DPJ, Eda criticized moving closer to the LDP as a betrayal of the party's founding principles (*Yomiuri*, December 2, 2013). He accused Watanabe of turning the YP into the Watanabe faction of the LDP (*Yomiuri*, December 10, 2013).

Watanabe sought to solve the crisis by reaffirming this leadership. He got a unanimous vote of Diet members supporting his leadership (*Yomiuri*, August 6, 2013), kicked one of his critics out of the party (*Asahi and Yomiuri*, August 23, 2013), and replaced Eda as secretary general with Keiichirou Asao. He said he was not interested in forming another "cut-and-paste" party (*Yomiuri*, October 5, 2013). Eda was upset with Watanabe's domineering methods and lack of institutionalization within the party. He responded, "Even if the leader says something a million times that does not make it party policy. It must be an institutional decision" (*Yomiuri*, October 6, 2013).

In November, Eda and two other Diet members absented themselves from the vote on Abe's state secrets law, which Watanabe supported (*Yomiuri*, November 28, 2013). Fearing defections, the party decided not to punish the offenders (*Yomiuri* December 3, 2013), but by this time a split had become inevitable. Watanabe moved toward expelling the rebels while Eda prepared for a new party. The Unity Party (Yuinotou) was founded on December 18, 2013, with the explicit goal of promoting the reorganization of the opposition into a single large party (*seikai saihen*). Unity would later move toward that goal by merging with part of the JRP to form the JIP (the Japanese name changed marginally from *Ishin no Kai* to *Ishin no Tou*), a story we shall pick up below. YP for its part continued to see its role as making policy suggestions to the Abe government (*Asahi*, December 28, 2013) and delayed formal recognition of the new party as long as it could (*Yomiuri*, January 7, 2014).

Then Watanabe's legal troubles began. A weekly magazine, the scandal sheets of Japanese politics, reported that Watanabe had borrowed 800,000,000 yen from a company and failed to report it properly. When the national newspapers picked up the story it became a serious scandal (*Asahi*, March 26, 2014). Watanabe claimed it was a personal loan, but when evidence indicated the money might have been used to finance the election campaign, the legal system got involved (*Yomiuri*, April 1, 2014) and Watanabe was forced to resign from his party leadership position (*Asahi*, April 7, 2014). His legal troubles continued until after the election returns were in.

Secretary General Asao was selected as Watanabe's temporary replacement, but, like Eda before, Asao also began discussing cooperation with the JRP creating yet another rift with Watanabe, leading to talk of another split (*Yomiuri*, June 20, 2014). Soon Watanabe was demanding that Asao resign (*Yomiuri*, September 11, 2014) arguing instead for cooperation with the governing parties (*Asahi*, September 13, 2014). Watanabe held talks with Shintarou Ishihara, former co-leader of the JRP who had by this time left and formed the PFG, which, as we shall describe below, held similar attitudes toward cooperation with other opposition parties (*Asahi*, September 22, 2014).

The rift could not be repaired. Almost half of the party's Diet members signed a petition requesting the dissolution of the party (November 18, 2014). Many YP candidates sought refuge in the DPJ, a few going to the JIP. With no time to organize a new party, Watanabe ran as an independent and lost his seat, a seat he or his father had held since 1963.

The failure of the JRP

The JRP was the big winner in the 2012 election. After the election it failed to solve a series of problems common to new parties, squandered its political capital, and, like the YP, split apart.

The JRP was founded from a merger of a local party led by Tooru Hashimoto, mayor of Osaka Japan's second city, with the Sun Party led by Shintarou Ishihara, then governor of Tokyo (Reed, *JD 2012*). Hashimoto remained in Osaka while Ishihara moved back into the Diet. The two joint leaders shared a conservative agenda with Prime Minister Abe. However, Ishihara, like Watanabe, had no interest in cooperation with other opposition parties while Hashimoto, like Eda, wanted to form a large party capable of competing with the LDP. Like YP, it would be this issue that split the party before the 2014 election.

Institutionalization of Hashimoto's role also proved difficult. Hashimoto participated in party meetings via the Internet, but when the party in the Diet did something he disagreed with, he also sent angry emails (*Yomiuri*, February 28, 2013). The media was soon calling this the "east-west conflict" (*touzai tairitsu*, meaning Tokyo vs Osaka).

Hashimoto was the face of the party during the election, but Ishihara led the party in the Diet and thus tended to become the face of the party after the election. The contrast between the young and energetic Hashimoto and the octogenarian Ishihara was stark. With Ishihara running the Diet delegation, other octogenarians dominated leadership roles (*Asahi*, December 22, 2012). Then Hashimoto tarnished his own public image with a gratuitous comment on the comfort women issue (*Yomiuri*, May 14, 2013), costing the party support among women (*Yomiuri*, June 11, 2013). The JRP won only two seats in the Tokyo Prefectural Assembly election in 2013, followed by a disappointing result in the House of Councillors (HC) election (*Yomiuri*, July 31, 2013). Hashimoto took the blame (*Yomiuri*, June 24, 2013) and withdrew from active participation in national politics to focus on Osaka (*Yomiuri*, July 28, 2013).

Hashimoto had built a strong base in the Osaka city and prefectural assemblies. His primary goal in Osaka was to merge the municipal governments of Osaka and Sakai with the prefectural government and turn Osaka into a "metropolitan prefecture" (*to*) like Tokyo. In order to accomplish this goal, he had resigned as governor to run for mayor against an incumbent who opposed the project, simultaneously running his second-in-command for governor, winning both elections. The next big showdown was the Sakai mayoral election pitting Hashimoto's candidate against the incumbent. The old magic simply did not work this time. The issue was the metropolitan prefecture, and Hashimoto's candidate lost (*Asahi*, September 30, 2013). Hashimoto was popular in Osaka but his pet project was not (*Asahi*, November 19, 2013). With his string of stunning electoral victories ended, Hashimoto began to hear grumbling within his own party (*Yomiuri*, October 5, 2013), finally losing his majority in the prefectural assembly to defections and expulsions (*Yomiuri*, December 16, 2013). Since no other party supported the metropolitan idea, Hashimoto's vision was in jeopardy. The only path remaining was to hold a local referendum, bypassing the assemblies and going directly to voters, but Hashimoto could not pass an ordinance enabling such a referendum without the support of another party. As we shall see below, he found a way of using the 2014 election to gain that support.

When the Eda left YP to form Unity, both he and Hashimoto moved toward merger, an idea opposed by Ishihara (*Yomiuri*, December, 23, 2013). Ishihara began hinting that he might leave the JRP over the nuclear issue, even suggesting that a merger with the LDP was possible (Kyodo Tsushin, January 23, 2014). Compromises were made and differences papered over, but when Unity refused to accept a plank promising a new made-in-Japan constitution (*jishu kenpou*, a term implying that the current constitution was imposed upon Japan by the United States), Ishihara could compromise no longer (*Asahi*, May 24, 2014). Such a constitution was Ishihara's goal when he resigned his post as governor of Tokyo and re-entered national politics (*Yomiuri*, May 25, 2014). The decision to split was accomplished amicably. Ishihara founded the PFG and Hashimoto began negotiating a merger with Unity, the result of which was the JIP.[1]

The Third Force parties reorganize

The PFG

Ishihara's new party looked much like the Sun Party he led before merging with the JRP. The constitution was still at the top of the agenda, but another theme gained prominence: the need for a stronger defense. In this, the Abe administration was seen as an ally and Komeito as the primary enemy. Ishihara declared, "I rate the Abe administration very highly" and "I will not allow Komeito an unfettered hand" (*Yomiuri*, May 20, 2014).

The party attracted a new high-profile candidate, Toshio Tamogami, a decorated and outspoken retired Chief of Staff of the Air Defense Force. Tamogami ran against Komeito's Akihiro Oota in Tokyo 12th district, charging Komeito with preventing Prime Minister Abe from doing what was needed to protect national security (*Yomiuri*, December 4, 2014). The clearest statement came after the election. Tamogami said, "If we cannot replace the LDP–Komeito coalition with a coalition between the LDP and PFG, we will never be able to save Japan" (*Asahi*, December 20, 2014).

When the votes were counted, however, Tamogami had finished fourth out of four with less than half the Komeito vote. It must have been particularly galling that the PFG finished behind the Japanese Communist Party (JCP). The far left won over six times the vote of the far right in the PR tier (Scheiner, Smith, and Thies, this volume). The PFG won only two seats, both elderly candidates with strong personal bases in their districts who could have won without any nomination. In other words, the party label won exactly zero seats – zero in PR and no contribution to the two SMD victories. Ishihara-style conservatism has little appeal to Japanese voters, and the PFG is not an attractive alternative to Komeito as the LDP's coalition partner. The 2014 election also seems to have removed Ishihara as an important player on the national stage.

The JIP

In July 2014, the JRP and Unity formed a joint Diet fraction in the Diet surpassing the DPJ fraction for total number of seats (*Yomiuri*, July 9, 2014). Negotiations toward merger did not go smoothly as conflicts emerged over the new party name, the location of party headquarters, and the selection of the party leader (*Asahi*, September 3, 2014). In the end, Hashimoto prevailed (*Yomiuri*, September 21, 2014). JRP absorbed Unity, although the party changed its official name to JIP. Hashimoto and Eda would serve as joint leaders but, for the purposes of receiving party subsidies, the official leader would be Hashimoto. Finally, the headquarters would be in Osaka.

Eda was also much more interested in cooperating with the DPJ than was Hashimoto. Hashimoto's aversion to labor unions and the fact that the DPJ opposed his plans to merge Osaka municipal and prefectural governments stood in the way. Yet Eda was more prominent as the face of the party during the election than Hashimoto. The campaign theme was also Eda's, a proposal for reducing the number of representatives in the Diet. In most of the country, though not in Osaka, JIP also pursued electoral cooperation with the DPJ, moving candidates to other districts to avoid competing with each other in order to defeat the LDP.

The JIP lost only one seat from their number at the time of dissolution but won 13 fewer seats than the JRP had won in 2012. The JIP also won only 15.7% of the PR vote as compared to 20.4% for the JRP in 2012. Because the DPJ won 11 more seats than they had at the time of dissolution and 16 more than they had in 2012, the JIP could no longer claim to be the largest opposition party.

After the election, Hashimoto resigned from his position as joint party leader (*Yomiuri*, December 22, 2014). He made it clear, however, that his resignation was *not* permanent. He was taking leave from those duties to concentrate on Osaka's affairs. Leading up to the 2014 election, Hashimoto threatened to run a candidate against every Komeito incumbent in Osaka, even threatening to resign as mayor to run himself and having the governor do the same. In the event, however, JIP did not challenge Komeito in Osaka and Komeito agreed to vote for having a referendum on his merger proposal, though Komeito would continue to campaign for a "no" vote in the referendum (*Asahi*, December 27, 2014) (Figure 6.1).

Should the JCP be considered a Third Force party?

A big winner in the 2014 election was the JCP. The party gained 2,339,841 votes over 2012 in the SMDs and increased its seats from 8 to 21. Yet the JCP cannot be considered a Third Force party for two reasons. First, JCP policy positions are far from any of the large parties and it has little interest in compromising any of those positions in order to participate in reorganizing an alternative to the LDP. Second, we see the JCP success in 2014 based less on support for the party than on voter dissatisfaction with the choices offered by all the other parties. Voters thus used a JCP vote to express that dissatisfaction. If any of the other opposition parties were to offer a more attractive alternative to the LDP

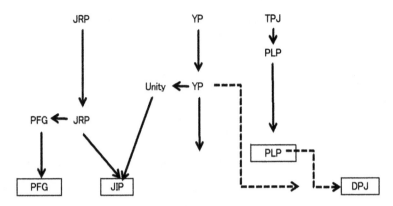

Figure 6.1 Reorganization of Third Force parties
Source: Authors.

at the next election, we should expect those JCP gains to vanish without a trace. Historically, the JCP has served as an evergreen receptacle for protest votes, but never as a Third Force.

Conclusion: From Third Force to third party

As the election approached, four legitimate Third Force parties occupied the Japanese political party scene: JRP, YP, PLP, and PFG. When the returns were tallied, however, all were essentially gone. Only those that merged, JRP and the YP splinter Unity, survived in the form of JIP. The other three parties totalled only four seats among them. YP disintegrated and the other two won two seats each, and those wins were all predicated on candidates with strong *kouenkai*, not on party organization or popularity.

Beyond the individual stories of the parties related above, there are two possible and related larger patterns. First, party leaders more interested in cooperation with the LDP generally lost out to those seeming to prefer forming an opposition capable of opposing the LDP. This is not universal, as the future of Tooru Hashimoto is unclear. However, the case of YP is instructive. The YP party leader who wanted to form an opposition, Kenji Eda, now helps to lead the third party JIP. The party leader more interested in cooperating with the LDP, Yoshimi Watanabe, saw his party disappear along with a seat his family had held for over 50 years. Second is of course the consolidation of several Third Force parties into a third party. This coalescence into the JIP reflects the type of consolidation we might expect from the cold logic of Duverger's Law. The hard resource allocation choice forced upon the opposition resulting in fewer candidates and better de facto opposition coordination (Smith, this volume) also may reveal another aspect of this same pattern.

How far will this go? We could imagine Japan returning to a 2 ½ party system, with the erstwhile Third Force merging or coordinating with the DPJ and Komeito surviving mostly due to the PR vote. The Third Force consolidation into a third party is a way stage to a LDP vs DPJ/JIP mostly two-party system but this is not the only possibility. Japanese might see continued estrangement among the opposition parties (meaning DPJ and JIP, as JCP will remain aloof). Or, another round of party births, splinterings, and recombinations could begin anew. However, if the DPJ and JIP settle their differences enough to present a more or less unified alternative to the LDP, then the 2014 election has been an important turning point in the transition.

Note

The authors thank Axel Klein, Ethan Scheiner, and Daniel Markham Smith for their useful comments on an earlier version of this chapter.

1. See Pekkanen, Reed, and Smith, this volume, for more detail. Also see Pekkanen and Pekkanen (2015) for a closer tracking of the, in their words, "telenovela-like" gyrations of these parties in 2014.

Bibliography

Klein, Axel (2013). Komeito – the First Third Force. In Robert Pekkanen, Steven R. Reed and Ethan Scheiner (eds) *Japan Decides 2012: The Japanese General Election.* London: Palgrave Macmillan.

Pekkanen, Robert J. and Saadia M. Pekkanen (2015). Japan in 2014: All about Abe. *Asian Survey* 55(1): 103–118.

Reed, Steven R. (2013). Challenging the two-party system: Third force parties in the 2012 election. In Robert Pekkanen, Steven R. Reed and Ethan Scheiner (eds) *Japan Decides 2012: The Japanese General Election.* London: Palgrave Macmillan.

Strausz, Michael and Robert J. Pekkanen (2014). The rise and fall of Your Party. *Paper presented at the Annual Meeting of the Association for Asian Studies.* pp. 27–30.

7
Komeito – Rock "n" Row the Coalition Boat

Axel Klein

When at 9:15 pm on election night Komeito's Secretary General Yoshihisa Inoue appeared on national television to comment on the results, he seemed quite content. His party had secured 35 seats, more than ever before under the current electoral system. All nine Komeito candidates in single-member districts (SMDs) had been successful and 7.3 million votes in the proportional representation (PR) tier meant another 26 seats. Just a few weeks after Komeito's 50th anniversary (cf. McLaughlin, 2014) and 15 years after the coalition with the LDP had begun, things looked good for the party.

Inoue duly thanked Komeito's voters for their support and emphasized the party's main tasks: welfare, peace, human rights, and the introduction of a reduced consumption tax for daily necessities (*NHK*, December 16, 2014). While the first three issues had always been part of Komeito's core program, the reduced consumption tax (hereafter RCT) was a comparatively new policy by which Komeito tried to reconcile its core voters with a tax the party had strongly rejected in the 1980s, unwillingly accepted in the late 1990s, and in 2012 even agreed to raise twice.

The debate and negotiations surrounding these two hikes are one piece of evidence to assess how Komeito fared as junior coalition partner during the two years under examination. A second central issue is collective self-defense (CSD), actively pushed by the Liberal Democratic Party (LDP) but at odds with Komeito's pacifist principles. Here and more than in any other policy area, the party found itself politically squeezed between its coalition partner and its main support group Souka Gakkai.[1]

But the key question of this chapter not only refers to Komeito's achievements in terms of policies but also to those on the electoral front. Judging only from the number of seats, both the House of Councillors

(HC) election in 2013 and the House of Representatives (HR) election in 2014 made the party's performance look like a success. The number of votes for the party, however, has not grown. Instead, low turnouts and an opposition in disarray (introductory chapter, this volume) were the causal factors behind the increase in Komeito's parliamentary seats. What is more, during the second half of 2014, Souka Gakkai increasingly showed signs of dissatisfaction with the party (see below).

As these introductory paragraphs forebode, a precise cost/benefit analysis for this coalition would be a very complex task, too complex in fact for the volume at hand. It may therefore be admissible to begin this chapter with a few simple reminders of what life looks like as a junior coalition partner (cf. Hasunuma and Klein, 2014). First, no party wins them all; compromise is unavoidable. Second, a junior partner like Komeito often scores fewer points than its bigger counterpart. Third, Komeito continuously needed to maneuver between the expectations of its core supporters and their political ideals on the one side and the LDP with its often diverging demands on the other. As the next pages will show, this resulted in periods of cooperation and periods of opposition between both parties. Komeito sometimes rowed and sometimes rocked the coalition boat.

This chapter will proceed with a look at Komeito's endeavors in the policy arenas of consumption tax and CSD, followed by short summaries on the party's efforts regarding social policies, "Abenomics," and foreign relations. These policy fields are crucial to understand what the party gained from its partnership with the LDP. The chapter then turns to elections, including the 2013 HC elections and, in more detail, the 2014 HR elections. The data this chapter is based upon stem from party publications, official election results, reports in Japan's mass media, and interviews with politicians.

Consumption Tax

From Komeito's perspective, the story of the consumption tax (hereafter CT) is a tale of promises, disappointments, and repeated struggle for compensation. While in opposition, the party flatly rejected the introduction of the tax. While in government, it tried to channel as much of the revenue to low-income households and into the social security systems. In 2012, then Prime Minister Yoshihiko Noda suggested a first CT hike to 8% in April 2014 and a second raise to 10% in October 2015. Because the opposition had a majority in the HC, he needed the cooperation of the LDP and Komeito. While the LDP was willing to agree in exchange for general elections, Komeito initially rejected the plan (*Asahi*, January 6, 2012). After a few months of bargaining, however, the party agreed in exchange for concessions. To its supporters Komeito explained it had won the guarantee that (1) the additional tax revenue would only be used for social security, (2) a reduced consumption tax on daily necessities would be introduced, and (3) further measures would be taken to help low-income households (*Asahi*, June 16, 2012).

In Komeito's manifesto for the 2012 election, the party stated that it was working hard for the introduction of the RCT along the CT hike (Komeito, 2012), and a week after the LDP–Komeito coalition had regained power, the LDP's General Secretary Shigeru Ishiba came out in support of the RCT (*Asahi*, December 23, 2012). It did not take long, however, until Komeito's expectations were disappointed. Arguing that the necessary administrative preparations could not be completed in time, the Ministry of Finance and the LDP postponed the RCT.

After this first setback, Komeito demanded the introduction for October 2015 when the second CT hike was due. The LDP's tax experts, however, warned that time was too short to agree on what consumer goods would be considered "daily necessities" and thus fall into the range of application of the RCT. Eventually, Komeito was left without any guarantee but only with the LDP's promise that "we will strive to introduce the RCT alongside the second consumption tax hike to 10%" (*Asahi*, January 24, 2013).

As compensation, Komeito successfully pushed for a cash allowance for low-income households to take effect shortly after the first CT hike, a measure that also originated from the 2012 negotiations.[2] Although Komeito's initial demand was considerably cut by the LDP, the law stipulated that households exempted from municipal tax would receive a one-time cash allowance of 10,000 yen per person, low-income pensioners would be allotted an extra 5,000 yen. Households receiving child allowance would also find 10,000 yen per child in their bank account. People living on social welfare (*seikatsu hogo*), however, would receive nothing (*Yomiuri*, March 18, 2014).[3]

Then the issue of the RCT was moved to the backburner until November 2014 when Prime Minister Abe called the snap election and delayed the CT hike by 18 months. As a consequence, Komeito had to wait at least another year and a half until its election promise from 2012 would be realized. All the party got from the LDP was agreement to include a sentence into its manifesto that would stress the coalition's strive to introduce the RCT by October 2017.[4] During the 2014 election Komeito presented itself as the only party to push for the introduction of the RCT. The LDP, on the other hand, mostly ignored the issue.

As a consequence, at the end of 2014, the RCT still was as much a thing of the future as it had been in 2012. Komeito's efforts so far had resulted in a one-time cash allowance and in keeping the issue on the agenda. While Abe left no doubt about the date of the second CT hike in April 2017, the wording with regard to the RCT still left a backdoor open for another delay. What was more, neither the list of target items nor the rate of an RCT had been decided upon, leaving more room for maneuvering between the coalition partners.

CSD

The negotiations about the second core issue under examination also remained unfinished. Out of the debate on constitutional revision developed the less complex but still controversial question of whether Japan's self-defense forces (SDF) would be allowed to conduct CSD even outside of Japanese territory and when close allies were under attack. A "yes" would mean a break with the way the constitution had been interpreted by all Japanese governments since 1972.

During the campaign for the HC election of 2013, Komeito took a passive stance on constitutional revision. In its manifesto this issue did not feature prominently. While the LDP was actively campaigning for an "autonomous constitution adequate for Japan" (*nihon ni fusawashii jishu kenpô*), Komeito considered the existing constitution to have been of great merit for the positive development of Japan. Instead of an all-out constitutional revision the party campaigned only for additional contents (*kaken*) along three basic principles: respect for basic human rights, sovereignty of the people, and permanent peace. Komeito was also willing to add two clauses to Article 9: (1) acknowledging the SDF as the smallest (possible) military organization necessary for defending the country and (2) stating that Japan's contributions to the international community should be based on the ideal of pacifism (Komeito, 2013: 33). Party head Natsuo Yamaguchi expressed strong opposition to any form of CSD (*Asahi*, December 1, 2014). It was this clear stance and the self-portrayal as the "party of peace" (*heiwa no tou*) that Komeito was measured against when the LDP pushed toward CSD in 2014. Opponents of CSD, like Souka Gakkai or the daily *Asahi*, expressed their hope that Komeito would stop Abe (*Asahi*, January 25, 2014), and the party itself reminded the public that slowing down hawkish and nationalist initiatives of the LDP was a major reason for being part of the coalition government (KHI, 2014: 262–279).

What followed was about half a year of negotiation, during which Komeito negotiated with the LDP, demanding a more defensive stance,

bargaining for concessions, and protracting the decision-making process (cf. *Asahi*, June 25, 2014). Eventually, both parties agreed on
the following conditions that would have to be met before any CSD
outside Japanese territories could be allowed. The cabinet decided to
interpret Article 9 to permit the minimum military defensive action
needed if

(1) a military attack is directed against Japan or against a close ally, and
    the existence of Japan is threatened, and if a clear danger arises that
    the life, right to freedom, and pursuit of happiness of the people will
    be fundamentally undermined;
(2) there is no other appropriate measure to maintain the country and
    protect the population from this threat.

Yamaguchi and other party representatives expressed their conviction
that hardly anything had changed in terms of constitutional interpretation. On its English website[5] Yamaguchi was quoted: "Our success maintaining the basic logic of the government's interpretation
expressed in 1972, which has served as the basis for subsequent government interpretations of Article 9, was key in ensuring logical consistency
[...] So-called collective self-defense, in which the purpose is to defend
another country, is neither recognized now nor in the future."

Komeito politicians on the subnational level, however, lamented that
it was hard for them to convince voters, among others because the content of the conditions and the issue itself were complicated.[6] Lower
House member Isamu Ueda summarized in his email newsletter (July 7,
2014) that the decision was based on a "realism that strikes the right
balance of a complicated issue." Critical reporting in the mass media
was not helpful as it contradicted Komeito's view and raised doubts as
to whether the "party of peace" image was still justified (*Asahi*, June 25,
2014; September 22, 2014; November 23, 2014).[7]

What made it even more difficult for the party was that over the following months Abe showed a different way of interpreting the cabinet
decision. While Komeito considered economic reasons to be insufficient to dispatch SDF, Abe wanted the Strait of Hormuz to be cleared
from sea mines to ensure safe oil supplies (*Asahi*, October 7, 2014).
While Komeito insisted it was virtually impossible to let SDF defend any
third country, Abe contradicted (*Shukan Asahi*, July 25, 2014: 18; *Asahi*,
November 23, 2014; December 4, 2014).

Still, so far the coalition only had a cabinet decision but no law. As was
the case with the consumption tax, the compromise the coalition had

agreed upon left enough leeway to challenge Komeito's understanding of the agreement. Just as the date of the RCT introduction, its percentage, and the range of application were still open for further discussion, so was the concrete meaning the conditions Komeito had celebrated as a pacifist victory were to take.[8]

Social policies

In its 2012 manifesto, Komeito had proposed a typical list of welfare policies that catered mostly to its main constituencies: housewives and their families in low- and middle-income households (cf. Ehrhardt, 2014; Klein, *JD* 2012). After the 2012 election, however, Komeito managed to leave its mark in a new and pronounced form by establishing a fourth major pillar to social policies. Next to pension, long-term care, and health services, the party pushed child-rearing as a comprehensive social policy field. Based on the expectations of extra tax revenue coming from the CT hike, the party had successfully demanded to channel parts of the larger social budget to childcare and families, an extension to the otherwise mostly senior recipient groups of social benefits.

The LDP had grown an interest in extending childcare facilities in order to make it easier for mothers to enter the labor market and consequently even agreed to waive kindergarten fees for three- to six-year-olds (Komeito, 2013: 20). Komeito, on the other hand, presented these policies as part of its efforts to help families with children. The party also presented a "new child-rearing system" (*kosodate shin seido*) which featured prominently on its website and publications.[9] The LDP did not mention this key policy of its coalition partner at all (see also Gaunder, this volume).

In the 2013 negotiations with Komeito, the Ministry of Finance as well as the LDP had managed to delay most of that spending to the second CT hike originally scheduled for October 2015. When that hike was postponed to April 2017 Komeito's campaign seemed to run aground, but in January 2015, the coalition agreed to still increase support for families with children. Of the 8.2 trillion yen expected from the first CT hike 1.35 trillion (ca. 15%) was allotted to childcare and other family policies, with an additional 140 billion yen coming from an increase in co-payment from users of nursing care facilities (*JT*, January 11, 2015).

Other decisions on social policy may have reminded voters that the previous DPJ government had been considerably more generous. Even though the LDP–Komeito coalition agreed to waive high school tuition fees for low-income families (*Yomiuri*, September 6, 2013), the DPJ had decided in 2010 to waive tuition fees for *all* families. Now only about one-fifth of all households with high school children would profit from the new policy. The same was true for the DPJ's benefits for single mothers that the LDP–Komeito coalition drastically cut and repackaged as "support for self-help." Economist Noriko Hama (2013) called these decisions "the largest cut ever in welfare assistance." Komeito justified the cuts (which it called "suitable adaptations") with lower costs of living due to deflation and the necessity to keep social benefits lower than wages (Komei Shinbun, January 30, 2013).[10]

Abenomics

In general, Komeito supported the LDP's economic policy but neither did it mention the term "Abenomics" in its 2013 and 2014 manifestos nor did it elaborate on the negative effects of Abe's "three arrows" (another term that was missing from the 2014 manifesto) on Komeito's core clientele (Noble, this volume). For one, Abe's labor policies reduced the low level of protection of irregular workers even further and made it easier for companies to lay off employees. While companies were quickly granted substantial tax reductions, the ordinary consumer had to accept a higher consumption tax with another one yet to come.

The biggest problem for Komeito, however, was that the desired "trickle down" effect hardly materialized and especially low- and middle-income households seemed to profit little if at all from Abenomics. Since Komeito's economic growth strategy relied exclusively on higher wages and more private consumption, it became increasingly difficult for the party to argue its case. All it did was evoke a "positive [economic] spiral" (*koujunkan*) and economic recovery from which families should profit (Komeito, 2014).

Foreign policy

Even though foreign policy had never been Komeito's strong suit, the party has a long history of mending and grooming relations with China. As early as 1969 the party convention passed a resolution demanding the normalization of relations with the People's Republic, spurred on by Souka Gakkai's then president Daisaku Ikeda. Over the next years Komeito, albeit in opposition, played an important role in Japan's rapprochement toward the PRC. In 1971, the party sent a mission to Beijing to meet Prime Minister Enlai Zhou, a move that was later credited with having been vital in restoring diplomatic relations between both countries (KHI 2014: 102–118; *Yomiuri*, January 26, 2013).

During the Abe years, Yamaguchi took the lead in improving relations with China. In January 2013, Yamaguchi was the first Japanese politician to meet President Jinping Xi. Komeito's party leader was chosen by Abe to deliver a handwritten letter asking for a meeting with his Chinese counterpart. Even though Xi stressed the importance of a dialogue between both countries when he met Yamaguchi on January 25, 2013, Chinese military planes still flew over the disputed Diaoyu/Senkaku islands. Nevertheless, Komeito's role as intermediary between Abe and Xi was clearly welcomed by both sides and was an asset the party contributed to the coalition (Krauss, this volume).

Elections

Next to the HR elections of 2014, three other elections need to be mentioned first. The most important one doubtlessly was the 2013 HC election. Almost 7.6 million voters cast their ballot for Komeito in the PR tier, resulting in seven seats, one more than before. All four Komeito candidates running in multi-member districts were elected. Together with its nine uncontested seats the party now had 20 members in the HC, compared to 115 of the LDP. The major consequence of this election was that it ended the *nejire kokkai* (introductory chapter, this volume).

A second election worth mentioning here was the gubernatorial election in Saga Prefecture (see Pekkanen, Reed and Smith, this volume). Both LDP and Komeito endorsed Takashi Koriya, a former bureaucrat from METI, who – according to an LDP survey – led his competitors by ten percentage points before campaigning started. Over the next two weeks, however, this margin vaporized and on July 13, 2014, Taizou Mikazuki, a former Lower House member for the DPJ, won. According to an exit poll conducted by the daily *Asahi*, more than half of Komeito's supporters did not vote for Koriya. The paper reasoned that the cabinet decision on CSD may have been a major cause for this unwillingness to follow Komeito's candidate recommendation (*Asahi*, August 01, 2014).

The gubernatorial election in Okinawa displayed a conflict between Komeito's headquarter and its local branch. While the national level of the party supported the relocation of US military facilities from Ginowan to Henoko, the prefectural chapter rejected the plan (Kagotani, this volume). As a result, party headquarters decided in October 2014 not to endorse any candidate and instead call a "free vote" (*jishu touhyou*) when the incumbent Hirokazu Nakaima ran against the former mayor of Naha, Takeshi Onaga. Nakaima, supported by Komeito's head-quarter and the LDP, lost. The prefectural Komeito's candidate Onaga became governor and repeatedly angered the national government (cf. *Asahi*, March 27, 2015).

Preparations for the HR elections in 2014 were short and uncontroversial. As soon as rumors spread regarding general elections, Komeito and Souka Gakkai representatives met on November 11, 2014, to prepare for the coming campaign (*Asahi*, November 12, 2014). Candidate selection was simple. All 31 incumbents ran again. The nine candidates who had won SMDs in 2012 were re-nominated, including former party head Akihiro Oota (Tokyo 12), who had already been too old by Komeito's own statutes in 2012 but now even exceeded the maximum nomination age by two more years.[11] On the 11 PR lists, all 22 incumbents were nominated on the same list positions as in 2012. Among the 20 additional candidates, ten were new (Smith, this volume). Komeito reduced the number of PR candidates from 45 in 2012 to 42, adapting to the vote share they expected to win.[12]

Like in 2012, the cooperation between Komeito and the LDP meant that both parties would maintain the division of labor: none of the 283 LDP candidates running in SMDs would compete against a Komeito politician and about 200 of them were officially endorsed by the junior coalition partner. Estimates ran from 10,000 to 25,000 votes Komeito could mobilize for Liberal Democrats in SMDs, apparently depending on the mutual trust and commitment of LDP candidates toward local Komeito branches (*Shukan Asahi*, December 12, 2014: 18; Klein and Reed, 2014: 36).[13] In return, the nine Komeito candidates running in SMDs would enjoy Liberal Democratic support. Another part of the cooperation was that LDP candidates in SMDs were supposed to ask their supporters to vote Komeito in PR, a strategy that in the past had not produced as much for Komeito as the well-mobilized voters of Souka Gakkai had contributed to the LDP's successes (Klein, 2013: 93–94).

With national aggregate data not available, media reports on exit polls in certain prefectures can only tell parts of the story. These spotlights show a variety of ways electoral cooperation between the LDP and Komeito would work (or not). In Miyagi Prefecture, for example, 63–84% of those who voted Komeito in PR also voted for the LDP candidates in the five SMDs. In Nara 1, 76% of Komeito PR voters also voted for the Liberal Democrat. Kagoshima 3, however, saw a majority of Komeito supporters (56%) chose the incumbent independent candidate over the new Liberal Democrat (40%). Kagawa 2 saw a 55%/36%

split of Komeito supporters between the LDP and the DPJ candidate. In Yamanashi 2, Komeito voters were almost evenly divided between the LDP (47%) and the independent candidate (45%). In Hokkaido 10, Asahi's exit polls showed that 75% of LDP supporters voted for Komeito's Inatsu.[14]

A second measure to raise electoral chances was Komeito's successful attempt to avoid direct competition with the Japan Innovation Party (JIP). In spite of temporary confrontation between both sides (Smith; Pekkanen and Reed, both this volume), only one JIP candidate, Youichirou Aoyaki, ran against a Komeito competitor, Isamu Ueda (Kanagawa 6), and ended up second (see Table 7.1).

In Komeito's manifesto for the 2014 HR campaign the party featured the idea of "regional revitalization" (*chihou sousei*) to meet the challenges of the country. A long list of issues should be dealt with, the party argued, by focusing on rural and semi-urban areas: economic growth, deflation, shrinking population, energy, employment of young people and women, education, child-rearing, health, long-term care, and pensions (Komeito, 2014). The nine candidates running in SMDs mostly built their campaigns on these issues and – compared to Liberal Democrats – addressed fewer local issues (Arai, this volume). Still, some could be found: Hisashi Inatsu (Hokkaido 10) saw new chances for coal from Hokkaido to solve the energy problems of his country; Kazuyoshi Akabane (Hyogo 2) presented policies "for our beloved Kobe"; Isamu Ueda (Kanagawa 6) demanded better noise protection for the neighborhood of the Hodogaya Bypass.

As a result of its electoral cooperation with the LDP and its truce with the JIP, the competitive situation for Komeito in SMDs became less challenging. In Osaka 3, 5, and Hyogo 8 the only competitors were Communists, who on average took home 41.5% of the votes and could not defeat Komeito's candidates.[15] In Osaka 6, a third but unpromising PLFP candidate entered the race, mostly taking votes from the Communist. Komeito's Shin'ichi Isa won this SMD with more than 50% of the vote. In Hyogo 2 and Hokkaido 10, a DPJ candidate joined the competition next to the Communist. Compared to the SMDs with only one competitor, Komeito's vote share dropped here by about 10%. Finally, there were three districts with four candidates. In all of them Komeito won with an average of 41.5% (cf. Table 7.1).

The party contributed 10.74% of all coalition seats in the HR and 14.81% in the HC. According to Gamson's law (cf. Gamson, 1961; Browne and Franklin, 1973), Komeito could have been expected to fill

Table 7.1 Distribution of vote shares in SMDs with a Komeito candidate

SMD, candidate, vote share	Candidate from …				
	JIP	DPJ	PLFP	PFG	JCP
Hokkaido 10 H. Inatsu 48.5%		39.8%			11.6%
Tokyo 12 A. Ota 41.6%			18.9%	18.5%	21%
Kanagawa 6 I. Ueda 39.9%	26.5%	22%			11.6%
Osaka 3 S. Satou 57.2%					42.8%
Osaka 5 T. Kunishige 57.5%					42.5%
Osaka 6 S. Isa 56.3%			18.4%		25.3%
Osaka 16 K. Kitagawa 43.2%		24.8%		17.2%	14.8%
Hyogo 2 K. Akaba 49.3%		30.8%			19.9%
Hyogo 8 H. Nakano 60.9%					39.1%

Source: Election data from Yomiuri Online (www.yomiuri.co.jp/election/shugiin /2014/?from=ycnav2; accessed February 15, 2015).

two cabinet positions. As with all other previous coalition cabinets, however, the party only filled one (Oota kept his position as Minister of Land, Infrastructure, Transport, and Tourism). As Linda Hasunuma and I argue (2014), Komeito's disclaimer may have been compensated with other concessions. In addition, it is plausible to assume that cabinet positions are of much more importance to the LDP than to Komeito (see, e.g., *Shukan Asahi*, July 25, 2014: 20).

Conclusion

This chapter tried to draw a rough picture of how Komeito fared as junior coalition partner of the LDP. The result is ambivalent. One key characteristic of the coalition (and probably most other coalitions) is that those measures that partners agree upon may be labeled differently by the parties but are still easily passed. That was true for the massive public construction budget to rebuild the Northeast as it was true for the extension of childcare facilities. While the LDP could continue its pork barrel politics and entice women to ease the country's labor shortage, Komeito framed the same policies as restoration of life lines and support for families with children.

Controversial policies like the RCT or CSD, however, led to confrontation and prolonged negotiations. Here, Komeito repeatedly switched to the mode of a ruling opposition that tried to represent and defend the interests of its core voters against the much bigger coalition partner. Still, with complex issues at hand, it sometimes proved difficult for the party to convince its own voters of the rightness of its actions. As parts of the media criticized Kōmeitō for not behaving like a "party of peace," many supporters apparently suspected their political representatives to have abandoned core ideals. Finding itself between a rock (LDP) and a hard place (voters) surely was no new experience for the party, but it was one that always entailed the danger of losing electoral support.[16]

Next to permanently explaining its policy choices and compromises to voters, Komeito also tried to prime or redirect voters' attention. Articles and topics in the party's daily *Komei Shinbun* or the monthly *Koumei Geppou* reflected this attempt. From the party's point of view it was destructive when newspapers and television kept controversial issues center-stage. Yamaguchi, for example, claimed that the people expected economic recovery, reconstruction of the northeast, and better social security. Only 10% of the population, he asserted, were interested in the CSD issue (*Shukan Asahi*, July 25, 2014: 18).

Clearly, Komeito preferred rowing the coalition boat over rocking it, but after the 2014 elections the key question for the party seemed to be how far its core voters would be willing to accept compromises on military engagement of Japan's self-defense forces. Back in 2001, when Komeito agreed to the Peace Keeping Operation law that would make the SDF part of the "war against terror," the backlash within Souka Gakkai was considerable (cf. Fisker-Nielsen, 2012). Now, the coalition was again navigating toward an increase in military activity, and as in

2001, Komeito's voters were considering a third option of dealing with the coalition boat: jumping it.

Notes

Many thanks to Steven Reed for his data collections and to all editors and Dan Smith for their helpful comments.

1. Souka Gakkai (literally, the "Value Creation Study Society") is a Japanese lay Buddhist movement (cf. McLaughlin 2009, 2012). Its then president Daisaku Ikeda was the key figure in founding Komeito.
2. One-time cash allowances are a typical policy instrument of Komeito (see, e.g., Hasunuma and Klein 2014: 56–58).
3. More on Komeito's social welfare policies below; see also Komeito's website at www.komei.or.jp/more/understand/keigenzeiritsu2.html (accesed February 20, 2015).
4. Komeito's website at www.komei.or.jp/more/understand/keigenzeiritsu2.html (accessed February 20, 2015).
5. www.komei.or.jp/en/policy/stands/20140702.html (accessed February 23, 2015).
6. Personal interview with Masanari Takahashi, member of the Fukuoka prefectural assembly, on November 11, 2014, Fukuoka; cf. also *Asahi*, May 18, 2014 (Nagoya edition), May 21, 2014 (Akita edition), and *Shukan Asahi* July 25, 2014.
7. See also Pekkanen and Pekkanen (2015).
8. When Abe was pressed in parliament to elaborate on what an "evident danger" (*meihaku na kiken*) would be, he replied: "An evident danger is evident so there is nothing vague about it" (*meihaku na kiken to iu no ha meihaku na no de aimai na mono deha nai*) (*Asahi*, October 7, 2014).
9. Among others in various issues of the monthly Komei Geppou, see also www.komei.or.jp/news/detail/20140313_13488 (accessed February 28, 2015).
10. These examples and the above-mentioned exemption from one-time payments of those living on social welfare are evidence that Komeito's social policies are far less generous than those of Western European Socialist or Social Democratic Parties.
11. Komeito's statutes excluded candidates from nomination if they turned 69 while in office but Oota was not the only exception to the rule. Secretary General Yoshihisa Inoue (age 67, No. 1 on the Tohoku list) and Yoshio Urushibara (age 70, No. 1 on the Hokuriku Shinetsu list) also exceeded the age limit. Komeito justified their nomination with the lack of time for finding successors (Yomiuri, November 19, 2014; Smith, this volume).
12. The party fielded two candidates less in Kita-Kantou and one less in Chugoku (source: www.komei.or.jp/campaign/shugiin/hireiku.php (accessed February 15, 2015)).
13. Also, personal interviews with Masanari Takahashi, member of the Fukuoka prefectural assembly, on November 11, 2014, Fukuoka, and Katsuei Hirasawa, member of the lower house for the LDP, on November 11, 2010, Tokyo.

14. Sources: Respective prefectural editions of *Asahi* from December 16, 2014. Not all local editions carried these data and those that did published different bits and pieces from the exit polls.
15. In Hyogo 8, turnout reached a low with 45.87%. A little over 10% of the ballot sheets were either left blank or made invalid (*Asahi*, December 16, 2014, Hyogo edition).
16. In his interview with me, Masanari Takashi explained how difficult it was for him and most other Komeito politicians on the subnational level to argue against the mass media story line that Komeito had given in to hawkish LDP demands (*Fukuoka*, November 11, 2014).

References

Browne, Eric C. and Mark N. Franklin (1973). Aspects of coalition payoffs in European parliamentary democracies. *The American Political Science Review* 67: 453–469.

Gamson, William A. (1961). A theory of coalition formation. *American Sociological Review* 26: 373–382.

Ehrhardt, George (2014). Housewive voters and Kōmeitō policies. In George Ehrhardt, Axel Klein, Levi McLaughlin and Steven R. Reed (eds) *Kōmeitō – Politics and Religion in Japan*. pp. 187–211. Berkeley: Institute of East Asian Studies, University of California.

Fisker-Nielsen, Anne-Mette (2012). *Religion and politics in contemporary Japan*. New York: Routledge.

Hama, Noriko (2013). Abe's 15-month reversal budget fudges cost of swapping people and butter for concrete and guns. *Japan Times*, February 4, 2013.

Hasunuma, Linda and Axel Klein (2014) Kōmeitō in coalition. In George Ehrhardt, Axel Klein, Levi McLaughlin and Steven R. Reed (eds) *Kōmeitō – Politics and Religion in Japan*. pp. 240–267. Berkeley: Institute of East Asian Studies, University of California.

KHI (Komeitoshi hensan iinkai) (2014). *Koumeitou 50nen no ayumi* [The 50 year walk of Komeito]. Tokyo: Komeito kikanshi iinkai.

Klein, Axel (2013). Komeito – The first third force. In Robert Pekkanen, Steven R. Reed and Ethan Scheiner (eds) *Japan Decides 2012. The Japanese General Election*. pp. 84–98. London: Palgrave.

Klein, Axel and Steven R. Reed (2014). Religious groups in Japanese electoral politics. In George Ehrhardt, Axel Klein, Levi McLaughlin and Steven R. Reed (eds) *Kōmeitō – Politics and Religion in Japan*. pp. 25–49. Berkeley: Institute of East Asian Studies, University of California.

Komeito (2012). *Manifesto 2012. Nihon saiken* [Rebuilding Japan]. Tokyo: Komeito.

Komeito (2013). *Manifesto 2013*. Tokyo: Komeito.

Komeito (2014). *Manifesto 2014*. Tokyo: Komeito.

LDP (2014). *Keiki kaifuku, kono michi shika nai.*[Economic Recovery, there is no other way]. Tokyo: Liberal Democratic Party.

McLaughlin, Levi (2009). *Sōka Gakkai in Japan*. PhD dissertation, Princeton University.

McLaughlin, Levi (2012) Sōka Gakkai in Japan. In Inken Prohl and John Nelson (eds) *Brill Handbook of Contemporary Japanese Religion.* pp. 269–307. Leiden: Brill.

McLaughlin, Levi (2014). Electioneering as religious practice: A history of Sōka Gakkai's political activities to 1970. In George Ehrhardt, Axel Klein, Levi McLaughlin and Steven R. Reed (eds) *Kōmeitō – Politics and Religion in Japan.* pp. 51–82. Berkeley: Institute of East Asian Studies, University of California.

Pekkanen, Robert J and Saadia M. Pekkanen (2015). Japan in 2014: All about Abe. *Asian Survey* 55: 103–118.

Shūkan Asahi = first published in 1922, is a weekly magazine published by the Asahi Shimbun with a circulation of about 170,000 (2015) (source: Nihon zasshi kyōkai at: www.j-magazine.or.jp/magadata/index.php?module= list&action=list&cat1cd=1&cat3cd=2&period_cd= (access: June 2015)

Part III

Campaigning, Candidates, Districts

8

The Abe Cabinet and Public Opinion: How Abe Won Re-election by Narrowing Public Debate

Yukio Maeda

Prime Minister Shinzo Abe successfully managed his second premiership from December 2012 until his first cabinet overhaul in September 2014. Abe shuffled his cabinet in order to consolidate his power and to accelerate efforts to achieve his policy goals. No one expected that he would call a snap election just two months later. Unfortunately for Abe, two ministers were forced to resign just a month after joining the cabinet due to scandals, an embarrassment ominously reminiscent of the nightmare of successive ministerial resignations in his first premiership (2006–2007). Early in November 2014, a preliminary report on third-quarter GDP growth was unexpectedly disappointing, signaling that "Abenomics" had not accelerated the sluggish economic recovery. Abe decided to postpone the scheduled hike of the consumption tax from October 2015 to April 2017. In this unpromising political context, he abruptly called a general election in order to hear "the voice of the people" (see Pekkanen, Reed, and Smith, this volume for the general context of this election). Using various opinion polls reported by Japan's news agencies, this chapter examines how people viewed the second Abe premiership and reacted to his unexpected calling of a general election.[1]

Why do people approve of Abe and why not?

Numbers from public opinion polls are difficult to interpret without a baseline for comparison. In order to see how people evaluated Abe's second premiership, I turn to approval ratings of prime ministers published by Jiji Press, which has conducted monthly public opinion polls using

Table 8.1 Cabinet approval from Ikeda to Abe (2nd)

Prime Minister	Months	Average	Highest	Lowest	Initial month	Last month
Ikeda	52	41.0	54.4	31.1	33.8	43.4
Sato	92	35.0	46.5	17.3	46.5	17.3
Tanaka	29	28.6	61.0	10.6	56.0	10.6
Miki	25	30.6	41.9	19.4	41.9	19.4
Fukuda, T	23	27.4	34.3	22.7	29.6	34.3
Ohira	19	29.4	35.0	20.9	35.0	27.3
Suzuki	28	31.2	41.6	15.8	41.6	15.8
Nakasone	59	40.7	51.8	24.7	34.5	40.6
Takeshita	19	30.3	41.5	4.4	37.5	4.4
Uno	2	14.8	19.5	10.1	19.5	10.1
Kaifu	27	43.1	54.2	27.5	27.5	44.2
Miyazawa	21	25.6	47.6	10.3	47.6	10.3
Hosokawa	9	59.0	67.4	46.2	62.9	46.2
Hata	2	40.8	40.9	40.7	40.9	40.7
Murayama	18	34.9	41.9	28.1	29.7	28.9
Hashimoto	31	38.1	46.8	23.4	46.8	23.4
Obuchi	20	33.2	47.6	19.4	24.8	32.4
Mori	13	19.8	33.3	9.6	33.3	10.8
Koizumi	65	47.2	78.4	34.0	72.8	43.2
Abe, 1st	12	36.5	51.4	22.6	51.3	25.5
Fukuda, Y	12	29.2	44.1	15.6	44.1	15.6
Aso	12	22.3	38.8	13.4	38.6	13.4
Hatoyama	8	39.8	60.6	19.1	60.6	19.1
Kan	15	26.0	45.6	12.5	41.2	13.3
Noda	16	27.1	50.1	17.3	50.1	18.2
Abe, 2nd	24	52.9	62.1	43.5	54.0	

Source: Jiji Opinion Poll, July 1960–December 2014.

the same methodology since June 1960. Table 8.1 shows the number of months each prime minister since Hayato Ikeda served and their average, highest, and lowest approval ratings. It also shows approval ratings during their first and final months in office.

The average approval rating for the Abe cabinet since December 2012 is a remarkably high 52.9%, second only to the very popular but short-lived Morihiro Hosokawa cabinet (59%) and higher than the cabinet of Jun'ichiro Koizumi (47.2%), who effectively exploited public opinion polling to his political advantage. As Abe remains in office, his average score may yet fall. Still, an average approval rating above 50% is unusually high after serving two full years.

It should be noted that Abe is the only person, since the LDP was founded, who returned to office as prime minister after once being ousted. It is interesting to see the contrast between his first and second terms in office. Abe's first term in office was marred by several scandals among his cabinet members, one of whom eventually committed suicide in May 2007. In that same month, a huge scandal in the Social Insurance Agency, the "lost pension records" problem, broke out and was exhaustively reported in the mass media. Abe's first term tarnished his image very badly. Thus, it is very surprising that Abe scored high approval ratings in his second try. Abe may have learned from his mistakes (Endo and Pekkanen, this volume), but the public can evidently be much more forgiving than scholars may have assumed.

One way to make sense of Abe's current popularity is to compare his first and second terms, and Kyodo Opinion Polls provide an illuminating contrast between the two. Though most opinion polls ask people why they approve or disapprove of prime ministers, Kyodo prompts respondents by explicitly referring to policy areas. For the first Abe cabinet, the most common reason respondents supported Abe was "he is better than the other politicians." On average, 15.1% of the entire electorate supported Abe for this reason. His personality comes next. In total, 11.2% of people approved of Abe because they trusted him. Policy reasons rank only in the third place. Yet, it was not Abe's economic policies but rather his foreign policies that appealed to voters. On average, 5.6% of the entire electorate supported the Abe cabinet because they "have hope for Abe's foreign policy" (*gaikō ni kitai dekiru*).

The reason why people approve of Abe in his second term is very different from his first term. The driving force of approval is faith in Abe's economic policy (Abenomics). A few months after his second inauguration, roughly a quarter of the entire electorate supported his cabinet because they "have hope for Abe's economic policy" (*keizai seisaku ni kitai dekiru*). The number of respondents motivated by economic policy during Abe's first term was just 5% at most. In the first year of his second tenure, 13.3–27.0% of the entire electorate supported the Abe cabinet because they had "hope for Abe's economic policy." However, this number gradually but steadily declined, and dipped to 7.1% in July 2014.

There is another interesting difference in the public's attitudes toward the first and the second Abe cabinets. Supporters of the second Abe cabinet are far more likely to be male than the supporters of the first (Endo and Pekkanen, this volume). Mainichi publishes its polling results

Table 8.2   Gender gap in cabinet approval

	Koizumi	Abe (1)	Fukuda	Aso	Hatoyama	Kan	Noda	Abe (2)
Mean Difference	0.6	−4.2	−4.3	0.6	3.4	0.4	0.4	8.0

Source: Mainichi Opinion Poll, April 2001–December 2014.

for men and women separately, which enables us to observe gender gaps in public opinion. Table 8.2 shows the difference between men's and women's approval levels since Koizumi. Positive numbers indicate that men rate an administration more highly than women and negative numbers indicate the reverse. On average, men's approval ratings of the second Abe cabinet exceed women's ratings by 8 percentage points, while men's approval trailed 4 percentage points behind women's in the first Abe cabinet. Furthermore, the popular base of the second Abe cabinet is also more skewed toward men than those of other prime ministers. This stark gender difference in approval implies that Abe sent very different messages to the Japanese people during his first and second premierships.

The reason for this gender gap becomes apparent when we look at the reasons men and women give for backing a prime minister. Using the Kyodo Opinion Poll from December 2012 to October 2014, I calculate Abe's approval based on economic policy separately for men and women.[2] On average, men's and women's approval based on Abe's economic policy differs by 8.5 percentage points and reaches 12 percentage points a few times. It seems that the gender gap in public opinion toward the second Abe cabinet and the very high approval based on economic policy are interrelated.

However, high approval based on economic policy does not necessarily mean that people feel the economy is doing well. The Yomiuri Opinion Poll studied people's evaluation of the economy using two questions: "Do you approve or disapprove of the economic policy of the Abe cabinet?" and "Do you feel the economy is improving under the Abe cabinet?" The positive answer to the first question (approving economic policy) and the negative answer to the second question (do not feel the economy is improving) are displayed in Figure 8.1. While 50–60% of people expressed their approval of Abe's economic policy, more than 70% of people did not feel the economy was improving. Apparently, some people endorsed Abe's economic policy without feeling its positive influence on the economy.

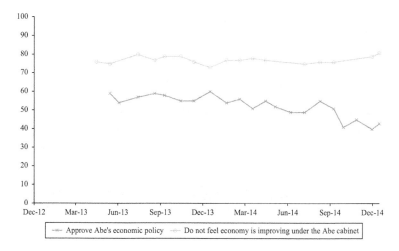

Figure 8.1 Public opinion on Abe's economic policy
Source: Yomiuri opinion poll, May 2013–January 2015.

It is puzzling as to why people evaluate Abe's economic policy positively even though they admit it has not been working so far. Without access to the micro data, any explanation remains speculative. One reasonable explanation is that people approve Abe's economic policy prospectively without regard to its actual performance. In this scenario, as long as Abe can generate good expectations for the future, his past performance does not matter (see, e.g., MacKuen et al., 1992). Indeed, on average, only 18% of people feel the economy is improving under the Abe cabinet.

However, hope will not sustain approval forever. Eventually, expectations have to be tested against economic reality or expectations need to adjust. While there is neither an upward nor downward trend for those who do not feel the economy is improving, those who approve of Abe's economic policy declined slowly but steadily and were outnumbered by those who disapprove of Abe's economic policy in October 2014. Perhaps this transition point prompted Abe to reschedule the timing of the consumption tax hike and call a snap election. Then, during the subsequent election campaign, Abe focused on the issue of the economy to rekindle the public's faith in his economic policy (see Noble, this volume).

Issues in election campaigns

In its special feature articles (December 3–5, 2014), the Asahi lists eight policy areas: (i) economic policy, (ii) diplomacy and collective defense, (iii) nuclear power plants and energy policy, (iv) employment and empowering women, (v) reducing the number of lower house seats, (vi) education and childrearing, (vii) public works projects, and (viii) agricultural policy and the Trans-Pacific Partnership (TPP). In addition to those eight policy areas, the Yomiuri published special feature articles on three more issues: revitalizing localities, social security, and constitutional revisions (December 1–2 and 4–12, 2014). While the classification of policy areas differs across newspapers, these 11 policy areas cover most of the debates between the government and the opposition during the 2014 election campaign.[3]

However, not all issues were treated equally. The government and the opposition seek votes by framing policy issues to their electoral advantage. Prime Minister Abe tried to appeal to voters through his economic policy. For example, 40% of his speech at the official start of the election campaign was devoted to Abenomics (Asahi, December 3, 2014).

His emphasis on the economy is also clear from a content analysis of newspapers. I compiled the 507 Yomiuri news articles that refer to Prime Minister Abe in the main text from November 8, 2014, the first day dissolution of the lower house was mentioned, to December 14, 2014, election day. These articles were then machine-coded into policy areas and topics in political affairs.[4] As news articles can include many different policy areas, coding categories are not mutually exclusive and one article can be counted more than once. Table 8.3 shows the result of this classification.

Among the articles in which Prime Minister Abe appeared, roughly 40% refer to Abenomics, and 55% of the articles mention either Abenomics or the consumption tax hike. Clearly, Abe's economic policy dominated the discussions during the election campaign. The government defends and the opposition attacks Abenomics by referring to whatever economic statistics best advance their arguments (Asahi, December 7, 2014). In contrast, revitalizing localities was mentioned in 11% of the articles, and empowering women was mentioned in only 3%, even though Abe himself emphasized these two issues at the press conference held when he reshuffled his cabinet in September (Asahi, September 4, 2014). Collective defense showed up in 20% of the news articles, and nuclear power plants and energy policy appeared in 12%,

Table 8.3   Issue coverage by the Yomiuri (November 8–December 14, 2014)

Issues	Number of articles	Percentage
Consumption Tax	205	40.4%
Abenomics	202	39.8%
Election and Strategy	159	31.4%
Economic Policy	115	22.7%
China–Japan Relations	106	20.9%
Collective Defense	99	19.5%
Social Security	91	17.9%
Business Condition	84	16.6%
Exchange Rate	77	15.2%
Nuclear Power Plant/Energy Policy	62	12.2%
Fiscal Policy	58	11.4%
Revitalizing Localities	58	11.4%
Political and Electoral Reform	50	9.9%
Okinawa	44	8.7%
South Korea–Japan Relations	39	7.7%
Monetary Policy	37	7.3%
Inequality	37	7.3%
APEC	36	7.1%
The Great East Japan Earthquake	34	6.7%
TPP	33	6.5%
Agricultural Policy	31	6.1%
Stock Market	25	4.9%
Education and Childrearing	25	4.9%
Scandal	25	4.9%
Russia–Japan Relations	23	4.5%
Constitutional Revision	22	4.3%
US–Japan Relations	16	3.2%
Empowering Women	15	3.0%
North Korea	14	2.8%
Total Number of Articles	507	

Source: Yomidasu (Yomiuri Shinbun Database). If "Prime Minister Abe" or "Prime Minister Shinzo Abe" is included in the main body of the articles, these articles are selected. The coverage is limited to the National Edition.

but Abe avoided taking clear stances on these divisive issues in his campaign speeches (Asahi, December 15, 2014). Thus, it seems fair to say that Abe succeeded in framing the entire election campaign as a referendum on Abenomics. This communications strategy worked very effectively, not because Abenomics was widely applauded, but because it prevented the other issues from being a focus of debate before the election.

Table 8.4(a)   What is most important for your voting decision in this election?

	November 19–20	November 28–29	December 10–11
Economic Policy such as Business Condition and Employment	34.8	35.1	30.9
Fiscal Reconstruction	10.1	10.4	9.1
Trans-Pacific Partnership (TPP)	1.7	2.7	1.9
Atomic Energy/Energy Policy	7.7	8.2	7.7
Social Security Policy such as Pension and Low Fertility Rate	26.1	27.4	29.4
Constitutional Reform	2.8	4.1	4.1
Recovery from the Great East Japan Earthquake	2.8	1.8	2.0
Security and Diplomacy	4.7	3.3	5.2
Revitalizing Localities	3.7	3.8	6.6
Others	2.5	1.2	1.2
DK/NA	3.1	2.0	1.9
	100.0	100.0	100.0

Source: Kyodo Opinion Poll, Kyoto, November 21 and 30; and December 12, 2014.

What issues proved to be really important for voters? Most opinion polls ask which issues people consider important in deciding how to vote. Technical details of how a poll is designed, such as how a list of policy areas is constructed and whether people can choose more than one policy area, strongly influence how people respond (Hijino, this volume). It is illuminating to examine the responses to two different question formats to understand which policy was important from the voters' perspective. The Kyodo Opinion Poll asks respondents to choose only one important issue. The responses to this question, asked in three waves of the survey, are shown in Table 8.4 (a). The issue that concerned people the most was economic policy, which was chosen by roughly one-third of the respondents. This result is consistent with the messaging from the Abe campaign. But it is unclear whether the government was successful in transmitting its priorities to the voters because roughly the same number of people chose economic policy as the most important issue for the 2009 and the 2012 general elections in Kyodo Opinion Polls.[5] The second most important issue is social security policy. Less than a tenth of the respondents consider other issues foremost when casting their ballots, including nuclear power and collective defense.

Table 8.4(b)   Most important issues (multiple answer)

For this House of Representative Election, which policy or issue do you consider important in deciding your candidate or party choice? Please choose from the following nine issues (MA).

Business Condition and Unemployment	70
Consumption Tax Hike	47
Recovery from the Great East Japan Earthquake	54
Energy Policy	46
Diplomacy and Security	51
Constitutional Revision	29
Electoral Reform	31
Revitalizing Localities	56
Money and Politics	46

Source: Yomiuri Opinion Poll, Yomiuri, November 23, 2014.

On the other hand, the responses to a similar question posed in the Yomiuri Opinion Poll are shown in Table 8.4(b). In the Yomiuri poll, the respondents can choose as many policy areas as they consider important. While the economy is again the most important issue (70% of the people selected "business conditions and unemployment"), the percentages for the other issues are very much different from those in Table 8.4(a). While recovery from the Great East Japan Earthquake was chosen only by 2% of the people in the Kyodo Opinion Poll, it was chosen by 54% of the people in the Yomiuri poll. While the numbers in the two tables are both meaningful, it seems that the numbers from the Kyodo Opinion Poll reflect people's priority more straightforwardly than those from the Yomiuri Opinion Poll. Though social security is another issue of great concern for the ordinary electorate, it received less attention from the government (17.9% in Table 8.3), and it is fair to say that it was pushed onto the sidelines during the election campaign.

Policy and voting in the 2014 general election

The economy was the only issue that was considered very important by both the government and the people, but did it really influence individual voting decision? And did it make a difference in the final outcome of the election? The FNN-Sankei Opinion Poll, conducted on December 6 and 7, provides a clue to this question (Table 8.5).[6] Respondents were asked whether they would choose a candidate who clearly endorses or

Table 8.5   Issues and voting decision

In this House of Representative Election, with the following policies, for which candidate do you vote? Please choose the one most close to your idea.

A) Abenomics	
Candidate who endorses Abe's economic policy	38.1
Candidate who opposes Abe's economic policy	19.9
Do not consider Abe's economic policy in deciding vote	38.4
DK/NA	3.6
B) Collective Defense	
Candidate who supports collective defense	30.5
Candidate who opposes collective defense	33.7
Do not consider collective defense in deciding vote	30.2
DK/NA	5.6
C) Nuclear power plant	
Candidate who supports restarting reactors and sustaining nuclear power plants in the future	13.1
Candidate who supports restarting reactors but in favor of closing down the nuclear power plants in the future	50.6
Candidate who supports immediate close down of the nuclear power plants	24.0
Do not consider nuclear power plants in deciding vote	9.9
DK/NA	2.4
D) Constitutional Revision	
Candidate who supports constitutional revision	31.9
Candidate who opposes constitutional revision	32.6
Do not consider constitutional revision in deciding vote	30.9
DK/NA	4.6

Source: FNN-Sankei Opinion Poll (December 6 and 7, 2014) http://www.fnn-news.com /yoron/inquiry141208.html, date accessed 26 March 2015.

opposes particular policies proposed by Prime Minister Abe. The question covers four policy areas: economic policy (Abenomics), collective defense, nuclear power, and constitutional revision.

For example, with regard to economic policy, people were asked whether they will vote for a candidate sympathetic to Abe's economic policy, a candidate unsympathetic, or do not consider economic policy in deciding their votes. In the answer to this question, 38% were willing to vote for a candidate who endorses Abe's economic policy, 20% were willing to vote for a candidate who opposes Abe's economic policy, and 38% do not factor Abenomics into their voting decisions. The distribution is two-to-one in favor of Abe, a higher margin for him than in the other policy issues. In fact, in regard to collective defense and constitutional revision, which are the classic left-right ideological issues in Japan, voters are divided into three groups of roughly the same size: those who choose a candidate who endorses Abe's position, those who choose a candidate who opposes Abe's position, and those who do not consider the issue at all in deciding how to vote. While some individuals may care about those issues greatly, they do not make a large difference in the aggregate outcome of the election as the votes of supporters and opponents cancel out. In the case of nuclear power, most people endorse restarting the existing reactors even though the majority prefer shutting down nuclear power plants in the future, so it makes hardly any difference in voting over a short time frame.

On election day, the Asahi Exit Poll asked whether voters consider Abenomics to be a success or a failure.[7] Of the respondents, 26% thought it was a success, 29% saw it as a failure, and 39% could not say either way (don't know).[8] While 62% of those who viewed Abenomics as a success voted for the LDP, only 9% of those who thought Abenomics was a failure voted for the LDP. And 37% of those who had no clear evaluation of Abe's economic policies voted for the LDP.[9] The relationship between voters for the opposition and their evaluation of Abenomics is exactly reversed. It is clear that evaluation of Abe's economic policy is linked to individual vote choice, but its positive and negative impacts on the aggregate outcome of the election were canceled out as there were roughly equal numbers of voters who were positive and negative toward Abenomics.

Four decades ago, in the context of a British general election, Butler and Stokes (1974) discussed the conditions under which a policy issue has a strong influence on the outcome of an election. According to their argument, the following three conditions have to be satisfied. First, a large pool of voters need to be aware of issues and have formed opinions toward them. All issues have their constituents, but those of interest to only a fraction of voters will have no net impact on election outcomes. Second, the distribution of opinions has to be one-sided. Otherwise, the impact of those holding opposing views will be canceled out. Third, the positions of political parties on the issues must be clearly differentiated and well recognized by voters.

Applying Butler and Stokes' framework to the issues in the 2014 general election, the third condition was clearly met. The LDP and the opposition parties obviously took different stances on Abe's economic policy. However, the other two conditions are not met. For the first condition, 39% of the electorate lacked a clear opinion regarding Abenomics. Those who had formed an opinion were equally divided into supporters and detractors and therefore the second condition was not met. Abenomics was by far the most prominent issue in the 2014 election, but it did not have a net impact on the final outcome. Ironically, economic policy mattered not because it was an important determinant of how people voted, but because it kept other issues that could have undermined LDP support out of political discourse. This crowding out may have been Abe's strategy from the start.

Discussion

Very few people foresaw that a general election would take place in December 2014. The House of Representatives did not need to have an election for two more years and Abe's approval ratings were very high. Unlike the 2005 and 2009 general elections, there was no emergent political reason to call for an election. Yet, Abe's surprise move paid off politically. The LDP and Komeito together won 325 seats, and Abe effectively silenced his rivals within the LDP and the opposition in the Diet. He can now claim a new mandate for pursuing his policy goals for another few years.

However, people did not necessarily welcome having a general election at that particular time. Many opinion polls indicated that people were not convinced by Abe's explanation for having the election. For example, 65% of the respondents negatively evaluated the prime minister's decision to call a general election in a Yomiuri Opinion Poll (Yomiuri, November 23, 2014). In an Asahi Opinion Poll, 62% of people opposed having a general election in December 2014 (Asahi, November 21, 2014). In the same poll, people also showed little interest in the election; 21% of the respondents indicated that they were very much interested in the election, a number much lower than in the previous three elections.[10] Indeed, the voting turnout was 52.66%, 6.66% percentage points lower than the 2012 general election and the worst turnout in history.

Likewise, with regard to the outcome of the election, people think that the LDP won more seats than it deserved to. In another Asahi Opinion Poll, 59% of the respondents answered that the LDP and Komeito had won too many seats (Asahi, December 17, 2014). In a Yomiuri Opinion Poll, 55% of the respondents wished that the LDP had won fewer seats than they actually obtained, and 45% wished that the DPJ had won more seats (Yomiuri, December 17, 2014).

If people were unconvinced of the reason for and the timing of the election, and regretted how many seats the LDP actually won, why did the 2014 general election end up with another landslide for Prime Minister Abe? The reason is simple. People felt they had no effective alternative to choose. An Asahi Opinion Poll asked respondents which of two reasons best explained why the LDP won far more seats than a simple majority: "People evaluated Prime Minister Abe's Policy (positively)" or "The opposition parties were unattractive" (Asahi, December 18, 2014). Of the total respondents, 72% chose the latter. In response to a similar question posed in a Yomiuri Opinion Poll, 65% chose "People thought the LDP was better than the other political parties" as a reason for its victory (Yomiuri, December 17, 2014). Only 7% chose "economic policy was (positively) evaluated." Clearly, the LDP's landslide victory was a consequence of passive choice and the withdrawal of many citizens from voting.

Looking at the number of seats, Prime Minister Abe gained a very solid majority in the Diet. However, being unconvinced of the need for an election and deprived of viable alternatives, people were far from enthusiastic. Prime Minister Abe's popularity may evaporate quickly once people lose faith in his economic policy.

Notes

1. Most of the poll results cited in this chapter are publicly available either on paper or on the web. However, some of the findings were made available to the author by news agencies. I appreciate the generosity of the polling sections of the Asahi Shinbun and Kyodo News.
2. The gender breakdown was not published but was made available by Kyodo News to the author.
3. Mainichi also published special feature news articles on policy, which refer to (a) economic policy, (b) nuclear power plants and energy policy, (c) empowering women and childrearing, (d) revitalizing localities, (e) diplomacy, (f) collective defense, and (g) constitutional revision (December 4–13, 2014). All these issues are covered either by the Asahi or Yomiuri.
4. For coding news articles, I used free text-coding software KH Coder (Higuchi, n.d.).
5. The average score for 2014 is 33.6%, while it is 30.6 for 2009 and 29.7 for 2012, respectively. It seems that people are concerned about the economy whoever is in the government.
6. The results are available at http://www.fnn-news.com/yoron/inquiry141208.html
7. The question wording is "Do you think Prime Minister Abe's economic policy in the past two years has been a success or a failure?" The entire question

was not published but supplied to the author from the polling section of the Asahi Shinbun.
8. The results of the Asahi exit poll were published on December 15 and 16, 2014. However, some numbers referred to in the main text were not published but made available to the author by the polling section of the Asahi Shinbun.
9. The number for those who had no clear evaluation of Abe's economic policy was not published but made available by the Asahi Shinbun.
10. 47% for the 2005 election, 49% for the 2009 election, and 39% for the 2012 election.

References

Butler, David and Donald E. Stokes. (1974). *Political change in Britain: The evolution of electoral choice* (2nd ed). London: Macmillan.

Higuichi, Koichi. n.d. (April 2, 2015). KH Coder. http://khc.sourceforge.net/en/, date accessed

MacKuen, Michael B., Robert S. Erikson and James A. Stimson (1992). Peasants or bankers? The American electorate and the U.S. economy. *The American Political Science Review* 86(3): 597–611.

9
Did Abe's Coattails Help the LDP Win?

Kenneth Mori McElwain

Introduction

The LDP strolled to victory in the 2014 House of Representatives snap election, buoyed by support for its "Abenomics" policy agenda (Maeda, this volume) and the opposition parties' difficulties in mustering competitive candidates (Pekkanen, Reed, and Smith, this volume). As Kingston (this volume) argues, the LDP's campaign centered on its credentials as economic managers, even as contentious issues such as the resumption of nuclear reactors (Hughes, this volume) and constitutional reform loomed over the postelection calendar. The divisiveness of these topics presents a challenge for moderate LDP legislators, and hence for the party overall. On the one hand, a larger majority in the House of Representatives (HR) would fortify the party's control over the Diet. On the other hand, many new pickups would be moderate legislators representing urban swing districts, who are less enamored of the leadership's conservative agenda.

This chapter examines how the LDP utilized its campaign resources to balance these two goals: winning more seats in aggregate and ensuring that relatively conservative candidates were victorious. I do so by analyzing the pattern of party leader campaign visits, or *"yuuzei."* The study is motivated by growing evidence that popular leaders can generate electoral coattails, whereby voters support a particular candidate because of their affinity for the party leader. In earlier work on the 2005 HR contest (McElwain, 2009), I showed that campaign stops by then Prime Minister Junichiro Koizumi raised the vote share of LDP candidates by 3–5%. While Shinzo Abe – the prime minister of Japan and LDP president – may not have been the charismatic equal of Koizumi, his Cabinet approval rating in the month before the election was 45.5%, higher than Koizumi's 39.9% in August 2005.[1] As such, it is quite possible that Abe was able to help his preferred candidates by stumping for them personally. This leaves us with the question, "Who does the LDP want to help the most?"

My analysis focuses on the campaign schedules of six senior LDP figures, including Prime Minister Abe. First, LDP leaders favored districts where the race was expected to be close. Second, they targeted candidates who were more conservative, specifically those who *supported* prime ministerial visits to Yasukuni Shrine and *opposed* affirmation action programs for women. This latter finding is counter-intuitive, insofar as Abe has tried to soften the LDP's social conservatism by promoting a "Womenomics" platform. However, it is consistent with Kingston's argument (this volume) that Abe sends subtle signals about his conservative beliefs to his core partisan supporters, even as the party trumpets a moderate socioeconomic agenda to the public.

How do leaders influence elections?

Electoral campaigns try to sell two things: the candidate's personal merits and his or her party's collective virtues. For much of the postwar period, Japanese elections hinged on the personal dimension, and the LDP's dominance rested on its ability to recruit better candidates (Scheiner, 2006). Until the 1990s, the reelection rates of Japanese incumbents hovered above 80%, even as the popularity of individual parties waxed and waned. Since the introduction of the mixed-member majoritarian (*heiritsu-sei*) system in 1994, however, electoral emphasis has shifted to the "party vote." Candidates no longer rely on their personal popularity to insulate them from turbulent political winds, and the average reelection rate dropped to below 50% in the 2009 and 2012 HR elections (McElwain, 2012). The rise and fall of Third Force parties (Pekkanen and Reed, this volume) speaks to the growing willingness of legislators to abandon damaged party brands lest their own electoral survival be threatened.

That said, voters do not appear to be enamored of any of their party options. According to a monthly survey data from the Jiji Press, the proportion of respondents claiming to be "independent," or lacking party affinity, has climbed from an average of 33% in the 1980s to 58% between 2005 and 2014. Instead of deep, enduring partisan identification, voters seem to be judging parties by their *leaders*. In parliamentary systems, a party's president or chairman is its de facto nominee for prime minister, making the leader's charisma and competence an important facet of the party's brand. Indeed, parties are increasingly making their leaders the focal point of their campaigns – a process often dubbed the "presidentialization" of parliamentary politics (Poguntke and Webb, 2005). In the Japanese context, Krauss and Nyblade (2005) and Krauss and Pekkanen (forthcoming) attribute this to the rising number of independent voters who obtain political information and election news from television, where the focus on leaders is stronger than in print. McElwain and Umeda (2011) show that media coverage of parties increases during internal presidential primaries, suggesting public appetite for observing and evaluating potential leaders. This is more than media-driven pageantry. Administrative reforms since the late 1990s have strengthened the prime minister's policymaking capacity and autonomy (Estevez-Abe, 2006; Takenaka, 2006), making the choice between party leaders consequential to actual governance.

From an electoral perspective, leaders are valuable resources because they can generate "coattails" that influence voter assessments of the party's candidates. A charismatic leader may induce independent voters to back his party in the hope of making him prime minister, while a lackluster one may turn off even partisan supporters. For example, Kabashima and Imai (2002) find that survey respondents who held negative views of gaffe-prone Prime Minister Yoshiro Mori were less likely to vote for the LDP in the 2000 HR election. Indeed, fear of contesting the 2001 House of Councillors (HC) election under Mori prompted the LDP to stage its first primary election to select its president in decades, leading to the ascendance of Junichiro Koizumi, one of the most popular prime ministers in postwar Japan (Lin, 2009).

Leaders can do more than raise the popularity of the party as a whole. This chapter follows McElwain (2009) and examines the ability of leaders to elevate the profile of *specific candidates* through campaign visits. When a popular leader visits a candidate's district and publicly proclaims his support, constituents have the opportunity to form an emotional association between support for the leader and voting for that candidate. This effect is stronger among independent voters, who are more likely to internalize and act on new information than are diehard partisans.

The strategic dilemma for parties is deciding *where* to send their leaders. Japan's Public Office Election Law restricts active campaigning on behalf of individual candidates to only 12 days before the election (McElwain, 2008). While Japan is not a geographically large country, transportation time – by car, train, or air – forces parties to ration leader visits among the 295 single-member districts (SMDs). I posit two competing strategic motives for the LDP. The first is *electoral util-itarianism*. The LDP's victory in the preceding 2012 election rested on narrow victories in many SMDs. While 237 of its 289 candidates won outright, 39 came in second and needed to be "resurrected" in the proportional representation (PR) tier; 120 were first-time winners who could be vulnerable in the 2014 HR contest. To the extent that Prime Minister Abe could marshal coattail benefits for LDP candidates, he should favor districts where the opportunity to flip a narrow loss into victory is greater, such as where the race is expected to be close (Hypothesis 1) and where there are more independent voters up for grabs (Hypothesis 2).

The second motivation is *ideological loyalty*. LDP leaders should back candidates who share their conservative views on policy, thereby con-solidating Prime Minister Abe's hold on power and averting postelection internal conflict over the legislative agenda. As Krauss (this volume) argues, the passage of the Special Secrecy Law, the LDP's revisionist views on Japan's wartime history, and the reinterpretation of Article 9 to permit collective self-defense, all reflected Abe's hawkish agenda on foreign policy. While these initiatives consolidated the party's support among its conservative base, the LDP downplayed these issues in the election, making economic revitalization and Abenomics its campaign cornerstones (Kingston, this volume). It also made gender, particularly promoting women in the workplace and improving childcare facilities, part of its "Womenomics" message, breaking from the party's socially conservative DNA. Constitutional reform, which had been emphasized in the LDP's 2012 campaign (Winkler, *JD* 2012), was relegated to five short lines on the last page of its 2014 manifesto (LDP Election Policies, 2014). That said, the temperance of the LDP's campaign message does not indicate its actual moderation on controversial issues. For example, the party revived its internal commission on constitutional reform in February 2015, and Abe has declared that constitutional amendment would be one of his top priorities after the 2015 House of Councilors (HC) election (*Asahi*, February 27, 2015).

The ideal outcome for the LDP would be to win a unilateral two-thirds in the election, allowing it to propose constitutional amendments in the HR without relying on its coalition partner, Komeito, which has tradi-tionally opposed revisions to Article 9 (Kingston, this volume; Klein, this volume and *JD 2012*).[2] Failing that, it would be in Abe's interests to have more conservative LDP candidates win their seats, as it would minimize intra-party discord over contentious policies and streamline agenda-setting in the Diet. From an ideological perspective, then, I predict that party leaders will favor districts whose candidates are more conservative (Hypothesis 3).

Leaders target conservatives in close races

Party elites cannot afford to be homebodies during the hectic 12-day campaign period. *The Yomiuri Newspaper* (December 14, 2015) reports that Prime Minister Abe campaigned in 25 prefectures for a total travel distance of 14,000 kilometers, while Banri Kaieda, president of the DPJ, traveled 9,000 kilometers. I gathered data on the locations and dates of leader visits from the LDP homepage, which allowed users to browse the campaign schedules of more than a dozen legislators.[3] I restricted my search to the six most active and popular LDP legislators: Shinzo Abe (prime minister), Shigeru Ishiba (special minister for local revitalization), Taro Aso (deputy PM and minister of finance), Sadakazu Tanigaki (LDP secretary general), Yoshihide Suga (chief cabinet secretary), and Shinjiro Koizumi (vice-minister for national reconstruction).[4] Table 9.1 lists the distribution of their visits by different district characteristics, as well as that of Banri Kaieda (president) and Katsuya Okada (deputy president) of the DPJ as comparisons. A few informative patterns emerge. First, Abe visited more districts than did his DPJ counterpart Kaieda.[5] One reason is that Kaieda had fewer potential targets, as the DPJ only nominated 178 candidates, far fewer than the LDP's 283 (Smith, this volume). Equally important, DPJ frontbenchers were forced to defend their own turfs. The *Yomiuri* (December 14, 2014) reports that Kaieda spent more time in his own district (Tokyo 1st) after newspaper surveys showed him in a dead heat against the LDP challenger. In fact, the LDP seems to have purposefully targeted DPJ elites.[6] The constituency that received the most total visits by LDP and DPJ leaders – five times each – was Saitama 5th, the home of Yukio Edano, the popular DPJ secretary general and former chief cabinet secretary. Overall, the six top LDP leaders campaigned in the districts of DPJ elites nine times, compared to only once in the opposite direction.

Second, the LDP sent its headliners to different *types* of districts, based on each leader's attractiveness to conservative partisans or independent swing voters. An interesting distinction can be found between the schedules of Shinjiro Koizumi, an immensely popular young politician and son of former Prime Minister Junichiro Koizumi, and that of more senior legislators. For example, former Prime Minister Taro Aso was only sent to visit LDP incumbents, while Koizumi Junior supported more challengers.[7] Koizumi also went to Okinawa, the home of US military bases and a controversial location for LDP hawks (Kagotani, this volume), while Abe, Ishiba, and Aso did not. He was also more likely to stump in districts where the LDP had endorsed candidates of the more centrist and pacifist Komeito. In fact, the LDP made sure to take care of its coalition partner: collectively, the six LDP frontbenchers visited Komeito districts an average of 1.9 times, as opposed to 1.2 times for their own candidates.

To estimate the determinants of LDP leader visits more systematically, I use statistical tests to analyze the campaign locations of Shinzo Abe, as well as the total number of visits by the six LDP elites identified in Table 9.1. For *Abe Visits*, I use a logistic regression model, where the dependent variable equals "1" when Abe made a campaign stop and "0" otherwise. For *LDP Visits*, I use a negative binomial regression model, where the dependent variable is the total count of leader visits by the six LDP elites. Of the 295 SMDs, 130 were never visited, 57 were visited once, and 108 were visited twice or more.[8] Table 9.2 presents these results.[9]

As discussed earlier, there are two lines of reasoning regarding the LDP's strategic allocation of leader visits.[10] The first is electoral utilitarianism: leaders will go to marginal constituencies where the race is expected to be tight, so that even a small positive bump can flip the final outcome (Hypothesis 1). This is confirmed by the negative coefficient on *Margin2012*, the district-level difference between the LDP and DPJ's vote

Table 9.1　Locations of campaign visits (December 2–13, 2014)

	LDP*						DPJ*	
	Abe	Ishiba	Aso	Koizumi	Tanigaki	Suga	Kaieda	Okada
No. of districts visited	77	58	21	63	70	57	41	55
Visited twice	0	0	0	2	2	0	3	9
With incumbents	56	54	21	51	62	57	13	20
With Komeito**	8	1	0	6	2	0	–	–
Prefectures visited	25	20	15	27	19	18	18	16
Candidate performance (%)								
SMP Win	49	70	76	56	51	61	11	22
Resurrected (PR)	42	25	19	39	43	33	26	27
Lose	9	5	5	5	7	5	63	51

Notes: *The LDP ran 283 candidates, of whom 267 were incumbents. The DPJ ran 178 candidates, of whom 61 were incumbents.
**In 9 districts, the LDP endorsed a Komeito candidate instead of nominating its own candidate.
***The win/loss designation for the LDP includes both its own and endorsed Komeito candidates.

Table 9.2 The determinants of LDP visits

Model 1: Logistic regression[1]
Model 2: Negative binomial regression[1]

	(1) *Abe Visit*	(2) *LDP Visit*
Hypothesis 1		
(Electoral Competitiveness)		
Margin 2012	−7.456***	−3.535***
	(1.758)	(0.463)
Incumbent	−3.648*	0.547
	(1.419)	(0.310)
Hypothesis 2		
(Potential Coattails)		
Independents	26.73*	13.15***
	(11.24)	(3.781)
Abe Popularity	−6.354	4.458*
	(6.735)	(1.778)
Hypothesis 3		
(Ideological Loyalty)[2]		
Women's Employment	0.541*	0.181*
	(0.241)	(0.0758)
Yasukuni Visits	−0.581**	−0.0790
	(0.214)	(0.0673)
Observations	253	253
Pseudo-R^2	0.338	0.151

Notes: [1]Robust standard errors in parentheses: *** $p < 0.001$, ** $p < 0.01$, * $p < 0.05$
[2]Measured on five-point scale, where higher values indicate greater opposition.

shares in the preceding election.[11] Where the two parties were tied in 2012 (*Margin2012* = 0), Model 1 estimates a 47.1% probability of an Abe visit. Whether the vote margin was 20%, however, the same probability falls to just 16.7%. The predicted number of total LDP visits (Model 2) similarly drops, from 2.2 to 1.1 occasions.[12] Abe was also 53% less likely to stump for *incumbent* candidates, who have had two years to cultivate constituency networks and burnish their legislative credentials, than for newcomers or previous losers, who lack that advantage.[13]

A related strategy is to target independent voters, who are more likely to be swayed by new information or impressions gleaned from leader visits (Hypothesis 2). I use prefectural-level opinion polls from the Yomiuri (December 6, 2015; local editions) to measure the share of *Independents* who claimed no affinity for any party. Figure 9.1 plots the

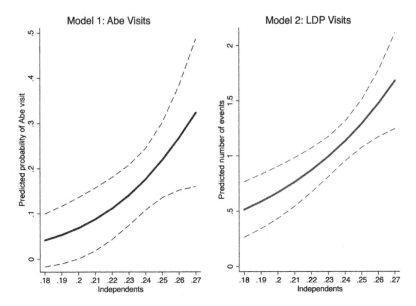

Figure 9.1   Leaders target independent voters
Source: 95% confidence intervals shown as dashed lines.

simulated effect of a change in *Independents*, with the left panel showing changes in the probability of an *Abe Visit* and the right panel displaying the estimated number of visits by all LDP elites. A one standard deviation increase in *Independents* from 24% to 26% raises the predicted probability of an *Abe Visit* by over 10%, from 17.7 to 27.8. The same change increases the collective number of *LDP Visits* from 1.1 to 1.5 incidences.

I also estimate the potential length of Abe's coattails, or *Abe Popularity*. This is the proportion of respondents who support Abe minus the proportion who support the LDP, such that a positive difference indicates that Abe's coattails extend beyond LDP partisans. As discussed in McElwain (2009), the marginal value of a party leader's visit should be greater – and hence the probability of a visit should be higher – where the leader's coattails are expected to be longer. However, this variable is not a strong predictor of Abe visits (Model 1), although it is statistically significant for the total number of LDP visits (Model 2). That said, a 1% increase in *Abe Popularity* only raises the frequency of *LDP Visits* by 0.05 incidences. This substantively small effect suggests that the LDP focused on sending its leaders to appeal to independents, regardless of the overall popularity of the Abe cabinet.[14] In that sense, the purpose of

LDP visits may have been to raise the profile of the Abenomics message generally, rather than to rely on Abe's individual ability to mobilize or persuade voters. I will return to this point in the next section, where I evaluate the effects of leader campaigning.

The second motivation for leader visits is to reward and secure the election of conservative candidates who are more likely to support the LDP's post-election legislative agenda. The Asahi-Todai Elite Survey asked every election candidate to rate their support or opposition (five-point scale) to 30 different policies or statements, with questions ranging from foreign affairs and economic growth to social norms and gender.[15] I focus on two ideological issues that Prime Minister Abe has prioritized, even as they have proved divisive among LDP candidates. The first is *Yasukuni*, the candidate response to the question, "I want the Prime Minister to worship (*sanpai*) at Yasukuni Shrine." The second is *Women*, which scores candidates on the question, "The government should establish special institutions (*seido*) to increase the number of women in higher status or better occupations."[16]

Figure 9.2 plots the predicted probability of Abe visits, with higher values in both *Yasukuni* (left panel) and *Women* (right panel) denoting

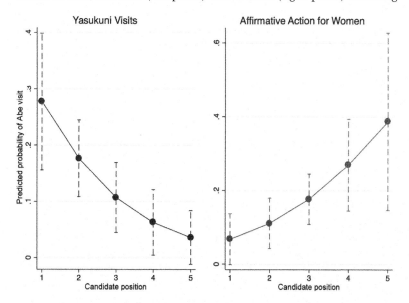

Figure 9.2 Abe visits more conservative legislators

Notes: Vertical bars denote 95% confidence intervals around the point estimate.
Source: Predicted probabilities calculated from Table 9.2, Model 1 coefficients. Candidate positions are scaled so that higher values denote greater disapproval of that issue.

greater opposition. The prime minister was more likely to visit a strong supporter of Yasukuni worship (27.8%) than he was to visit a neutral LDP candidate (10.7%). More intriguing, opposition to affirmative action for women actually increased campaign support. A candidate who was strongly opposed to the program had a 38.7% chance of an Abe visit, compared to 17.7% for a neutral candidate. The frequency of total *LDP Visits* similarly fell from 1.6 to 1.1 incidences. This finding speaks to the LDP's explicit decision to temper its campaign platform (Kingston, this volume). While the Abe cabinet has advocated the promotion of women in the labor market, the party has historically defended a gendered breakdown of home and work responsibilities. The results shown in Figure 9.2 indicate that the party leadership was willing to reward ideological conservatives, even those that opposed Abe's "Womenomics" agenda.[17]

Did Abe visits improve the LDP's performance?

The big question, of course, is whether any of this made a material difference in the election. The political parties certainly believe so, or they would not spend that money and time sending their leaders to the far corners of the archipelago. However, the magnitude of the effects could vary substantially, based on the underlying motivation for those campaign visits. If the LDP's strategy was driven by electoral utilitarianism, then we would expect leader visits to improve the party's vote share. If ideological cohesion mattered, however, then the electoral effects could be more ambiguous. The previous section found evidence in support of both motivations. Here, I examine the effect of Prime Minister Abe's campaign visit by using a two-step Heckman selection model, which allows us to account for underlying factors that predict the likelihood of an *Abe Visit* in the first place, such as district competitiveness or candidate ideology.[18]

My main dependent variable is the vote share (0–1) of the LDP's candidate in each district, and the primary explanatory variable is *Independents*, or the proportion of nonpartisan voters. The preceding section showed that Abe was more likely to visit districts with a larger segment of independents. If the party's strategy were successful, then we would expect LDP vote share to increase where an *Abe Visit* occurred and where *Independents* is high. In my statistical model, I control for the conditional relationship between these variables with an interaction term, *Abe Visit * Independents*, which is expected to have a positive impact on *LDP Votes*.

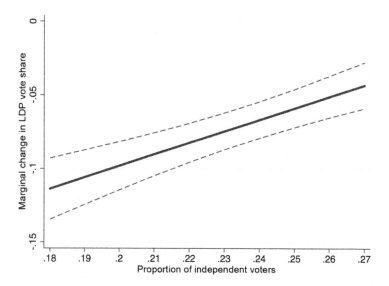

Figure 9.3   Marginal effect of an Abe visit
Source: 95% confidence intervals shown as dashed lines.

In lieu of presenting the full results, which are available upon request, Figure 9.3 displays the marginal effect of an *Abe Visit* at different levels of district partisanship. It shows the *difference* in vote share between districts that Abe visits and those that he passed over. The positive slope suggests that Abe's visits were successful in converting more independent voters to the LDP's side. In districts that Abe visited, a 1% increase in the proportion of independents raised the LDP's vote share by 0.5%. However, the net effect of an Abe visit is negative, as seen by the predicted values all lying below "0." The most straightforward interpretation, then, is that Abe visits did *less harm* in districts with more independents but were not actually helpful on average.

Conclusion

With the LDP expected to retain, if not extend, its substantial majority in the HR, the party deployed one of its main campaign resources – leader visits – to buoy the prospects of candidates battling in tight races. Prime Minister Abe also favored more conservative candidates, even those that were opposed to one of the pillars of his "Womenomics" policy agenda. That said, evidence of Abe's ability to actually improve the fate of LDP candidates is elusive. In general, independents were more likely to vote for the LDP when Abe visited their districts, but the net effect of his campaign stops were neutral to negative.

These findings are consistent with what Kingston (this volume) calls the "Abe conundrum": Abe's ability to remain popular despite strong public opposition to the conservatism of his signature policies. Kingston and Maeda (this volume) both attribute this to the LDP's campaign emphasis on "Abenomics," which trumpeted inoffensive priorities such as economic revitalization and gender neutrality, even as the party's actual legislative achievements leaned more ideological. In fact, the "Abenomics" platform can be seen as a successful strategy to secure Abe's policy mandate. It will be very difficult for LDP legislators who oppose the party's legislative agenda to do so publicly, given the centrality of Abenomics during the 2014 campaign. At the same time, the LDP's allocation of campaign visits seems to have emphasized ideological purity, possibly sending a message to other legislators that loyalty will be rewarded. In fact, the party's strategy mirrors Prime Minister Junichiro Koizumi's decision to make postal privatization the foundation of his 2005 HR campaign. The issue was highly polarizing at the time, but by focusing his support on candidates who pledged allegiance, Koizumi was able to deter any opposition to political reform after the election. While Abe's visits may not have directly helped LDP candidates – most of whom would have won regardless – he may have successfully insulated himself from an early leadership challenge and retirement as prime minister.

Notes

1. Public opinion data were compiled by the author from monthly survey reports by the *Jiji Press*.
2. The ratification of constitutional amendments in Japan requires an absolute two-thirds in both the HR and HC, followed by a majority in a voter referendum.
3. Unfortunately, the subsection of the LDP website that listed campaign locations was made private after the election. The link https://special.jimin.jp /speech is now password protected, but screen grabs are available from the author upon request. The DPJ's webpages are active as of February 20, 2015. See for example, http://www.dpj.or.jp/article/105829.
4. Designated cabinet and party positions are those at the time of the 2014 HR election.
5. By comparison, in the 2005 election, then DPJ leader Katsuya Okada visited more districts (75) than did Junichiro Koizumi (72 districts) (McElwain, 2009).
6. For this analysis, I define DPJ elites as Kaieda and Okada, as well as Goshi Hosono (former secretary general), Seiji Maehara (former party president), and Yukio Edano (secretary general).

7. The average 2012 vote margin between the LDP and DPJ was 14.4% in districts that Aso visited, but only 8.9% where Koizumi visited. The greater propensity of Aso, Ishiba, and Suga to visit incumbents also meant that those candidates had a higher probability of winning than more vulnerable candidates visited by Abe and Koizumi.

8. More specifically, 53 districts were visited twice, 36 were visited three times, 16 were visited four times, and 3 were visited five times.

9. In both models, I follow McElwain (2009) and control for non-political determinants of leader visits by including proxies for the geographical remoteness of districts. Given the short campaign period, districts that are more difficult to reach should be targeted less frequently. I use two related variables: *distance_log*, or the logged distance in kilometers between the most populated municipality in the constituency and Nagatacho, the location of the Japanese Diet, and *distance_sq*, the square of *distance_log*. Districts close to Tokyo (which can be easily reached by train) and those far away (accessible by airplane) require shorter travel time, and thus should be visited more frequently. I also include a dichotomous variable for whether the district houses the largest train station in that prefecture, which should increase the probability and frequency of visits. These results are omitted from Table 9.2 but are available from the author upon request.

10. All election outcome data for the 2012 and 2014 HR elections come from Ko Maeda's public dataset, which draws on the Yomiuri Newspaper's post-election vote counts. His dataset can be downloaded from: http://politicalscience.unt.edu/~ maeda/

11. While the DPJ coordinated candidates with the Japan Innovation Party in 2014 to avoid splitting the opposition vote (Smith, this volume), it was the primary non-LDP party in 2012, making its competitiveness vis-à-vis the LDP a reasonable metric for the expected closeness of the election.

12. All predicted probabilities are estimated by altering the value of a specific independent variable while holding all others at their median values.

13. *Incumbent* is only moderately correlated (0.37) with *Margin2012*, but given the LDP's big victory in 2012, the vast majority of its 2014 candidates (267 out of 283) were incumbents.

14. The weak result for *Abe Popularity* is not due to collinearity; its correlation with *Independents* is a negligible 0.02.

15. On many issues, there were minimal differences among LDP candidates. For example, when asked whether they supported constitutional reform, 263 were in favor and none were opposed. The survey results, organized by electoral district, can be found on the Asahi website http://www.asahi.com /senkyo/sousenkyo47/asahitodai/ (accessed February 25, 2015). Summaries of candidate responses were reported in the December 2nd, 2014 edition of the Asahi. Not all candidates responded to the full battery of 30 questions. As a result, the sample for the statistical analysis is less than the total number of LDP candidates.

16. For *Yasukuni*, 53% were strongly or weakly in favor, 38% were neutral, and 9% were strongly or weakly opposed. For *Women*, 32% were in favor, 61% were neutral, and 7% were opposed.

17. One alternative interpretation is that the LDP leadership favored conservatives because their ideological extremity made them electorally vulnerable. However, the empirical correlation between *Women* and *Margin2012*

is effectively zero (–0.002), making electoral utilitarianism an unlikely explanation.

18. I first tested for the possibility of endogeneity between *Abe Visit* and *LDP Vote* by taking the residuals from Model 1 in the previous section and including it as a covariate in an OLS regression predicting LDP vote share. The residual variable was statistically significant in the OLS, indicating that we must explicitly model the probability of an Abe campaign stop in a two-stage process. In the Heckman model, I first analyze the probability that Abe visits a district using Model 1 (Table 9.2) and then estimate the predicted effects of a visit conditional on that probability. In the latter stage, I control for a battery of other factors linked to election outcomes, such as the LDP's performance in 2012 (*Vote2012*) and the total number of district candidates in 2014 (*Candidates*).

Bibliography

Estevez-Abe, Margarita (2006). Japan's shift toward a westminster system: A structural analysis of the 2005 lower house election and its aftermath. *Asian Survey* 46: 632–651.

Kabashima, Ikuo and Ryosuke Imai (2002). Evaluation of party leaders and voting behavior: An analysis of the 2000 general election. *Social Science Japan Journal* 5: 85–96.

Krauss, Ellis S. and Benjamin Nyblade (2005). "Presidentialization" in Japan? The Prime Minister, Media, and Elections in Japan. *British Journal of Political Science* 35: 357–368.

Krauss, Ellis S. and Robert Pekkanen. (Forthcoming). Japan: Partial presidentialization of parties. In Gianluca Passarelli (ed.) *The Presidentialization of Political Parties. Organizations, Institutions, and Leaders.* London: Palgrave Macmillan.

LDP Election Policies [Jimintou Jyuten Seisaku]. (2014). https://www.jimin.jp/news/policy/126585.html, accessed February 25, 2015.

Lin, Chao-Chi (2009). How Koizumi won. In Steven R. Reed, Kenneth Mori McElwain and Kay Shimizu (eds) *Political Change in Japan: Electoral Behavior, Party Realignment, and the Koizumi Reforms.* pp. 109–132. Palo Alto: Walter H. Shorenstein Asia-Pacific Research Center.

McElwain, Kenneth Mori (2009). How long are koizumi's coattails? Party-leader visits in the 2005 election. In Steven R. Reed, Kenneth Mori McElwain and Kay Shimizu (eds) *Political Change in Japan: Electoral Behavior, Party Realignment, and the Koizumi Reforms.* pp. 133–156. Palo Alto: Walter H. Shorenstein Asia-Pacific Research Center.

McElwain, Kenneth Mori (2008). Manipulating electoral rules to manufacture single party dominance. *American Journal of Political Science* 52: 32–47.

McElwain, Kenneth Mori (2012). The nationalization of Japanese elections. *Journal of East Asian Studies* 12: 323–350.

McElwain, Kenneth Mori, and Michio Umeda (2011). Party democratization and the salience of party leaders. *Journal of Social Science (Shakai Kagaku Kenkyu)* 62: 173–193.

Palmer, Harvey D. and Guy D. Whitten (2000). Government competence, economic performance and endogenous election dates. *Electoral Studies* 19: 413–426.

Poguntke, Thomas and Paul Webb (eds). (2005). *The Presidentialization of Politics: A Comparative Study of Modern Democracies*. Oxford: Oxford University Press.

Scheiner, Ethan (2006). *Democracy without Competition in Japan: Opposition Failure in a One-Party Dominant State*. Cambridge: Cambridge University Press.

Takenaka, Harukata (2006). *Shushou shihai – nihon seiji no henbou*. Tokyo: Chuo Kouron Shinsha.

Winkler, Christian G. (2013). Right rising? ideology and the 2012 house of representatives election. In Robert Pekkanen, Steven R. Reed and Ethan Scheiner (eds) *Japan Decides 2012: The Japanese General Election*. pp. 201–212. New York: Palgrave Macmillan.

10

Candidates in the 2014 Election: Better Coordination and Higher Candidate Quality

Daniel M. Smith

At first glance, candidate recruitment and nominations for the 2014 House of Representatives (HR) election appeared relatively unexciting compared to the 2012 election. In 2012, there were a record number of candidates (1,504) from 12 registered parties, and nearly half of the candidates were running for the very first time in an HR election. Many of these new candidates were recruited through open recruitment (*koubo*) contests that promised to deliver new blood to a system dominated by members of political dynasties, such as current Prime Minister Shinzou Abe, and other traditional elites (Smith, *JD 2012*).

However, most of those new candidates were unsuccessful in 2012, and half of them did not return. In 2014, only 1,191 candidates entered the contest, and of these, only 278 were first-time candidates (Table 10.1). Among the rest were 470 incumbents, 117 former incumbents hoping to win back their seats, and 13 who had previously served in the House of Councillors (HC). The percentage of candidates who were either incumbents or past incumbents from either house (–50.4%) was the highest since the current electoral system combining single-member districts (SMDs) and proportional representation (PR) was adopted in 1994 (for details on the electoral system, see Scheiner, Smith, and Thies, this volume).

Legislative turnover was also dismally low. Only 43 (9%) of the 475 elected members were newcomers. This marks the second lowest turnover in postwar Japanese history, behind only the 1980 election (7% turnover), which was held just seven months after the 1979 election. Moreover, as Scheiner, Smith, and Thies (this volume) note, the

Table 10.1 Parties and candidates in the 2014 election

	LDP	Kom	DPJ	JIP	PFG	JCP	SDPJ	PLP	Other	Total
Incumbent	289	31	62	41	18	7	2	5	15	470
	82%	61%	31%	49%	38%	2%	8%	25%	15%	39%
Former incumbent	6	0	83	12	2	1	1	9	3	117
	2%	0%	42%	14%	4%	0%	4%	45%	3%	10%
First-time candidate	36	10	41	14	16	105	14	2	40	278
	10%	20%	21%	17%	33%	33%	56%	10%	41%	23%
SMD only	12	9	1	1	3	273	1	1	49	350
	3%	18%	1%	1%	6%	87%	4%	5%	51%	29%
Dual-listed	272	0	177	76	36	19	17	12	0	609
	77%	0%	89%	90%	75%	6%	68%	60%	0%	51%
PR only	69	42	20	7	9	23	7	7	48	232
	20%	82%	10%	8%	19%	7%	28%	35%	49%	19%
Female	42	3	29	9	3	79	1	3	29	198
	12%	6%	15%	11%	6%	25%	4%	15%	30%	17%
Median age	56	49	48	45	51	49	53	50	48	53
Total	353	51	198	84	48	315	25	20	97	1,191

Notes: Incumbent includes both SMD and PR list incumbents. Past losing candidates do not count as first-time candidates—only individuals who have never run for the HR before are included. Party abbreviations: LDP = Liberal Democratic Party; Kom = Komeito; DPJ = Democratic Party of Japan; JIP = Japan Innovation Party; PFG: Party of Future Generations; JCP = Japan Communist Party; SDPJ = Social Democratic Party of Japan; PLP: People's Life Party. Other includes (number of new candidates in parentheses): Happiness Realization Party (42); New Renaissance Party (4); other minor parties (7); and independents (44).

Source: Coded by the author based on *Asahi*, *Mainichi*, and *Yomiuri* candidate data.

major opposition parties did not even nominate a single candidate in 48 (16%) of the 295 SMD races.

It may therefore be tempting to interpret the 2014 election simply as a strengthening of the incumbent political elite – particularly within Prime Minister Abe's Liberal Democratic Party (LDP), which nominated 61% of the incumbent candidates – and a retrenchment of the opposition parties' efforts to challenge the ruling LDP–Komeito coalition. However, a closer inspection of the opposition parties' candidate nominations reveals an improved level of coordination following the chaos of 2012, and some promising growth in candidate quality. This chapter details the coordination that took place within parties (particularly the LDP) following redistricting and between parties in the opposition seeking to challenge the ruling coalition. In addition, the chapter explores the biographical characteristics of new candidates, including their party and career backgrounds, prior political experience, gender, and family ties. Despite the challenges of the snap timing of the election, the ever-changing partisan affiliations of opposition incumbents, and redistricting that eliminated five SMDs, the opposition managed to produce a relatively coherent candidate nomination strategy. In fact, the snap timing may have even helped to prevent the opposition coordination failures witnessed in 2012, when parties had ample time to find candidates to run in SMDs.

The candidate selection process in Japan

There are relatively a few legal eligibility restrictions on running for office in Japan (see Fukui 1997), but it is costly. In order to register as a candidate for the HR, a candidate (or her party) must pay an election deposit (*kyoutakukin*) of ¥3,000,000 (roughly $25,500 at the 2014 exchange rate) to run in an SMD, plus another ¥3,000,000 if she also wants to be included on her party's PR list. Parties must also pay ¥6,000,000 for each "pure PR" candidate. The SMD deposit (¥3,000,000) is returned only if the candidate secures one-tenth of the vote in her district; the PR supplement (¥3,000,000) for a dual-listed candidate is returned only if she wins her SMD race. Additionally, the party receives a reimbursement of ¥12,000,000 for each PR seat it wins. Historically, this hefty deposit requirement has not dissuaded fringe candidates from running in hopeless district races, but it *has* influenced the nomination strategies of the more serious office-seeking parties, which tend to avoid wasting party resources (Harada and Smith, 2014).

When it comes to the actual process of candidate selection, each of the parties uses its own method of recruitment. Traditionally, the weak central leadership of the LDP abdicated the candidate selection process to prefectural-level party organizations and the support groups (*kouenkai*) of outgoing candidates (e.g., Shiratori, 1988; Ishibashi and Reed, 1992; Fukui, 1997), which often favored local politicians, former bureaucrats, and the sons and personal secretaries of the outgoing candidate. However, the party has increasingly made use of an open recruitment system and party primaries at the local level in an attempt to revitalize the process, centralize control over candidates, and avoid criticisms of political nepotism (Asano, 2006; Seko, 2006; Tsutsumi, 2012; Smith, *JD 2012*).

The Democratic Party of Japan (DPJ) and other new opposition parties, including the so-called "Third Force" parties from the 2012 election – the Japan Restoration Party (JRP), Your Party (YP), and Tomorrow Party of Japan (TPJ) – have similarly recruited from local politicians where possible (such as the JRP's stronghold in Osaka), but they have also aggressively conducted nationwide, centralized open recruitment contests to seek new candidates (Smith et al., 2013; Smith, *JD 2012*). In fact, a big reason for the use of open recruitment contests in these parties was the lack of a pool of high-quality local politicians to challenge the LDP in national elections (Scheiner, 2006; Uekami and Tsutsumi, 2011; Smith et al., 2013). Candidates selected through open recruitment contests have thus tended to be of lower quality (in terms of political experience) but exhibit more moderate policy stances than their counterparts recruited through traditional channels (Smith and Tsutsumi, 2014). In contrast to the other main parties, the central leaderships of the Japan Communist Party (JCP) and Komeito exercise greater control over the selection of all candidates (Shiratori, 1988; Smith, 2014).

Candidate selection in 2014: Abe caught the opposition off guard

Part of the explanation for lackluster candidate entry in 2014 was the surprise timing of the election. When Prime Minister Abe signaled his intention to call an early election in mid-November, the DPJ and other opposition parties, still in disarray following the LDP landslide in 2012, had less than a month to prepare for the December 2014 poll.

The DPJ had gone from a 308 seat majority after the 2009 election to just 57 seats after 2012 and had maintained a low media profile as it licked its wounds (Ikeda and Reed, this volume). Meanwhile, the Third Force parties underwent a number of dizzying reorganizations

(Pekkanen and Reed, this volume). Ichirou Ozawa's TPJ rebranded itself the People's Life Party (PLP). Yoshimi Watanabe's YP split in 2013, with Kenji Eda and his followers founding the Unity Party; YP ultimately disbanded completely just before the 2014 election. The JRP also split – with former co-leader Shintarou Ishihara forming the Party of Future Generations (PFG) and the remaining members merging with the Unity Party and rebranding themselves as the Japan Innovation Party (JIP) just a few months before the election. After some of its members decided to rejoin the DPJ, PLP leader Ozawa announced that his party's few remaining members could "do as they please [and] select the road needed to survive" (*Yomiuri*, November 21, 2014).

Thus, the 2014 election continued the trend since electoral reform in 1994 of frequent party switching (e.g., Kato and Kannon, 2008; Nyblade, *JD 2012*), especially among opposition party candidates seeking to provide a credible alternative to the long-dominant LDP. Table 10.2 shows the previous party affiliations of all candidates (at the time of the most recent prior HR election in which they ran) in order to illustrate the party switching that occurred before the 2014 election. Most (842) of the returning candidates who ran in 2014 had also been candidates in 2012. A number of JCP candidates and a handful others had not run in 2012, but rather were returning from past elections. Some of the non-JCP candidates had previously run under the banner of parties that no longer exist, such as the New Frontier Party (NFP) or Liberal Alliance. Among the candidates who abandoned the TPJ/PLP, many returned to the DPJ or joined the JIP. When YP split, several members went to the JIP or ran as independents; a few joined the DPJ.[1]

After Abe signaled his intention to dissolve the HR, opposition party leaders clumsily scrambled to find new candidates and decide nominations. JIP co-leader Tooru Hashimoto and JIP Secretary General Ichirou Matsui both considered running in Osaka 3rd District and Osaka 16th District, respectively, against Komeito incumbents (*Asahi*, November 15, 2014), but ultimately gave up the idea. PFG co-leader Ishihara had initially announced that he would retire from politics, but he was ultimately placed ceremoniously on the party's PR list in Tokyo (in last place). None of the opposition parties had yet conducted any major candidate recruitment effort to prepare for the next election.

The snap election also took many individual candidates in the governing LDP–Komeito coalition by surprise. With its huge majority win in 2012, the LDP had less reason to be concerned with finding candidates to run in each district. In addition, the party had excess incumbents in the prefectures that experienced a reduction in seats due to redistricting.

Table 10.2 Previous party affiliation of candidates in the 2014 election

	LDP	SDPJ	Kom	JCP	DPJ	JIP	PLP	PFG	Other	Total
LDP	314	0	0	0	0	0	0	0	2	316
SDP	0	11	0	0	0	0	0	0	0	11
Kom	0	0	41	0	0	0	0	0	0	41
JCP	0	0	0	210	0	0	0	0	0	210
NFP	1	0	0	0	1	0	0	0	0	2
DPJ	0	0	0	0	146	2	0	0	3	151
Lib. All.	0	0	0	0	0	0	0	0	1	1
YP	0	0	0	0	4	12	0	0	7	23
JRP	0	0	0	0	0	46	0	29	3	78
TPJ	0	0	0	0	5	7	18	2	4	36
Other	2	0	0	0	1	3	0	1	37	44
First-time	36	14	10	105	41	14	2	16	40	278
Total	353	25	51	315	198	84	20	48	97	1,191

Notes: Does not capture all party switching that occurred between elections, only differences in party labels at the time of the 2014 election and the most recent prior election contested by the candidate. Party abbreviations: LDP = Liberal Democratic Party; Kom = Komeito; DPJ = Democratic Party of Japan; JIP = Japan Innovation Party; PFG: Party of Future Generations; JCP = Japan Communist Party; SDPJ = Social Democratic Party of Japan; PLP: People's Life Party. NFP = New Frontier Party (1996); Lib. All. = Liberal Alliance (2000). Other includes (number of new candidates in parentheses): Happiness Realization Party (42); New Renaissance Party (4); other minor parties (7); and independents (44).
Source: Coded by the author based on *Asahi, Mainichi, and Yomiuri* candidate data.

Even so, several veteran LDP incumbents who had intended to retire before the next election were compelled to run again due to the short notice, and Komeito relaxed its age limit (69) for candidacy (*Yomiuri*, November 21, 2014; see also Klein, this volume).

Coordinating nominations in redistricted prefectures

For the 2014 election, the boundaries of 42 SMDs in 17 prefectures were redrawn to address the problem of malapportionment across districts (see Pekkanen, Reed, and Smith, this volume). The redistricting eliminated five rural SMDs – one each in Fukui, Yamanashi, Tokushima, Kochi, and Saga prefectures. In each case, the prefecture went from three to two SMDs. The LDP solved the problem of having excess incumbents by promising the incumbents from eliminated districts a safe position on the party list above dual-listed SMD candidates. For example, in Fukui Prefecture, where the new 2nd District was made up mostly of the old 3rd District, the LDP kept incumbent Tsuyoshi Takagi as its candidate, and the former 2nd District incumbent Taku Yamamoto was given a safe position on the party list. The 1st District LDP incumbent, Tomomi Inada, remained as her party's candidate in the new 1st District.

In Tokushima and Kochi, the LDP's incumbents from eliminated districts were also given safe list positions to solve the nomination problem following redistricting. The incumbent from the old Tokushima 1st District, Mamoru Fukuyama, was given the number two position on the party list for the Shikoku region. The 2012 Tokushima 3rd District candidates for the LDP and DPJ ran in the new Tokushima 1st District, with LDP candidate Masazumi Gotouda again winning the seat. The DPJ's veteran candidate in the old Tokushima 1st District, Yoshito Sengoku, retired from politics after losing his seat in 2012. The LDP's incumbent candidate in Tokushima 2nd District, Shunichi Yamaguchi, again won re-election. In Kochi Prefecture, 1st District LDP incumbent Teru Fukui was given the top list position in the Shikoku region, above Mamoru Fukuyama from Tokushima Prefecture. The LDP's incumbents in Kochi 2nd and 3rd Districts continued on as the party's candidates in Kochi 1st and 2nd Districts.

Lastly, in Saga Prefecture, 2nd District LDP incumbent Masahiro Imamura was not given a guaranteed safe position on the party list in the Kyushu region, but nonetheless won the election at the 31st position, because the LDP won enough seats to elect all of its SMD nominees. The LDP's incumbent from the old 3rd District, Kousuke Hori, retired and was replaced by former Saga Governor Yasushi Furukawa in the new 2nd District. In Yamanashi Prefecture, an opposition stronghold, 3rd District incumbent Hitoshi Gotou from the DPJ resigned his seat in November (prior to Prime Minister Abe calling the snap election) in order to prepare to run for governor of Yamanashi in January 2015. Former YP candidate from Yamanashi 3rd District, Katsuhito Nakajima, joined the DPJ and ran successfully in the 1st District, where the DPJ's 2012 candidate, Tsuyoshi Saitou, retired. The JIP's candidate from 2012 in Yamanashi 1st District, Sakihito Ozawa, was given the top position on his party's list in the Kinki region (Ozawa lost his SMD race in 2012 but won a PR seat as a dual-listed candidate).

The opposition learned (or was forced) to coordinate

One benefit of the snap election timing is that it gave little time to each of the major parties in the fragmented opposition to find a candidate to run in every district. Moreover, opposition party leaders were well aware that making an effort to find and nominate a candidate in each district (thus resulting in multiple opposition candidates) might again help the LDP, as it did in 2012 (Reed et al., *JD 2012*). Both the DPJ and JIP thus tried in many districts to refrain from nominating a new candidate where the other was stronger (i.e., already had an incumbent) or had a better chance to cut away at the LDP-Komeito majority. In Kumamoto 1st District, for example, the combined vote of DPJ candidate Ichirou Ikezaki and DPJ defector-turned-JRP candidate Yorihisa Matsuno in 2012 would have been higher than the winning LDP candidate. This time around, the DPJ stood down, and the party's local branch reluctantly threw its support behind Matsuno (*Yomiuri*, November 28, 2014).

In other districts, opposition coordination efforts were less successful. In Kanagawa 5th District, the DPJ's local party branch selected 48-year-old Yayoi Gotouda, the daughter of retiring DPJ candidate Keishuu Tanaka, who lost his seat in 2012. However, she was denied the official party nomination, partly because the party wanted to avoid splitting the anti-LDP vote with JIP former HC member Masashi Mito, who had already declared in the district (*Kanagawa Shimbun*, November 25, 2014; *Kanagawa Shimbun*, November 26, 2014).[2] Gotouda ultimately ran anyway as an independent and came in fourth place. Similarly, the DPJ denied the official nomination to Maki Ikeda in Hokkaido 2nd District so as not to interfere with DPJ-turned-JIP candidate Kenkou Matsuki's chances of winning a seat (*Hokkaido Shimbun*, November 25, 2014), but she ran anyway. In Osaka 10th District, coordination was never even considered (*Yomiuri*, November 28, 2014). There, LDP-turned-JIP candidate Kenta Matsunami and DPJ candidate Kiyomi Tsujimoto have been battling each other for control of the district since 2003, frequently alternating between winning the SMD and gaining a party list seat.[3]

Nevertheless, if we consider only candidates with official nominations from the DPJ and the Third Force (together the "Big Opposition"), the 2014 election displays much better coordination across SMDs than in 2012 (see Scheiner, Smith, and Thies, this volume). In 2012, only 76 of 300 SMDs had a single candidate from the Big Opposition. In 211 SMDs, the Big Opposition fielded two or more candidates, and in many of these races, the opposition candidates split the anti-LDP/Komeito vote to hand the governing coalition a number of seats that it might have otherwise lost (see Scheiner, Smith, and Thies, this volume).

In contrast, only 56 SMDs in 2014 featured more than one candidate from the DPJ, JIP, PLP, and PFG. This was no doubt in part because the parties lacked candidates to run in all districts and the time to recruit them, but was also in part the result of the directed effort by party leaders in the Big Opposition to avoid once again splitting the vote. In 73 (65%) of the 112 SMDs races where the Big Opposition combined had a greater number of votes than the winning governing coalition candidate, the parties only nominated a single candidate in 2014. Moreover, as Scheiner, Smith, and Thies (this volume) note, the decision to run no candidate at all in 48 SMDs may have also been strategically prudent. These were races with either a strong independent or Social Democratic Party (SDPJ) incumbent running against the LDP/Komeito coalition, or where the LDP/Komeito candidate was so popular that the likelihood of a victory was low, even for a coordinated opposition. Given the election deposit requirement described previously, and the tendency for SMD candidates to be dual-listed (thus costing ¥6,000,000 per candidate), nominating candidates in these additional races would have arguably been a waste of party resources for the opposition.

Backgrounds of new candidates in 2014

In addition to the improved coordination within the opposition, a few aspects of the career backgrounds of new candidates in 2014 stand out as promising of an opposition that will be capable of challenging the LDP's hegemony in future elections. Most notably, despite its major setback in 2012, the DPJ has continued to evolve from a party with a few quality candidates to one that now matches the LDP on this dimension.

A "quality" candidate is often defined as an individual with prior elected experience (e.g., Jacobson, 1983; Jacobson, 1990). Incumbents and former incumbents are thus considered high quality, but so are new candidates with backgrounds as local assemblymen, mayors, or governors, and former incumbents from the HC. Scheiner (2006: 137) argues that a "quality" candidate in Japan might be more broadly defined as an individual that has one or more of these backgrounds, or (1) candidates who "inherit" the SMD of a relative (a so-called "hereditary" or *seshuu* candidate), (2) former national-level bureaucrats, and (3) former TV news reporters. According to Scheiner, one of the key reasons that the DPJ was so slow to challenge the LDP's dominance between 1996 and 2003 was the party's lack of "quality" candidates. Weiner (2011) finds that the DPJ still suffered from a lack of quality candidates up until the 2009 election.

However, the percentage of prefectural and municipal assemblymen affiliated with the DPJ increased slowly beginning around 1999, and then more quickly after 2007, when the DPJ won control of the HC (Uekami and Tsutsumi, 2011). By the 2012 election, the party had begun to draw on these local "quality" candidates for new nominations (Smith et al., 2013). The 2014 election continued this trend, and featured the highest percentage of new quality candidates in the DPJ yet, at 63%. If we use the more broad definition of quality given by Scheiner (2006), nearly 70% of the DPJ's new candidates in 2014 were "quality" candidates, compared to less than 40% in the earlier years of party recruitment (Figure 10.1).[4]

Table 10.3 shows the career backgrounds and other characteristics of the 278 new candidates by party. In a promising change, although only 17% of all candidates in 2014 were women, women made up nearly a third of all new candidates, and nearly a half of the LDP's new candidates. This is a big increase from just 17% of all new candidates and 8% of new LDP candidates in 2012, though the percentage of women among elected candidates is still less than 10% (see Gaunder, this volume). Prior experience in local politics and serving as a Diet member's personal secretary continue to be common stepping-stones to candidacy, and a majority of candidates were born in the district or prefecture where they ran. Although former national bureaucrats once accounted for roughly a quarter of all new candidates in the LDP, in recent elections they have been less common – and just 11% of new LDP candidates in 2014.

Another common path to candidacy in the LDP, hereditary succession by family members, also continues to decline (Smith, *JD 2012*). The LDP nominated just three new "legacy" candidates (*nisei*), all of whom directly succeeded their relatives in the same district as "hereditary"

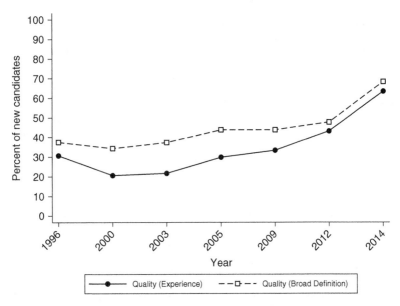

Figure 10.1 Quality of new candidates in the DPJ (1996–2014)

Note: Quality (Experience) includes any previous experience as a local assembly person, mayor, governor, or member of the HC. Quality (Broad Definition) includes the narrow definition plus hereditary candidates (*seshuu*), former national bureaucrats, and TV news announcers or commentators. It does not include legacy candidates (*nisei*) who did not directly follow their predecessors into office, local-level bureaucrats, print newspaper reporters, or other types of celebrities. Including these candidates would further increase the percent of "quality" candidates in the DPJ.

Source: Coded by the author based on *Asahi, Mainichi, and Yomiuri* candidate data.

candidates (*seshuu*) – a practice that the DPJ has prohibited but which the LDP cannot seem to completely overcome, despite much criticism in the media. In Yamagata 3rd District, long-time LDP veteran Kouichi Katou was one of the few LDP incumbents to lose his seat in 2012 – to an LDP-affiliated former mayor, Juichi Abe, who ran as an independent.[5] In 2014, the LDP nominated Katou's 35-year-old daughter, Ayuko Katou, in an uncontested open recruitment contest. Abe initially expressed interest in getting the official nomination of the party but decided not to enter the open recruitment contest after the LDP's prefectural branch decided to require any person seeking the nomination to agree to stand down if they did not win a vote among local party members. Katou was viewed as favored to win that vote. LDP HC member Yukari Satou also expressed some interest in the nomination (her grandfather was from the area), but ultimately decided to run from Osaka 11th District instead (*Kahoku Shinpou*, July 1, 2014).

Table 10.3 Backgrounds of first-time candidates in 2014

	LDP	Kom	DPJ	JIP	PFG	JCP	SDPJ	PLP	Other	Total
Local/HC experience	7 19%	2 20%	26 63%	6 43%	2 13%	30 29%	6 43%	2 100%	4 10%	85 31%
DM secretary	10 28%	2 20%	16 39%	4 29%	4 25%	0 0%	2 14%	1 50%	4 10%	43 15%
Bureaucrat	4 11%	0 0%	1 2%	0 0%	2 13%	0 0%	0 0%	0 0%	1 3%	8 3%
News media	0 0%	3 30%	3 7%	0 0%	1 6%	1 1%	0 0%	0 0%	0 0%	8 3%
Medicine	3 8%	0 0%	2 5%	0 0%	0 0%	6 6%	0 0%	0 0%	3 8%	14 5%
Law	3 8%	0 0%	0 0%	1 7%	0 0%	0 0%	0 0%	0 0%	1 3%	5 2%
Business	4 8%	0 0%	4 10%	3 21%	1 6%	4 4%	0 0%	0 0%	10 25%	26 9%
Education	8 22%	0 0%	5 12%	0 0%	1 6%	13 12%	4 29%	0 0%	3 8%	34 12%
Labor union	0 0%	0 0%	5 12%	0 0%	0 0%	9 9%	3 21%	0 0%	1 3%	18 6%
Agriculture	0 0%	0 0%	0 0%	0 0%	0 0%	2 2%	1 7%	0 0%	1 3%	4 1%
JSDF	0 0%	0 0%	0 0%	0 0%	3 19%	1 1%	0 0%	0 0%	1 3%	5 2%
Celebrity	0 0%	0 0%	1 2%	0 0%	0 0%	0 0%	0 0%	0 0%	2 5%	3 1%

Table 10.3 (Continued)

	LDP	Kom	DPJ	JIP	PFG	JCP	SDP	PLP	Other	Total
Legacy (nisei)	3	0	3	1	0	0	0	0	4	11
	8%	0%	7%	7%	0%	0%	0%	0%	10%	4%
Hereditary (seshuu)	3	0	0	0	0	0	0	0	1	4
	8%	0%	0%	0%	0%	0%	0%	0%	3%	1%
Born in district	23	7	21	3	4	54	9	0	22	143
	64%	70%	51%	21%	25%	51%	64%	0%	55%	51%
Born in prefecture	24	7	27	4	5	66	12	1	26	172
	67%	70%	66%	29%	31%	63%	86%	50%	65%	62%
Female	17	0	9	2	2	35	1	1	14	81
	47%	0%	22%	14%	13%	33%	7%	50%	35%	29%
Median age	47	47	51	40	53	55	56	69	44	50
Total no. of candidates	36	10	41	14	16	105	14	2	40	278

Notes: Each candidate can have multiple traits, and some past experiences may be missing if the candidate did not choose to report them. Local/HC experience includes service in municipal and prefectural assemblies, as well as service as mayor or governor, or in the HC. DM secretary is a private or public secretary to a member of the Diet. Bureaucrat is a national-level civil servant. News media includes television and print news media. Medicine includes doctors, nurses, and related fields. Business only includes persons with some kind of leadership title (e.g., *yakuin*), not simple employees (*shain*). Education includes everything from university professors to cram school teachers. Labor union includes anyone active in the union movement. Agriculture includes farmers and members of farming associations such as JA. JSDF are former enlisted members of the Japan Self-Defense Forces. Celebrity includes television and movie talent, as well as famous athletes, authors, and other notables. Legacy (*nisei*) candidates are related to a former member of the Diet; hereditary (*seshuu*) candidates are legacy candidates who directly succeed their relatives in the same district. Party abbreviations: LDP = Liberal Democratic Party; Kom = Komeito; DPJ = Democratic Party of Japan; JIP = Japan Innovation Party; PFG = Party of Future Generations; JCP = Japan Communist Party; SDP] = Social Democratic Party of Japan; PLP = People's Life Party. Other includes (number of new candidates in parentheses): Happiness Realization Party (15); New Renaissance Party (4); other minor parties (2); and independents (19).
Source: Coded by the author based on *Asahi, Mainichi, and Yomiuri* candidate data.

In Kagoshima 3rd District, veteran LDP incumbent Kazuaki Miyaji decided to retire. The party nominated his 34-year-old son, Takuma Miyaji (*Mainichi*, November 27, 2014). In Osaka 17th District, Nobuko Okashita had been the party's candidate since 2000, after the sudden death of her husband, Masahiro Okashita, who ran as the party's candidate in 1996, but died suddenly in 1998. Nobuko won election in the district twice, in 2000 and 2005, but lost in 2009 and 2012. In 2014, the party replaced her with her 39-year-old son, Shouhei Okashita, who had been gaining political experience in the Osaka Prefectural Assembly. Shouhei lost to JIP incumbent Nobuyuki Baba, but secured a seat through the PR list. In Gunma 1st District, the LDP prefectural branch initially considered replacing incumbent Genichirou Sata with former Prime Minister Yasuhiro Nakasone's 32-year-old grandson, Yasutaka Nakasone, but ultimately stuck with Sata (*Sankei*, November 20, 2014).

Summary

Like many other aspects of the 2014 election, candidate selection was a tame affair compared to the excitement of the 2012 election. However, Abe's decision to call the snap election may have been somewhat beneficial to the divided opposition's coordination strategy, even if it came before opposition parties could craft a convincing set of alternative policies. The main opposition parties ran fewer candidates against each other this time around, standing down in many SMDs where one party's candidate had a better chance of challenging the ruling coalition. In the districts where they ran no candidate at all, the opposition was likely to lose the contest anyway, and potentially waste scarce party resources.

Whether the opposition truly learned from its mistakes in 2012 or was simply caught off guard, the 2014 election featured much better coordination. In addition, the candidates that ran under the banner of the opposition parties, most especially the DPJ and JIP, no longer appear to suffer from the "quality" gap of years past. With the near demise of the PFG and PLP and the precedent of coordination achieved in this election, the DPJ and JIP may be more capable of challenging the LDP-Komeito dominance in future elections.

Notes

1. Of the 97 candidates grouped as "Other" in Table 10.2, 53 were affiliated with minor party movements. The remaining 44 independent candidates included

several individuals that were previously affiliated with a major political party (including 4 would-be DPJ and 3 would-be LDP candidates among the first-time candidates who ultimately ran as independents).

2. The DPJ also, in principle, has a ban on direct hereditary succession in nominations, though relatives may receive the nomination in later elections or from different districts.

3. The LDP also faced some issues in settling nominations (see Endo and Pekkanen, this volume). In Hyogo 12th District, the prefectural branch decided to recommend Shintarou Toida, the son of former LDP candidate Tooru Toida from neighboring Hyogo 11th District (*Sankei*, November 11, 2014; *Kobe Shimbun*, November 18, 2014). However, the district's independent incumbent, Tsuyoshi Yamaguchi also sought the LDP's nomination. The party withheld the official nomination from both, but Yamaguchi joined the LDP after winning the election. In Fukuoka 1st District, the LDP again faced internal division between two incumbents, Yuuji Shinkai and Takahiro Inoue (Smith, *JD 2012*). The party withheld the official nomination from both until it became clear Inoue would win. He was given the party's official nomination (*tsuika kounin*) the night before the election.

4. It should be noted, however, that at the same time that opposition candidates are increasing in quality, candidate quality is becoming less and less important to electoral success in an increasingly party-centered electoral environment (Reed et al., 2012).

5. Katou was not allowed to be dual-listed due to his advanced age (73), in accordance with LDP nomination principles.

References

Asano, Masahiko (2006). *Shimin Shakai ni okeru Seido Kaikaku: Senkyo Seido to Kouhosha Rikuruuto [System Reform at the Level of Civil Society: Electoral Reform and Candidate Recruitment]*. Tokyo: Keio University Press.

Fukui, Haruhiro (1997). Japan. In Pippa Norris (ed.) *Passages to Power: Legislative Recruitment in Advanced Democracies*. pp. 98–113. Cambridge: Cambridge University Press.

Harada, Masataka, and Daniel M. Smith (2014). You have to pay to play: Candidate and party responses to the high cost of elections in Japan. *Electoral Studies* 36: 51–64.

Ishibashi, Michihiro and Steven R. Reed. (1992). Second-generation diet members and democracy in Japan: Hereditary seats. *Asian Survey* 32: 366–379.

Jacobson, Gary C. (1983). *The Politics of Congressional Elections*. Boston: Little, Brown.

Jacobson, Gary C. (1990). *The Origins of Divided Government: Competition in the U.S. House Elections*. pp. 1946–1988. Boulder, CO: Westview Press.

Kato, Junko, and Yuto Kannon (2008). Coalition governments, party switching, and the rise and decline of parties: Changing Japanese party politics since 1993. *Japanese Journal of Political Science* 9(3): 341–365.

Nyblade, Benjamin (2013). Keeping it together: Party unity and the 2012 election. In Robert Pekkanen, Steven R. Reed and Ethan Scheiner (eds) *Japan Decides 2012: The Japanese General Election*. pp. 20–33. New York: Palgrave Macmillan.

Reed, Steven R., Ethan Scheiner, Daniel M. Smith and Michael Thies (2013). The 2012 election results: The LDP wins big by default. In Robert Pekkanen, Steven R. Reed and Ethan Scheiner (eds) *Japan Decides 2012: The Japanese General Election.* pp. 34–46. London: Palgrave.

Reed, Steven R., Ethan Scheiner and Michael F. Thies (2012). The end of LDP dominance and the rise of party-oriented politics in Japan. *Journal of Japanese Studies* 38(2): 353–376.

Scheiner, Ethan (2006). *Democracy without Competition in Japan: Opposition Failure in a One-Party Dominant State.* New York: Cambridge University Press.

Seko, Hiroshige (2006). *Jimintou Kaizou Purojekuto 650 Nichi [LDP Reform Project: 650 Days].* Tokyo: Shinchousa.

Shiratori, Rei (1988). Japan: Localism, factionalism, personalism. In Michael Gallagher and Michael Marsh (eds) *Candidate Selection in Comparative Perspective: The Secret Garden of Politics* pp. 169–189. London, UK: Sage.

Smith, Daniel M. (2013). Candidate recruitment for the 2012 election: New parties, new methods ... same old pool of candidates? In Robert Pekkanen, Steven R. Reed and Ethan Scheiner (eds) *Japan Decides 2012: The Japanese General Election* pp. 101–122. London: Palgrave.

Smith, Daniel M. (2014). Party ideals and practical constraints in Kōmeitō candidate nominations. In George Ehrhardt, Axel Klein, Levi McLaughlin and Steven R. Reed (eds) *Kōmeitō: Politics and Religion in Japan.* pp. 139–162. Berkeley, CA: The Institute of East Asian Studies at the University of California, Berkeley.

Smith, Daniel M., Robert J. Pekkanen and Ellis S. Krauss (2013). Building a party: Candidate recruitment in the Democratic Party of Japan, 1996–2012. In Kenji E. Kushida and Phillip Y. Lipscy (eds) *Japan under the DPJ: The Politics of Transition and Governance.* pp. 157–190. Stanford, CA: The Walter H. Shorenstein Asia-Pacific Research Center at Stanford University.

Smith, Daniel M. and Hidenori Tsutsumi (2014). Candidate selection methods and policy cohesion in parties: The impact of open recruitment in Japan. *Party Politics*, online first.

Tsutsumi, Hidenori (2012). Kouhosha Sentei Katei no Kaihou to Seitou Soshiki [Opening up the Candidate Selection Process and Party Organization]. *Senkyo Kenkyu [Election Studies]* 28(1): 5–20.

Uekami, Takayoshi and Hidenori Tsutsumi (2011). Minshutou no Kessei Katei, Soshiki to Seisaku [DPJ Formation, Organization, and Policy]. In Takayoshi Uekami and Hidenori Tsutsumi (eds) *Minshutou no Soshiki to Seisaku [DPJ Organization and Policy].* pp. 1–28. Tokyo: Touyou Keizai.

Weiner, Robert. (2011). The evolution of the DPJ: Two steps forward, one step back. In Leonard J. Schoppa (ed.) *The Evolution of Japan's Party System: Politics and Policy in an Era of Institutional Change.* pp. 63–98. Toronto: University of Toronto Press.

11
Women and the 2014 Lower House Election

Alisa Gaunder

Female candidacy in the 2014 lower house election was similar to past years. Moreover, the percentage of women elected only increased from 7.9% to 9.5%, despite the government's emphasis since 2010 on the goal of increasing female participation in the civil service sector, business, and politics. The Liberal Democratic Party (LDP) Prime Minister Shinzō Abe has frequently referenced the goal of increasing female leadership in management and politics to 30% by 2020. He even included a record tying five females in his second cabinet (although two female cabinet ministers had to resign shortly after their appointments due to questionable campaign and finance activities). Women also figure prominently in the third arrow of Abenomics, structural reform (see Noble, this volume). Specifically, Abe has emphasized the need for changes in workplace policies that will "create a society where women shine." The Democratic Party of Japan (DPJ) also highlighted women prior to the election, verbally committing to investigate an internal party quota for female candidates in early fall 2014. Neither party, however, managed to increase female candidacy (in any appreciable sense) in the 2014 lower house election. This chapter explores the effects of the electoral system and the snap election on female candidacy to explain this discrepancy between pre-election rhetoric and the reality of female participation in Japanese politics.

The effects of the electoral system and the snap election on female candidacy

The electoral system and snap election explain the dynamics of female candidacy in the 2014 lower house election. The electoral system for

---

I would like to thank Hikaru Oyashiki for her research assistance.

the lower house has 295 single-member district (SMD) seats and 180 proportional representation (PR) seats (see Scheiner, Smith, and Thies, this volume). The literature on women and politics maintains that PR systems are better for promoting female candidates (Rosen, 2013; Salmond, 2006). SMD systems deter female candidacy due to incumbency and other barriers to nomination (Darcy and Nixon, 1996; Schwindt-Bayer, 2005). In contrast, PR systems provide a comprehensive list of candidates and can promote parties to think in a more balanced way in candidate selection. PR systems also lend themselves to "positive action strategies" to promote female candidates, such as the adoption of legislative or party quotas (Norris, 2004).

In combined SMD/PR systems, women perform better in the PR tier (Moser and Scheiner, 2012). Japan tends to support this trend. The PR portion, however, is quite small. Moreover, ranking on PR lists can be and has been connected to candidates' performance in SMDs. For dual listing, open SMD seats are required for new women to enter. There also need to be a set of qualified women candidates in the pipeline. A large number of women are not found in the traditional occupations that feed the political pipeline, such as the civil service and local politics (Ogai, 2001). The trend toward open recruitment has mitigated this constraint to some extent (see Smith, this volume).

Informally, both the LDP in 2005 and the DPJ in 2009 promoted women candidates to bolster their reformist credentials by appointing several candidates to the PR list (Gaunder 2009, 2012). Koziumi put the candidates at the top of the list in most PR blocs; the DPJ put several women at the bottom of the list to capitalize on its overwhelming popularity. These informal efforts have led to a modest increase in female candidates and politicians since the implementation of the combined electoral system in 1996.

No party in Japan has successfully implemented a quota (Gaunder, 2015). Quotas by definition do not increase female representation. A certain percentage of female candidates could be mandated, for example, but if these women are not placed in winnable seats then the law would have little impact (Norris, 2004). Moreover, party-level quotas are often voluntary. If there are insufficient "sticks" to punish parties for failing to reach the quota, then the number of women elected might not change. Campaign finance and power within parties remain an issue even with quotas (Dahlerup and Freidenvall, 2005). Fast-tracking quotas can even lead to tokenism further stigmatizing women (Dahlerup and Freidenvall, 2005). Still, several countries have successfully implemented quotas (Krook, 2009). In some of these countries, a political party's successful implementation of a quota has reduced the reluctance of other parties to adopt quotas (Matland and Studlar, 1996). In Japan, the lack of opposition competition for the female vote has made it easier for the LDP to ignore calls to institutionalize the support of women (Gaunder, 2015).

Finally, the snap election impeded the recruitment of female candidates. Both the LDP and the DPJ struggled to find women candidates in the short time frame of Abe's snap election. The LDP had some success as 47% of new LDP candidates were women (Smith, this volume). The DPJ on the other hand could not implement a quota just two months after its commitment to investigate one.

Female candidacy by party

Due to the rigidity of incumbency in SMDs and the unanticipated nature of the election, female candidacy did not change dramatically in the 2014 lower house election. Out of the 1191 total candidates, 198 were women, or 16.6%. Of the 198 female candidates, 45 women were elected. That is, 22.7% of women candidates won seats in contrast to 43.3% of male candidates who won a seat. The number of women in the Diet increased from 38 to 45, but the total remains below the high of 54 women in the 2009 lower house election. Female representation at 9.5% in the 2014 election falls considerably short of Abe's 30% by 2020 rhetoric. This percentage of female representation also places Japan remarkably low in comparison to other countries. Japan currently ranks 113th for representation of women in the lower house. It continues to perform poorly regionwise where average female lower house representation in Asia sits at 19% (IPU 2015). This section considers female candidacy in the major parties (see Table 11.1) and compares the current electoral results to results of previous elections (see Table 11.2).

LDP

For the second election in a row the largest number of women elected came from the LDP. This result confirms the importance of party label in Japanese electoral politics. LDP women won because LDP candidates in general won (Gaunder, 2012; Martin Murphy, *JD* 2012). In the end, 42 of the LDP's 352 candidates were women, or 12%. Twenty-two female LDP candidates were dual listed in SMD races and on the PR list. Twenty women were only running on the PR list. The LDP had 17 first-time female candidates, 22 female incumbents, and 3 female former

Table 11.1 Women in the 2014 HR election

	# Women candidates (SMD only/PR only/dual listed)	# Women elected (SMD/PR)
LDP	42 (0/20/22)	25 (16/9)
DPJ	29 (0/1/28)	9 (2/7)
Komeito	3 (0/3/0)	3 (0/3)
Innovation Party	9 (0/0/9)	2 (0/2)
People's Life Party	9 (0/0/9)	0
Party for Future Generations	3 (0/2/1)	0
JCP	79 (64/8/7)	6 (0/6)
SDP	1 (0/1/0)	0

Source: Ministry of internal affairs and communications (MIC), http://www.soumu .go.jp/ senkyo/senkyo_s/data/, accessed February 1, 2015.

Table 11.2 Female members of the Japanese Diet (by share of women in party caucus)

	1996	2000	2003	2005	2009	2012	2014
LDP	4 (1.7%)	8 (3.4%)	9 (3.8%)	26 (8.8%)	8 (6.7%)	23 (7.9%)	25 (8.6%)
DPJ	3 (5.8%)	6 (4.7%)	15 (8.5%)	7 (6.2%)	40 (13%)	3 (5.2%)	9 (12.3%)
Komeito	n/a	3 (9.7%)	4 (11.8%)	4 (12.9%)	3 (14.3%)	3 (9.6%)	3 (8.6%)
JCP	4 (15%)	4 (20%)	2 (22%)	2 (22%)	1 (11%)	1 (12.5%)	6 (28.6%)
SDP	3 (20%)	10 (53%)	3 (50%)	4 (57%)	2 (29%)	0 (0%)	0 (0%)
Total*	23 (4.6%)	35 (7.3%)	34 (7.1%)	43 (9%)	54 (11.3%)	38 (7.9%)	45 (9.5%)

*Total includes women elected from all political parties, including smaller parties and independents not listed on the table. The percentage that follows represents the total percent of women in the Diet.
Source: Ministry of internal affairs and communications (MIC), http://www.soumu.go.jp /senkyo/senkyo_s/data/, accessed February 1, 2015; Interparliamentary Union, http://www .ipu.org/, accessed March 16, 2015.

incumbents. Twenty-five of the 42 women won election. Sixteen women were elected in SMDs and nine won in PR. Six of the nine women elected in PR had been dual listed and were "saved" by the PR list. Of the 25 female candidates who were elected, 20 were incumbents, four were first-time candidates, and one had been a former incumbent.

While the LDP did not come close to 30% female representation, it did increase its overall number of female candidates. In 2012, the LDP ran 27 women and 23 won. In 2014, it increased the number of female candidates from 27 to 42, but it only increased the number of women elected from 23 to 25. The 25 LDP women still fall short of the record 26 LDP women elected in 2005.

DPJ

Even though the DPJ ran fewer women candidates in the 2014 election than it had in the previous two elections, it saw more women elected. In 2014, the DPJ fielded 29 female candidates out of 198, or 15%. Twenty-eight of the candidates were dual listed and only one female candidate was listed in PR. There were nine first-time female candidates, six incumbents, 12 former incumbents, and two returning candidates who never won. Nine of the 28 women were elected. In 2012, the DPJ supported 37 women candidates but only three incumbents won in PR districts (Martin Murphy, *JD 2012*). Of the nine women elected in 2014, two women won in SMDs and seven women were elected in PR; all seven PR winners had been dual listed. Six of the successful female candidates were incumbents, one was a first-time candidate and two had been former incumbents.

The snap election impeded the DPJ's ability to explore a gender quota. In October 2014, the DPJ publicly announced that it would investigate implementing a quota system with 30% female candidates in time for the next lower house election (*Asahi*, October 16, 2014, web). Reaching the 30% goal would have been a stretch even if the DPJ had had more time to implement the quota. While 40 DPJ women won in the DPJ's landside victory over the LDP in 2009, women still only constituted 13.5% of sitting DPJ politicians (40 women to 296 total DPJ politicians). In the 2012 lower house election, 13% of the 267 DPJ candidates were women. In the 2013 upper house election, ten of the 55 candidates were women, or 18%. In the end, despite its desire to distinguish itself as a party that supports female candidates, the DPJ ran fewer female candidates than the LDP in 2014. The DPJ did support a slightly higher percentage of women candidates with its 15% female candidates versus the LDP's 12% female candidates.

The DPJ has had several non-quota resources in place for women prior to its commitment to investigate a quota (Gaunder, 2009). In addition to its open recruitment program, the DPJ has a program that provides female candidates a modest sum of money to start their campaign. It also has experimented with a party policy to support at least one female candidate in all upper house districts with more than three seats (personal interview, March 27, 2009). It will be interesting to see if the DPJ follows through with its commitment to a quota in the next lower house election.

Komeito

The LDP's junior coalition partner, the Komeito, continues to run a small number of female candidates. In 2014, the Komeito supported three female candidates out of 51 total candidates, or 6%. All three female candidates were incumbents fielded only on the PR list. The success rate of Komeito candidates is high. In 2014, all female candidates supported by the Komeito won. In 2012, the Komeito ran four women and three won. This high success rate is related to the coordination with the LDP in electoral districts as well as the party's ability to get out the vote (Klein, this volume).

Third Force parties

The Third Force parties did not make any significant changes in their support of female candidates. In 2012, the Third Force parties were new and had to scurry to find new candidates. In 2014, these parties ran both first-time and incumbent female candidates, but the newly realigned and renamed Japan Innovation Party was the only party to successfully see women elected.

Third Force parties experienced realignment between the 2012 and 2014 election cycles (see Pekkanen and Reed, this volume). Most notably, the Japan Restoration Party (co-led by former Osaka Governor Tōru Hashimoto and former Tokyo Mayor Shintarō Ishihara) split. Hashimoto's followers joined with the members of the Unity Party to form the Japan Innovation Party. Ishihara's group formed the smaller Party for Future Generations. The remaining Third Force party is Ichirō Ozawa's People's Life Party.

In general, these parties failed to capitalize on the momentum surrounding their initial creation in 2012. Since 2012 these parties have been plagued by internal divisions and a lack of policy coherence (Jain, 2014). Moreover, these parties could not cooperate with each other or the DPJ, further weakening their position (Pekkanen, Reed, and Smith, this volume).

Japan Innovation Party: The Japan Innovation Party had nine female candidates out of 84 total, or 11%. Four female candidates had never been elected, including two first-time candidates. There were also three incumbents and two former incumbents. All nine female candidates were dual listed. Two of the nine candidates won. One of the elected women was an incumbent; the other was a former incumbent.

Party for Future Generations: The Party for Future Generations had three female candidates out of 48 total candidates, or 6%. Two of the women were first-time candidates; the third was an incumbent. One female candidate was dual listed; the other two only ran on the PR list. None of the female candidates won.

People's Life Party: The People's Life Party had three female candidates out of 20 candidates, or 15%. Of the three women, one was a first-time candidate, one was an incumbent, and one was a former incumbent. Two of the three women were dual listed as SMD and PR candidates; the remaining female candidates ran on the PR list. None of the women were elected.

Traditional opposition parties

While significant party realignment has occurred after both electoral reform in 1994 and the splintering of the DPJ in 2012, a few smaller parties have remained intact, including the LDP's junior coalition partner, the Komeito (considered above), the Japanese Communist Party (JCP) and the Social Democratic Party (SDP). The JCP consistently has been committed to female candidacy. The case of the JCP, however, underscores the need for a more viable mainstream party to support women in larger numbers. The JCP is not a threat to the LDP, so its support of women largely goes unnoticed, leaving little hope for "contagion from the Left" (Matland and Studlar, 1996). The SDP traditionally has been a strong supporter of female candidates as well, but it has struggled to maintain its relevance. The SDP (then named the Japanese Socialist Party) oversaw the so-called "Madonna Boom" in 1989 when it successfully supported 10 female candidates for the upper house in 1989 under the leadership of the first female party head, Doi Takako. Shortly thereafter it lost its momentum, and currently it is close to extinction.

The JCP: The JCP had the highest percentage of female candidates with 79 female candidates out of 315 total candidates, or 25%. One incumbent female candidate ran; the remaining 78 females had never been elected, including 35 first-time candidates. Even though the JCP fields a large number of women, the success rate for all JCP candidates is low. When the JCP performs more strongly, women also do better. In 2014, the JCP more than doubled its total seats to 21 seats. Six women were elected compared to one woman in the previous election. Only one of the women elected was an incumbent; the five other women elected were newly elected.

In 2012, the JCP switched to a strategy of supporting candidates in SMDs and not dual listing. Even though some argued that this strategy decreased its ability to maximize its seat share (Martin Murphy, *JD 2012*), the party continued this strategy in 2014. This strategy is apparent in its support of women. The JCP fielded 64 women candidates exclusively in SMDs. It only dual listed seven female candidates, or 9% of its women candidates. Eight female candidates were placed only on the PR list. In the end, the JCP's representation came mainly from the PR list. Only one candidate won in an SMD; the remaining 20 winners were on PR lists. All six of the women elected won in PR. Two of the six women were dual-listed candidates who won a seat through PR.

The SDP: In 2014, the SDP fielded 25 candidates and only one woman, or 4%. The female candidate was a first-time candidate on the PR list. She did not win. Only two male SDP candidates won as the SDP continues to barely stay in existence.

Conclusion

While Prime Minister Abe and the LDP did not see a significant increase in female politicians elected, Abe did include four women in his third cabinet reshuffle following the election. The current female ministers include Yoko Kamikawa, Minister of Justice; Sanae Takaichi, Minister for Internal Affairs and Communication; Haruko Arimura, Minister of Gender Equality; and Eriko Yamatani, Minister of Disaster Management. Several of the female cabinet ministers are conservative. For example, Minister of Gender Equality, Arimura, opposes the dual surname legislation, as well as female imperial succession.

The rise of women to key posts in the LDP illustrates that having women in government does not necessarily result in progressive policies. In fact, conservative women often have been more successful attaining executive leadership precisely because they do not hold policy positions that challenge the status quo (Murray, 2010: 20).

Indeed, there is little evidence that the LDP will institutionalize support for female candidates. The party performs well in SMDs and thus has a large number of male incumbents it would be unwilling to replace. The DPJ's interest in pursuing quotas has some potential of influencing the political landscape for women. If the party is able to institute a quota which places women high on PR lists, it could indicate a real commitment to women that resonates with voters. The DPJ, however, is struggling to redefine itself following its time in government, despite the fact it has reestablished itself as the primary alternative to the LDP

(Ikeda and Reed, this volume). The women and politics literature does suggest that one party's successful support of women can in fact influence other parties' actions (Matland and Studlar, 1996). If the DPJ adopts a quota, this phenomenon might emerge in the future.

References

Dahlerup, Drude and Lenita Freidenvall (2005). Quotas as a 'fast track' to equal political representation for women: Why Scandinavia is no longer the model. *International Feminist Journal of Politics* 7(1): 26–48.

Darcy, Robert and David L. Nixon (1996). Women in the 1946 and 1993 Japanese house of representative elections: The role of the election system. *Journal of Northeast Asian Studies* 15: 3–19.

Gaunder, Alisa (2009). Women running for national office in Japan: Are Koizumi's female "children" a short-term anomaly or a lasting phenomenon? In Steven Reed, Kenneth Mori McElwain and Kay Shimizu (eds) *Political Change in Japan: Electoral Behavior, Party Realignment, and the Koizumi Reforms.* pp. 239–259. Washington, DC: Brookings Institution.

Gaunder, Alisa (2012). The DPJ and women: The limited impact of the 2009 alternation of power on policy and governance. *Journal of East Asian Studies* 12: 441–466.

Gaunder, Alisa (2015). Quota nonadoption in Japan: The role of the women's movement and the opposition. *Politics and Gender* 11(1): 176–186.

Interparliamentary Union (IPU) (2015). Women in national parliaments. http:// www. ipu.org/wmn-e/world.htm, accessed March 17, 2015.

Jain, Purnendra (2014). Election reveals the sorry state of Japan's political opposition. 18 December. http://www.eastasiaforum.org/2014/12/18/election -reveals-the-sorry-state-of-japans-political-opposition/, accessed December 29, 2015.

Krook, Mona Lena (2009). *Quotas for women in politics: Gender and candidate selection reform worldwide.* Oxford: Oxford University Press.

Matland, Richard E. and Donley T. Studlar (1996). The Contagion of women candidates in single-member district and proportional representation electoral systems: Canada and Norway. *Journal of Politics* 58(3): 707–733.

Martin Murphy, Sherry (2013). Women candidates and political parties in election 2012. In Robert Pekkanen, Steven R. Reed and Ethan Scheiner *(*eds*) Japan Decides 2012: The Japanese General Election.* pp. 170–176. New York: Palgrave Macmillan.

Moser, Robert G. and Ethan Scheiner (2012). *Electoral systems and political context.* New York: Cambridge University Press.

Murray, Rainbow (2010). Introduction: Gender stereotypes and media coverage of women candidates. In Rainbow Murray (ed.) *Cracking the Highest Glass Ceiling: A Global Comparison of Women's Campaigns for Executive Office.* pp. 3–27. Santa Barbara, CA: Praeger.

Norris, Pippa (2004). *Electoral engineering: Voting rules and political behavior.* Cambridge: Cambridge University Press.

Ogai, Tokuko (2001). Japanese women and political institutions: Why are women politically underrepresented? *PS: Political Science and Politics* 34(2): 207–210.

Rosen, Jennifer (2013). The effects of political institutions on women's political representation: A comparative analysis of 168 countries from 1992 to 2010. *Political Research Quarterly* 66(2): 306–321.

Salmond, Rob (2006). Proportional representation and female parliamentarians. *Legislative Studies Quarterly* 31(2): 175–204.

Schwindt-Bayer, Leslie A. (2005). The incumbency disadvantage and women's election to legislative office. *Electoral Studies* 24: 227–244.

12
Netizens Decide 2014? A Look at Party Campaigning Online

Joshua A. Williams and Douglas M. Miller

The December 2014 election was a digital milestone in Japan: political parties and politicians effectively became free to campaign online for the first time in a general election. Shortly after the 2012 general election, the Liberal Democratic Party (LDP) quickly pushed through a much-demanded and long-anticipated revision to the Public Offices Election Law (POEL), creating specific legal provisions allowing for previously prohibited online campaigning activities. While the new law came in time for the 2013 House of Councillors (HC) election, all indication was that online campaigning had minimal electoral impact. Can the same be said in 2014? This chapter provides a brief historical background on digital campaigning, looks at how political parties attempted to take advantage of digital campaigning resources, and contemplates the future of online campaigning in Japan. We find that parties were prepared to campaign online despite the relative suddenness of the election and that online behavior reflected offline patterns.

Online campaign background in brief

In Japan, all electoral campaigning is heavily regulated by the POEL, a law that came into being in its general current form in 1950 (Tkach-Kawasaki, 2011: 58–61). While the POEL was enacted in the name of electoral fairness, its rules which severely limit campaign spending and media access provided incumbents with de facto advantages, and have generally continued to do so despite numerous revisions (Krauss, 1996: 361; McElwain, 2008).

Like their Western counterparts, Japanese politicians started coming online in the mid-1990s as the Internet took off globally after the advent of the World Wide Web. However, unlike in the West, while online political communication in Japan flourished in the electoral off-season, it was stifled during election campaigns by bureaucrats strictly applying the pre-digital era POEL to digital activities – an incompatible mix. As early as 1998, opposition parties called for revision, but the LDP saw little reason to seek changes they felt might give opponents electoral advantages (Tkach-Kawasaki, 2011).

Revision of the POEL appeared inevitable after the Democratic Party of Japan (DPJ) took power in 2009, but it was not realized due to a confluence of events, including Prime Minister Yukio Hatoyama's resignation in 2010 and the triple disaster in 2011. However, the seeds of revision had been sowed within the LDP by pressure both internal from party members who had come to accept the potential of the Internet and external from opposition parties, young activists, and Internet business interests.

Passed in the spring of 2013, the POEL revision removed the de facto online campaigning ban with specific Internet-oriented regulation. Like their Western counterparts, parties and candidates gained nearly unrestrained online movement. At the same time, citizens gained partial freedoms – the prohibited use of email to promote a candidate is the most notable example of continued restriction. Regardless of the legal particulars, given various successful uses of the Internet in political communication around the world, high expectations flowed out of Japanese media for digital campaigning to revolutionize how politicians interacted with voters immediately prior to an election – expectations that failed to initially materialize (Williams, 2015).

2014 Election online campaigning particulars

Two major factors in 2014 provided a much different setting from 2013. First, while parties, candidates, and – particularly – citizens alike had little time to fully absorb the legal change in 2013, the law had been fully in effect for more than a year and a half for 2014. Second, despite the dismal results indicated above, general interest in the 2013 election was low because of the lack of potential to change administrations (Mie, 2013); 2014 provided this potential – no matter how remote. It must be noted that the suddenness of the snap election worked against this setting. At the same time, we find even judging strictly on websites, all parties were prepared to technically handle campaigning online.[1] Further and more importantly, parties undertook implementation of innovative digital strategies.

The LDP

The LDP implemented a three-pillared strategy for its online campaigns: the "Truth Team," the "Dashboard," and Apps (Public Relations Section, Liberal Democratic Party, 2015). The "Truth Team," a cross between a public relations department and cyber-security task force, was established within the headquarters to "listen" to chatter resulting from online campaigning, thereby allowing the party to give specific feedback to its candidates on their efforts. The Team also worked on monitoring for illicit online activities, such as the use of fake candidate profiles and accounts. The "Dashboard" was in-house software installed on tablet computers given to all candidates in order to more efficiently communicate real-time analytics of online activity. Further, the system provided a means of communicating methods for improving social media tactic. Finally, campaign-oriented apps for smartphones were created by the LDP, most notable of which was a small videogame with Prime Minister Shinzo Abe as its main character. The app – "Abe-pyon" – was released just prior to the 2013 elections and was downloaded over 300,000 times over the course of that election. While "Abe-pyon" garnered considerable user reaction and media coverage, LDP public relations officials stated the party decided that it was unnecessary to create additional apps for the 2014 election campaign as online campaigning had not been as prominently publicized.

Komeito

Whereas many of the political parties that ran candidates for the 2014 General Election utilized globally recognized social networking tools such as Facebook and Twitter, the Komeito stood out for using LINE[2] as its primary choice (Party Headquarters, Komeito, 2015). Komeito had much more to gain through its usage of particularized online communication tools; in creating online communication mechanisms through LINE, as well as through its website and other digital mediums, Komeito saw itself as being able to overcome any stigma attached to its well-known close affiliation with the religious organization Soka Gakkai International by fostering an environment where its supporters could share political information with their peers without necessarily being viewed as proselytizing a religious faith.

The JCP

The success of the JCP, particularly on proportional representation tickets in the 2014 election, was striking. In addition to the arguments raised in Scheiner, Smith, and Thies (this volume), we believe another factor could be the JCP's popular online campaigning strategy, first implemented in the 2013 election and updated for 2014 (Public Relations Section, Japanese Communist Party, 2015). Foremost, in order to combat a stigma attached to the Cold War legacy of its name and present its ideas to otherwise politically apathetic voters, the JCP created a team of *yurukyara* – mascot characters – to tout its messages. The characters – collectively dubbed the *Kakusanbu*, or literally "the Promulgation Department" – were designed and named to symbolize and promulgate policy stances of the party in an easy to understand and fun manner online.[3] Other tactics included national and regional online programming, which aired interviews with candidates.[4] Besides our own evaluation of the quality of these efforts, another indication that they could be linked to the JCP's success is the fervent belief by the JCP in this link. In particular, the JCP holds that these innovative measures influenced younger voters to vote for the JCP. The depth of the JCP's belief in this assertion is shown by the JCP continuing and expanding their online activity – the *Kakusanbu* gained several new characters for the 2014 election.

The DPJ

Contrary to the aforementioned three parties, the DPJ was conservative with innovation when it came to its online campaigning strategies in 2014 (Secretariat, Democratic Party of Japan, 2015). For example, the party had access to LINE as one of its tools for dissemination of information, but forewent its use (Kansai, 2014). This in no way means they were unprepared to campaign online however. According to a party official, the DPJ began such preparations as early as the summer of 2012, with regional public relations officers convening at the headquarters to discuss their online strategies under anticipation of the POEL revision. Leading up to the 2013 election, the party instructed its Diet members and their staff on various mechanisms for online communication, such as social networking.

Third Force and other parties

Beyond the four parties of focus above, it should be noted that all other political parties did utilize digital campaigning tactics. All parties had websites that were generally responsive to the election. Further, they used a variety of online tools, including Twitter, Facebook, YouTube, Google+, digital newsletters, and so forth. Some parties were even using more innovative techniques; the JIP, for instance, was broadcasting its stump speeches live via NicoNico Live and TwitCasting.[5] It is also worth pointing out the anomaly that was *No Party to Support*, an anti-establishment party which ran on the proportional representation ticket in Hokkaido. With almost no campaigning other than website, a few YouTube videos, and its trick name, it managed to gander more than 100,000 votes (Murai, 2014).

Online party patterns

Several patterns that emerged within online campaigning should be noted. First, one recurring theme arose through interviews with the four parties: they all felt that the POEL revision has indeed revamped communication between parties and candidates with their prospective voters during the campaigning period. Surveys support this self-assessment. One study indicated the total number of Facebook followers for each party rose from 2013 to 2014, as would be expected; and likes and comments to Facebook posts between the two elections rose slightly for the JCP, and several other minor parties, stayed the same for the LDP, though dropped significantly for Komeito and DPJ (Kansai, 2014). A separate survey of 444 individuals between the ages of 20 and 59 indicated that only one in four respondents did not know online campaigning had been unbanned; two in three respondents thought they wanted to use the Internet as a reference for election campaign information, of which 85.5% thought about homepages, 39% about social media sites, 27% about online ads, and 24% about video sites; and around 60% of respondents said they liked candidates that often updated blogs and social media services (Stage Group, 2014). It becomes quite understandable, then, why party officials' choices of *who most exemplified good online campaigners* during interviews were strongly reflective of their party's outcome: The LDP chose Prime Minister Shinzo Abe, Komeito chose two PR representatives, the JCP chose all 21 candidates who won seats, and the DPJ chose a representative who was not a candidate.

Second, parties actively sought to provide online campaigning assistance to their candidates. This is unsurprising given that candidates were undoubtedly utilizing online tools – 74% had homepages, 70% had Facebook pages, and 53% had Twitter accounts (Karibe, 2014). While use of these new tools provided new opportunities for political communication, the POEL revision created opportunities for legal errors as well. In order to negate any possible infractions of electoral guidelines, political parties' headquarter staff handed their candidates instruction manuals for online campaigning do's and don'ts, as well as basic social media use. Further, online platforms have themselves provided assistance to parties to promote usage. In 2013, for instance, Twitter published a brief, pictured-filled user guide aimed directly at parties, legislators, and candidates (Twitter, 2013).

Third, during the 2014 general election, the "tool" that stood out the most was *sharing*. With the POEL revision, messages, images, videos, and website links could now be shared to and by voters on multiple platforms, thereby giving parties what was effectively "endless" and "free" capability for information promulgation immediately prior to the election. As a JCP official stated, "The social media campaign has taken on the electoral campaign as a grassroots movement. While the party transmits information, it is the party members, *koenkai*, and supporters' networks that this information is spread on" (Public Relations Section, Japanese Communist Party, 2015).

Finally, parties have financially invested in digital methods, both in terms of online systems for the candidates and also in other forms such as paid banner advertisements – an action made legal for just political parties in the POEL revision.

Online campaigning in the future

While online campaigning was not a singular game changer in 2014, there is plenty of reason to bear in mind its influence on future Japanese elections. To start, younger adult generations show higher propensities for Internet use, at a rate of over 95% among 20- to 49-year-olds (Ministry of Internal Affairs and Communications, 2014).[6] As demographics change over the coming years, so will the likelihood of use of the Internet for information gathering.

Further, Japanese political parties show they are invested in online tactics. The LDP's creation of the *Truth Team* and *Dashboard* shows parties are concerned about their online campaign image and are willing to spend resources to protect it. Moreover, Abe Shinzo's continued online presence shows party leaders are invested in online activity, which will help ensure continuation. Komeito movement toward LINE shows parties are trying to follow their base supports through the notoriously fickle changes of digital technology use. Its use of Google-based ads shows parties' hard money is being spent on the medium. The JCP creating *yurukyara* specifically for online engagement shows parties are aiming toward digital methods to try and connect with younger generations and new audiences. The DPJ preparing for the deregulation from an early stage indicates that parties consider the Internet and the tools that become available with it to be vital to their own electoral success.

As online campaign activity grows among parties and candidates, previous research from other parts of the globe indicates we can expect more engagement from voters (Lilleker and Vedel, 2013: 411–412).

Finally, and potentially most importantly, the campaigning freedoms that the POEL revision provided may well affect how politicians feel regarding campaigning in general. It has been asserted that the digital political world and the real political world are influencing and shaping each other (Lilleker and Vedel, 2013,: 411–412).[7] It would not, therefore, be unexpected for politicians to question why they can freely campaign online but not on other mediums. This would potentially lead to calls for an overhaul of the entire POEL, which would then provide the chance to change the nature of Japanese campaigning entirely.

Notes

1. The following is a list of Japanese political parties and their accompanying websites: Liberal Democratic Party of Japan https://www.jimin.jp/; Komeito https://www.komei.or.jp/; Democratic Party of Japan http://www.dpj.or.jp/; Japanese Communist Party http://www.jcp.or.jp/; Japan Innovation Party https://ishinnotoh.jp/; People's Life Party http://www.seikatsu1.jp/; Party for Future Generations http://jisedai.jp/; Social Democratic Party http://www5.sdp.or.jp/; New Renaissance Party http://shintokaikaku.jp/; No Party to Support (Party) http:// shijinashi.com; and the Happiness Realization Party http://hr-party.jp/.
2. LINE is a messaging-based social networking system for electronic devices, most notably smartphones. Its largest user base is in Japan, followed by Thailand, Indonesia, Spain, and Taiwan (LINE, 2014).
3. For example, each of the characters was provided a unique Twitter account. One example is https://twitter.com/koyounoyooko, the account for the character "Koyou no Yoko," who represents "koyou" (employment) and is by far the most popular of the *kakusanbu* team – if one only considers Twitter followers.
4. Examples of JCP online video programming include *Tokoton Kyosanto* (JCP All-the-way), *Tomoko no Heya* (Tomoko's Room), and the *Daimon Zemi* (Daimon Seminar).
5. NicoNico Live http://live.nicovideo.jp/ is a livestreaming service of NicoNico, a Japanese-run video hosting service similar to YouTube. TwitCasting http:// twitcasting.tv is a livestreaming service of Moi Corporation, another Japanese company.
6. The baseline here is 20, as that is currently the voting age in Japan.
7. One notable example of this mirroring of the offline world by the online world was the DPJ's lack of a definitive party line for differentiation in the elections was reflected in its lackluster online campaigning efforts.

References

Kansai, T. (December 13, 2014). *[Sō senkyo 2014] Netto-jō no moriagari wa imaichi? Gurafu de miru Shūin-sen 2014: Politas "Sō senkyo" kara kangaeru Nihon no mirai* [General Election 2014: Online Campaigning not as Active? Examining the General Election with Graphs]. Retrieved February 23, 2015, from http://politas.jp/articles/295.

Karibe, M. (December 14, 2014). *Seitō-betsu, eria-betsu no Shūin-sen Rikkōhosha no Hōmupēji no hoyū jōkyō ya SNS no un'yō jōkyō* [General Election Candidate Website/SNS Usage: By Party and By Area]. Retrieved February 28, 2015, from http://www.katsuseijika.com/blog/details.php?p=1968.

Krauss, E. S. (1996). The mass media and Japanese politics: Effects and consequences. In S. J. Pharr and E. S. Krauss (eds) *Media and Politics in Japan*. Honolulu: University of Hawai'i Press.

Lilleker, D., and T. Vedel (2013). The Internet in campaigns and elections. In W. H. Dutton (ed.) *The Oxford Handbook of Internet Studies*. Oxford: Oxford University Press.

LINE (October 9, 2014). *Kōporēto LINE, jigyō senryaku happyō ibento "LINE CONFERENCE TOKYO 2014" wo kaisai* [Corporate LINE: "LINE CONFERENCE TOKYO 2014" Corporate Strategy Announcement Event Held]. Retrieved February 26, 2015, from http://linecorp.com/ja/pr/news/ja/2014/844.

McElwain, K. M. (2008). Manipulating electoral rules to manufacture single-party dominance. *American Journal of Political Science 52*(1): 32–47. http://doi.org/10.1111/j.1540-5907.2007.00297.x.

Mie, A. (July 20, 2013). Inaugural Internet campaigning not proving to be game-changer in poll. *The Japan Times Online*. Retrieved from http://www.japantimes.co.jp/news/2013/07/20/national/inaugural-Internet-campaigning-not-proving-to-be-game-changer-in-poll/

Ministry of Internal Affairs and Communications. (2014). *Heisei 26 nenban jōhō tsūshin hakusho* [2014 Whitepaper on Information Communications]. Retrieved February 28, 2015, from http://www.soumu.go.jp/johotsusintokei/whitepaper/ja/h26/pdf/index.html.

Murai, S. (December 16, 2014). Novelty party in Hokkaido shows that 105,000 voters want "none of the above." *The Japan Times Online*. Retrieved from http://www.japantimes.co.jp/news/2014/12/16/national/novelty-party-hokkaido-shows-105000-voters-want-none/.

Party Headquarters, Komeito (February 6, 2015). Personal communication.

Public Relations Section, Japanese Communist Party. (January 25, 2015). Personal communication.

Public Relations Section, Liberal Democratic Party. (February 16, 2015). Personal Communication.

Secretariat, Democratic Party of Japan. (February 17, 2015). Personal communication.

Stage Group (December 15, 2014). *Intānetto senkyo undō nitsuite no chōsa, netto jō no kōshiki jōhō ga "sankō ni naru – 85%" SNS katsuyō ni "kōkan ga moteru – 50%"* [Survey regarding Online Campaiging: "85% perceive official policy announcements online as beneficial" "50% think favorably towards SNS utilization"]. Retrieved February 20, 2015, from http://www.value-press.com/pressrelease/135384.

Tkach-Kawasaki, L. M. (2011). The internet and campaigns in Japan traditions and innovations. in Y. Tsujinaka and L. M. Tkach-Kawasaki (eds) *Japan and the Internet: Perspectives and Practices*. Center for International, Comparative, and Advanced Japanese Studies University of Tsukuba.

Retrieved from http://www.cajs.tsukuba.ac.jp/monograph/articles/01_201103/CAJS_Monograph_No1.pdf.

Twitter (2013). *Twitter Gaido: seitō, giin, kōho-sha no minasama e* [Guide to Twitter for Political Parties, Diet Members, and Candidates].

Williams, J. A. (February 2015). *Legal Tweets, Lawful Posts, and Licit Status Updates: Electoral Campaigning and the Internet in Japan in the 2010s [Dissertation Prospectus].* University of Washington Jackson School of International Studies. Retrieved from http://jwpolicy.com/research/publications/20150213-DissertationProspectus-JWilliams-Final.pdf.

Part IV
Governance and Policy

13
Abenomics in the 2014 Election: Showing the Money (Supply) and Little Else

Gregory W. Noble

Prime Minister Shinzo Abe's electoral platform in the December 2014 House of Representatives election cast continuation of "the three arrows of Abenomics" – monetary easing in the form of expanded purchases of bonds and other assets by the Bank of Japan (BOJ), "nimble" fiscal policy, and structural reforms to improve the flexibility and productivity of the economy – as the only way forward for Japan. This claim cleverly highlighted the lack of distinctive and convincing alternatives from the opposition. The opposition parties blamed Abenomics for falling incomes and increasing inequality, but they failed to put forth compelling alternatives. Two minor exceptions involved a symbolic conflict over opposition proposals to cut the number and remuneration of Diet members and bureaucrats, and the LDP's insistence on prompt restarts of shuttered nuclear generating plants. The 2014 election thus became a performance contest pitting the shaky status of the economy under the LDP–Komeito coalition government against the voters' complete lack of trust in the competence of the opposition parties. Many voters abstained, but enough showed up at the polls to give the LDP an overwhelming victory.

This chapter begins with a review of the economic context surrounding the election. Though Japan faces severe economic and demographic pressures, short-to-medium term prospects were more positive than generally recognized, making Abenomics more plausible and the alternatives less compelling. A brief overview of the previous stances of major parties, especially agreement to increase the consumption tax, is followed by an equally brief look at the LDP's framing of Abenomics as the centerpiece of the coalition's electoral appeal. The chapter then provides a more detailed look at the stances of the parties on taxes, spending and structural reform as seen in manifestos and slogans, candidate surveys, and campaign activities. An examination of the initial, quite limited, impact on policymaking gives way to a final evaluation of "Abenomics" as an electoral issue and implications for future elections.

Demographic and economic background

The immediate context of the election, and indeed Abe's pretext for dissolving the Diet and seeking a new mandate, was disappointing economic news, including an unexpected decline in gross domestic product (GDP) in the third quarter of 2014, as the economy failed to recover from the hit to spending caused by the increase in the consumption tax in April. The stubborn refusal of wages to rise and the failure of exports to expand despite the sharp depreciation of the yen added to the gloom and uncertainty.

Longer-term trends were even more ominous, and presented formidable challenges to the economic proposals and credibility of all parties. Demographic aging reduced economic growth and exerted inexorable pressure on pension and health care expenditures. Slow economic growth, in turn, restrained wages and household savings, and depressed the government's tax revenues, contributing to a world-leading gross national debt of over 230% of GDP. Slow growth in wages and national income received blame for a host of economic and social problems, including increases in inequality, poverty, and regional disparities. As growth continually slowed, Japan fell into a prolonged period of deflation and bumped into the "zero lower bound": with interest rates barely above zero, the BOJ had no room to cut interest rates further to stimulate demand.

Less widely noticed were two other disquieting trends: declines in household savings and terms of trade. During the post-war decades, Japanese households were hailed for their frugality. However, as the population aged and incomes declined, the household savings rate slid from 20% of GDP in 1974 to less than 2% in 2014, compared to 5% in the supposedly profligate U.S. (OECD, 2014). This decline in household financial capacity raised ominous questions about who would buy the flood of bonds that the Japanese government issued to cover yawning budget deficits. Similarly, after the mid-1990s, Japan's terms of trade – how many imports a dollar of exports can buy – steadily declined, led by Japan's imploding electronics industry (Nezu, 2011). As a result, even the sharp drop in the value of the yen following the aggressive monetary stimulus and quantitative easing programs urged by Abe and implemented by the BOJ failed (at least at first) to stimulate Japanese exports or to convince Japanese firms to bring off-shored production back home. In sum, long-term trends in the Japanese economy were deeply disconcerting, and help explain the reluctance of voters to express enthusiasm about Abenomics.

Some important recent events and mid-term trends, however, buttressed Abe's contention that Abenomics could work if given a little more time. First was a stunning collapse in the price of Japan's most important import. In July, Brent crude oil sold for $110 a barrel; by the election in mid-December, it had slid to $60, and soon after broke the $50 level. In October, the BOJ doubled down on its already aggressive purchases of financial assets, administering what Britain's authoritative *Financial Times* (October 31, 2014) dubbed "another dose of shock and awe," announcing plans to triple the acquisition of stocks and increase purchases of bonds by 60%.

At about the same time, the BOJ's widely watched *Tankan* survey of business conditions revealed continuing progress in working off Japan's glut of production capacity and excess workers (Bank of Japan, 2014). Fixed investment, far higher than necessary to support Japan's miniscule rate of growth after the bursting of the bubble, fell to sustainable levels seen in other advanced economies. An ever-increasing pile of retained earnings implied that if companies could be convinced that deflation was over they would have the wherewithal to hire workers and raise wages. Japan's unemployment rate dropped from 4.0% in 2013, Abe's first year in office, to 3.4% in the month of the election (*Nikkei*, January 30, 2015) while the ratio of job openings to job seekers reached 1.14 in December, the highest level in over 20 years (*Asahi*, February 27, 2015). The implication was clear: a quick push by Abenomics might boost Japan into position to begin tackling long-term problems.

Political context: The three-party agreement to increase the consumption tax

After the revision of the House of Representatives electoral system in 1994, the LDP faced a tension between its traditional catch-all centrism, with its heavy emphasis on clientelistic provision of public works and protection of producer groups (Scheiner, 2006), and neoliberal attempts to loosen the hand of government regulation, appeal to consumers and median voters, and restore fiscal discipline (Noble, 2014a). The Democratic Party of Japan (DPJ), another catch-all party, also wavered between protecting the status quo and embracing liberalization, though it displayed more concern for unions, workers, and social welfare, as epitomized in its winning campaign slogan in 2009: "from concrete to people." After difficult negotiations, the three leading parties reached an agreement in 2012 to increase the consumption tax (then 5%) to 8% in April 2014 and then to 10% in the fall of 2015 as a way to defray the rising costs of pensions and health care, and begin to repair Japan's tattered finances. Under pressure from backbenchers, the parties included a flexibility or "economic conditions" clause that would allow the prime minister to delay implementation if the economy failed to display sufficient vigor. After some hesitation, in the fall of 2013 Prime Minister Abe approved the initial increase (Noble, 2014b).

In the fall of 2014, however, Abe reacted to the surprisingly prolonged drop in consumption and GDP after the first tax increase by activating the flexibility clause and postponing the increase to 10% until April of 2017. During the election, Abe firmly ruled out the possibility of relying on a further flexibility provision; according to a senior journalist close to the LDP, Abe agreed to drop the economic conditions clause in order to win the support of the Ministry of Finance and fiscal conservatives within the ruling party (Tsutsumi, 2015: 41).

The claim that an election was necessary to ratify the delay in implementing the second tax rise and to demonstrate popular support for Abenomics met with widespread ridicule. Abe stoutly insisted, however, on seeking a specific mandate, and claimed that his three arrows represented the only way to escape from deflation and "the only path" forward for Japan. In contrast, he downplayed his well-known interest in revising the constitution and strengthening Japan's military capacity (see Kingston and Krauss chapters). The *Asahi* (November 28, 2014) calculated that in Abe's first major stump speech after announcing the election, Abenomics and the delay in the consumption tax increase accounted for nine out of 13 minutes.

Party stances toward Abenomics

Parties communicated their strategic appeals on Abenomics and other issues at several levels. Since the DPJ first introduced serious electoral manifestos to Japan in 2003, journalists and scholars have tended to focus on manifestos, but detailed manifestos were not the only way voters learned about party stances on policy, and arguably not the most important. At least as prominent were one or two sentence summaries from party leader debates and campaign posters. Most of these focused explicitly or implicitly on Abenomics, though the DPJ ("Now is the time to change the tide") and the Japanese Communist Party (JCP) ("Stop recklessness! Change politics") pitched their appeals more broadly.

Summaries by newspapers and news agencies of the party manifestos probably exerted the greatest impact on voters (cf. Horiuchi et al., 2014). The *Nikkei* (December 1, 2014), for example, compared policy proposals across five areas, three (or arguably four) of which involved Abenomics: growth strategy, employment, consumption tax, restart of nuclear power plants, and collective defense. The *Nikkei* (November 29, 2014) also provided an even simpler schema, highlighting the topic garnering the most space from each of the leading parties: the LDP manifesto was the most emphatic, devoting over half its volume to economics; the DPJ put social welfare first, closely followed by economics, while the Japan Innovation Party showed the most balance, devoting greatest attention to economics, followed by social welfare and then political and administrative reform.

Manifestos and longer newspaper articles covering them naturally went into greater detail. The opacity and vagueness of the 2014 manifestos, however, attracted criticism. As the *Asahi* (November 26, 2014) and others pointed out, the parties, especially the DPJ, felt burned when recent manifestos providing specific policy goals and numerical targets turned into millstones after the parties proved unable to meet the targets. A Waseda University team comparing the 2012 and 2014 manifestos found a universal decline in quality, as manifested in overall vision, coherence, specificity and implementability, and concern for average citizens. The larger parties scored noticeably better, but the DPJ policy proposals received by far the lowest marks for specificity, barely reaching half of the party's score in 2012 (Waseda RIM, 2014; see also Ikeda and Reed chapter). Finally, the major parties also produced detailed manifestos, usually called policy compilations (*seisaku shū*), ranging in detail from 20 pages for the JCP to a remarkable 95 pages for the LDP. No doubt these aimed mainly at specific interest groups. Leading news media almost uniformly ignored them; doubtless the vast majority of voters joined them.

The biggest clash involved evaluations of the state of the Japanese economy. The LDP (2014: 2) and Komeito (2014: 22) pointed to encouraging increases in corporate profits, employment, and nominal wages. Not surprisingly, the opposition parties took a much more critical view. The DPJ (2014: 2–3) started off its manifesto by noting that real wages had declined for 15 straight months, while GDP had declined for two quarters in a row (the conventional definition of a recession), then criticized the steady increase in the proportion of workers (over 37%

as of September 2014) relegated to low-paid and unstable "irregular" (*hi seiki*) employment. The Japan Innovation Party (JIP, 2014: 8) focused mainly on the need for reform, but also complained that high profits for big export-oriented firms had not diffused into more widespread growth. The Japanese Communist Party (JCP, 2014: 4), normally an ideological opponent of JIP, vociferously agreed, assailing "big companies and big shareholders," and decrying the loss of buying power suffered by the average worker as wages declined and the value of the yen shrank.

The parties differed less on actual economic proposals regarding taxes, monetary policy, and government expenditure levels. The leading parties agreed that Japan's fiscal problems were serious and that eventually it would be necessary to increase the consumption tax to 10% and beyond. They disagreed somewhat, however, on the LDP's proposal to cut corporate tax rates: the Komeito and JIP sided with the LDP, while DPJ candidates were slightly opposed (Asahi-Todai survey of candidates in *Asahi*, December 2, 2014).

Monetary policy proved less controversial than in the United States or Europe. Even in the full manifestos and "policy compilations" no party articulated an in-depth alternative. The LDP (2014: 2) was forthright in its defense of quantitative easing as "arrow number one" of Abenomics, but did not belabour the point. The Komeito ignored monetary policy altogether, and indeed the *kanji* character for "arrow" did not appear in the Komeito manifesto (see also Klein chapter). The DPJ (2014: 4) merely promised to ameliorate some of the less desirable consequences of quantitative easing, notably the hit to Japanese buying power following the depreciation of the yen, and to seek from the BOJ "a flexible monetary policy that pays full heed to the livelihoods of the citizenry." The JIP (2014: 8) basically upheld the validity of "arrow number one," though it complained that easy reliance on monetary and fiscal easing had seduced the LDP into avoiding painful but necessary reforms (JIP, 2014: 2) and claimed that the monetary arrow was losing momentum (JIP, 2014: 4). All in all, the aggressive monetary easing and major yen depreciation carried out by Abe's appointees to the Bank of Japan, with his constant rhetorical support and even pressure, remained surprisingly resistant to sustained criticism from the opposition parties.

Government expenditures attracted more controversy, perhaps because they were more tangible to the average voter. Much of the attention was rhetorical and symbolic, however. Not surprisingly, the neo-liberal JIP led the way, pledging as job number one to carry out "painful reforms" (*mi o kiru kaikaku*) by cutting the number and wages of Diet members by 30% (JIP 2014: 8). The JIP boasted of its record in slashing the salaries, bonuses, and pensions of mayors and local bureaucrats in Osaka (JIP, 2014: 5). The DPJ joined in, "aiming at" shrinking the total employment bill for civil servants by 20% and calling for unspecified cuts in the number of Diet members (DPJ, 2014: 10); in the NHK political talk shows leading up to the election, DPJ leaders repeatedly assailed the LDP for failing to make progress on its earlier promises to take action to reduce the size of the Diet, and for saddling the voters with the costs of an unnecessary election. The LDP and Komeito manifestos ignored these calls for exacting a pound of flesh from the politicians and bureaucrats, while the Communists (JCP, 2014: 7) and Social Democrats (SDP, 2014: 6) explicitly opposed them.

How important was this clash? Using an innovative "conjoint" survey and simulation of on-line voter preferences, Horiuchi et al. (2014) find that calls to make politicians and bureaucrats share in the voters' pain were surprisingly popular, attracting more support than "Abenomics." This appeal to popular resentments may have struck a chord, but it does not appear to have exerted much impact on voting behavior. The LDP and Komeito won over two-thirds of the seats despite ignoring the issue, while the JCP captured much of the protest vote, doubling its vote share and nearly tripling its seats in the 2014 elections, despite explicitly opposing cuts to the numbers and salaries of politicians and bureaucrats. Nor were the proposals realistic. Ousting 20% of the members of the Diet at a fell swoop was a political non-starter. Similarly, the courts had ruled that the ban on collective bargaining by civil servants was constitutional only because the salaries and bonuses of bureaucrats were based on recommendations by the National Personnel Agency designed to assure parity with the private sector. In television debates, the opponents of cuts noted that the ratio of civil servants to population in Japan was already much lower than in other advanced democracies. The news media paid little attention to the unrealistic calls for "painful reforms" of the Diet and bureaucracy.

As for overall expenditures, the LDP (2014: 6, 19) brandished its "second arrow" of "nimble" (*kidō-teki na*) fiscal policy, promising to compile a large supplementary budget and to support a "stable" and "sustainable" social welfare system, all while proclaiming its commitment to restoring fiscal rectitude. With the notable exception of the JIP, the other parties combined vague criticism of wasteful expenditures under the LDP with their own pledges to bolster various policy areas with additional spending. Komeito (2014: 3, 14), for example, promised to "enhance" (*jūjitsu o*) social welfare and education and to strengthen the functioning of the public pension system, while the DPJ claimed it would strengthen support for just about every policy area. Public works, long a focus of contestation between old-guard LDP spenders and would-be reformers, attracted relatively little criticism. After years of cuts, the share of public works spending in GDP was no longer particularly high compared to other advanced democracies. None of the parties objected to the LDP's (2014: 17) plans to upgrade infrastructure to prepare for the 2020 Tokyo Olympics. Nor did any of the parties except the Communists (2014: 3) call for cuts in defense spending. This was perhaps not a surprise, given Japan's relatively limited defense spending and the increasing perception of external threats; indeed, the DPJ (2014: 10) and JIP (2014: 14) both joined the LDP (2014: 25) in calling for enhancement of Japan's "defense power" (*bōei ryoku*).

Even in the controversial area of "structural reform," policy proposals varied relatively little. All parties agreed on the need to increase real wages, but they disagreed on the means to achieve that goal. The LDP (2014: 11–12) focused on the supply side: how to increase the flexibility, quality, and even (in the case of public works) the number of workers. Surprisingly for a nominally conservative party, the LDP promoted tripartite talks with corporations and unions and pressured employers to raise wages both directly and via paying higher prices to suppliers (*Nikkei*, December 16, 2014; Kantei, 2014). The noted economist Yukio Noguchi indignantly likened Abe's interventionist approach to Japan's mobilization for total war in the 1940s (Noguchi and Mikuriya, 2015: 72). The opposition, in contrast, highlighted the weakness of demand for high-quality jobs and the ever-rising proportion of workers relegated to "irregular" employment (see e.g. *Asahi*, November 28, 2014).

When it came to Japan's aging and uncompetitive agricultural sector, rhetorical commitment to reform was surprisingly widespread, but with one exception also exceedingly vague. By far the most explicit and aggressive approach came from the JIP (2014: 10), which proposed allowing corporations to enter the agricultural sector and called for weakening the power and monopoly position of the national agricultural cooperation association JA. In contrast, the LDP manifesto (2014: 14–15) mentioned possible reforms, but ignored JA and conveniently postponed any specific measures until June of 2015, after both the national and local elections, instead lavishing attention on governmental support. The DPJ (2014: 9), for its part, virtually abandoned talk of reform, instead highlighting plans to provide subsidies to individual farming households.

Proposals for reforms in immigration and trade and investment received limited support. The LDP (2014: 10) waffled, calling for creation of an environment in which skilled and experienced foreigners would be able to thrive but only "under the precondition that this would not constitute an immigration policy." The other parties simply ignored immigration as an issue, and only the LDP and Komeito called for increased support of foreign students. Stances toward participating in the demanding and "high-quality" Trans-Pacific Partnership (TPP) agreement advocated by the United States followed similar lines (see Katada and Wilbur chapter). JIP (2014: 14) firmly supported all international trade agreements. The manifestos of the LDP (2014: 24) and Komeito (2014: 21) each contained a single paragraph supportive of the TPP; the LDP's was noticeably brief and hesitant. The DPJ, similarly, expressed contingent and reluctant support. The Communists, Social Democrats, and PLF all firmly opposed.

The parties differed so little on two other important issues that voters could hardly base decisions on them. All parties firmly advocated the causes of local communities (especially in the calamity-struck northeast) and small and medium-sized enterprises. Similarly, all parties except the conservative Party for Future Generations (PFG) gave rhetorical support to women's issues, though the Social Democrats (SDP 2014: 6), Komeito (2014: 7) and LDP (2014: 8; 2016) devoted somewhat more attention than the others.

In health care, a major source of public expenditures, debate over structural changes focused primarily on whether to allow or expand "mixed billing" (*kongō shinryō*) – allowing patients to supplement national health insurance coverage with private payments, as opposed to the current requirement (with a few limited exceptions) to pick one or the other. Not surprisingly, the neo-liberal JIP (2014: 9–10) actively promoted mixed billing. The LDP advocated mixed billing as a way to provide more advanced (and costly) health care, but only in vague terms (LDP 2014: 8, 19), perhaps because the back benches of the LDP responded strongly to complaints from physicians running small clinics, who were ill placed to provide exotic and expensive new treatments (*Asahi*, August 25, 2013). As a result, most of the LDP's discussion of health care promised to enhance coverage rather than cut it. The DPJ and Komeito ignored mixed billing while citing numerous areas where they would bolster health care; the left-wing parties (JCP and SDP) expressly opposed mixed billing. As with agriculture, then, proposals for "structural reform" of health care that might cut expenditures or increase productivity received decidedly limited and lukewarm support, and provided only limited guidance in differentiating among the parties.

Nuclear power, particularly whether to restart existing plants, which were all shuttered in the aftermath of the Fukushima Daiichi disaster, *did* serve as an important differentiating issue. Restarting the nuclear plants would reduce Japan's bill for imported oil and gas and provide a significant boost to Abenomics. Yet even in the case of nuclear power, actual policy differences, and the degree of support for nuclear power even by its advocates, were more muted than the news headlines might have suggested (see Hughes chapter, this volume). Only the tiny PFG (2014: 4) stoutly and unapologetically promoted nuclear power. The LDP argued that existing nuclear plants, which it praised as a source of stable "baseload" power, should be allowed to restart once they had passed the new and more stringent safety tests promulgated after Fukushima, but its manifesto also accepted that the share of power generation from nuclear plants would gradually decline and expressed firm support for energy conservation and expansion of renewable energy, so that "reliance on nuclear energy ... should be reduced as much as possible" (LDP 2014: 11). JIP (2014: 12) largely agreed, calling for a "fadeout" to nuclear power rather than abrupt cessation, but also highlighting the importance of first solving the vexing problem of nuclear waste disposal, a stance that in practice might effectively stymie restarts. Komeito (2014: 22) called for a transition "toward a society without nuclear power generation," and advocated strict adherence to the rule that nuclear plants should be licensed for only 40 years, without allowing extensions. Similarly, the DPJ (2014: 9, 13–14) called for an end to nuclear power by the 2030s, and stressed the importance of first establishing "responsible evacuation plans" (DPJ 2014: 9). The JCP and remaining parties adamantly ruled out nuclear power. Even nuclear power, then, was only a partial exception to the broad pattern of limited articulation of differences on economic policy.

Abenomics after the election

The immediate impact of the election on economic policy was limited. The effort to use tripartite bargaining institutions to convince firms to increase wages seemed to have a modest impact on big businesses, which sounded amenable to increasing bonuses but remained reluctant to increase base pay, while most smaller companies denied that they were in a position to offer any pay increases at all (*Nikkei*, December 16, 2014). Many economists doubted that negotiations would have much effect. As the chief economist of a leading business think tank put it,

"For the prime minister of a country to lobby business executives to raise wages is problematic ... It is difficult to increase growth potential through government policies." (Suzuki 2015: 96).

As for mobilizing fiscal expenditures, far less actually happened than the average voter would have gathered from the LDP's aggressive campaign rhetoric about speeding the flight of the "second arrow." The big supplemental budget for the end of fiscal year 2014 consisted mainly of paying down outstanding debt and accumulating reserves to pay for future outlays (MOF 2015a). Total expenditures in the main budget for fiscal year 2015 increased less than half a percent. Despite all the talk of reconstructing the northeast and preparing for the 2020 Tokyo Olympics, spending on public works was flat and reached only half the level seen in the year 2000 (MOF 2015b), while the budgeted number of public school teachers fell by over 3,000, continuing the decline seen in 2014 and effectively reversing the previous policy of trying to reduce the student-teacher ratio in Japanese schools (*Asahi*, January 10, 2015). Tax revenues, on the other hand, were expected to grow a healthy 9%, following a robust 16% increase in 2014, as corporate profits recovered. This contrast between surging tax revenues and restrained expenditures was good (if belated and still inadequate) news for fiscal consolidation but directly contradicted Abe's avowed course of fiscal stimulus.

Nor was progress on Abe's plan to restart nuclear power plants rapid or extensive. Three months after the election, none of the shuttered plants was close to restarting even though some had passed the new safety inspections. Opposition from local communities and possible court injunctions cast a long shadow (*Chūnichi*, February 13, 2014; *JT*, February 17, 2015).

Finally, immediate post-election progress on various forms of "structural reform" was decidedly modest. Abe pledged to carry out "determined reform" of agriculture (especially JA), health care, employment, and energy (*Mainichi*, January 7, 2015), but faced strong opposition from interest groups and LDP backbenchers. After a stinging loss to a candidate backed by JA in the Saga Prefecture governor's election in mid-January, and with unified local elections looming in April, the Abe cabinet seemed unlikely to make swift progress in its reform efforts (*Asahi*, January 21, 2015). In late December, the LDP-Komeito tax commission confirmed the government's intent to reduce the top marginal rate for corporate taxation. The cut would in effect serve as a fiscal stimulus, but the commission also suggested changes to prevent unprofitable companies from avoiding all corporate taxes (*Shūkan Tōyō Keizai*,

January 17: 24–25). If implemented, this would count as a small but important structural reform, as it would reduce the number of "zombie" companies and encourage capital to flow to more productive uses.

Conclusion

Prime Minister Abe and his platform of "Abenomics" scored a decisive victory in the December 2014 House of Representatives election. Abe largely succeeded in keeping the focus on the economy and convincing voters that his was the only path to reform, even though economic conditions remained shaky. Electoral victory then allowed him to claim a mandate, or at least a permit, to pursue his broader policy agenda (see concluding chapter). Abe's success exposed the difficulty the DPJ and other opposition parties faced in devising plausible alternatives and persuading voters that they could implement them effectively. After gaining power in 2009, the DPJ was widely perceived, fairly or not, as having failed to provide effective leadership, leading to a disastrous electoral defeat in 2012 (Pekkanen et al., 2013). As a result, the DPJ's pathetic attempt in 2014 to buy support by promising to "enhance" government policy (and spending) in virtually every policy realm convinced few voters. Asked why the LDP and Komeito had won an overwhelming victory, only 11% of respondents credited Abe's policies, while 72% attributed it to the lack of appeal of the opposition parties. Asked if there were an opposition party that could be trusted with power, only 8% responded affirmatively (*Asahi*, December 18, 2014). The University of Tokyo's Masaki Taniguchi, who directs a joint venture with Asahi surveying candidates and voters during and after each Diet election, explained the LDP's victory as the result of a "negative, passive choice" (*shōkyoku-teki sentaku*) based on "performance evaluations" (*gyōseki hyōka*) (*Asahi*, February 1, 2015).

This conclusion is largely consistent with studies from other advanced democracies, which find that citizens tend to engage in performance or "valence" voting. Rather than searching in some policy space for the party whose proposals most nearly match their own preferences, they vote for the party in power if it has succeeded in attaining broadly shared goals such as economic growth and maintenance of social order, and punish it if it has not (Bermeo and Bartels, 2014; Clarke et al., 2009; on Japan, see Schoppa 2011; Reed et al., 2012). Japanese voters differ from citizens elsewhere primarily in the extent to which they distrust the opposition: even a mediocre performance by the LDP – as in the widespread perception that Abenomics had achieved only weak success in reviving the economy – is enough to assure its reelection (Cf. Scheiner, 2006).

The focus on performance, however, obscures some important ideological tensions that could take on greater salience in future elections. In 2014, the LDP proclaimed a bolder and more liberal platform than its policies actually justified. Abenomics touted fiscal stimulus, a nominally left-wing approach, and structural reform, a nominally rightwing approach, but actual policy depended heavily on monetary easing (hardly a conservative policy) to provide economic performance, flying on one engine (or arrow) rather than three. For its part, the DPJ failed to strike a clear ideological stance, attempting to buy votes with vague promises on every dimension. Only the Japan Innovation Party took a resolutely neo-liberal approach to structural reform, but its vote share failed to improve on the 2012 election.

Loose money, however, can take an economy only so far. Absent new policy measures, it seems unlikely and undesirable for the yen to sink much further, and the stock market could lose buoyancy if corporate profits fail to continue expanding. All the while, demographic aging continues to exert inexorable pressure on pensions and health care spending. Abe and the LDP may have won a decisive tactical victory in 2014 with only weak performance and muted debates over economic policy, but tougher choices loom even if Abenomics succeeds in pulling Japan out of deflation – and a potential financial crisis if it does not. Future Japanese elections may see more ideological contestation and even partisan restructuring.

References

Bank of Japan (2014). *Tankan* Summary (September 2014) at https://www.boj.or .jp/en/statistics/tk/gaiyo/2011/tka1409.pdf, accessed January 25, 2015.

Bermeo, Nancy and Larry M. Bartels (eds) (2014). *Mass politics in tough times: opinions, votes, and protest in the great recession.* New York: Oxford University Press.

Clarke, Harold D., David Sanders, Marianne C. Stewart and Paul F. Whiteley (eds) (2009). *Performance politics and the British voter.* Cambridge: Cambridge University Press.

DPJ (Democratic Party of Japan) (2014). *Ima koso, nagare o kaeru toki: minshutō no jūten seisaku* [Now is the time to change the time: The DPJ's major policies] http://www.dpj.or.jp/download/17761.pdf, accessed January 25, 2015.

Horiuchi, Yūsaku, Daniel M. Smith, Teppei Yamamoto and Mayumi Fukushima (2014). Shūin sōsenkyo, kinkyū kaiseki! Deeta ga akashita yūkensha no honne: Yūkensha no ma no kanshin wa 'abenomikusu' de wa nakatta. [Urgent analysis of the House of Representatives election! The real intention of voters as revealed by data: the real concern was not "Abenomics"]. *Nikkei Bijinesu* (December 19). http://business.nikkeibp.co.jp/article/topics/20141218/275309/?P=9, accessed January 26, 2015.

JCP (Japanese Communist Party) (2014). *Abe seiken no bōsō sutoppu! Kokumin no koe ga ikiru atarashii seiji o* (Stop the recklessness of the Abe administration! [Create] a new politics in which the voice of the citizenry can live). http://www.jcp.or.jp/web_policy/data/201411_sousenkkyo-seisaku.pdf, accessed January 25, 2014.

JIP (Japan Innovation Party) (2014). *Zōzei sutoppu de, mi o kiru kaikaku, minori no aru kaikaku* [Stop tax increases and [carry out] painful reforms, reforms that will bear fruit]. https://ishinnotoh.jp/election/shugiin/201412/pdf/manifest.pdf, accessed January 25, 2015.

Kantei (Prime Minister of Japan and His Cabinet) (2014). *Keizai no kō junkan jitsugen ni muketa seirōshi kaigi* (The government-labour-employer council on working toward realization of a virtuous economic cycle). At http://www.kantei.go.jp/jp/singi/seirousi/), accessed February 26, 2015.

Komeito (2014). *Manifesto 2014: Shūinsen jūten seisaku* [Manifesto 2014: Major policies for the House of Representatives election]. https://www.komei.or.jp/campaign/shuin2014/manifesto/manifesto2014.pdf, accessed January 25, 2015.

LDP (Liberal Democratic Party) (2014). *Keiki kaifuku, kono michi shika nai: Seiken kōyaku 2014* [Economic recovery – this is the only path: Electoral manifesto 2014]. http://jimin.ncss.nifty.com/pdf/news/policy/126585_1.pdf accessed January 25, 2015.

MOF (Ministry of Finance) (2015a). *The Draft Supplementary Budget for FY2014.* http://www.mof.go.jp/english/budget/budget/fy2014/03.pdf. January 9. Accessed February 23, 2015.

MOF (Ministry of Finance) (2015b). *Highlights of the Draft Budget for FY2015.* http://www.mof.go.jp/english/budget/budget/fy2015/01.pdf. January 14. Accessed February 23, 2015.

Nezu, Risaburo. (2011). Disturbing deterioration in Terms of Trade in Asia. *IIST World Forum.* August 31. http://www.iist.or.jp/en-m/2011/0198-0806/, accessed January 25, 2015.

Noble, Gregory W. (2014a). Koizumi's complementary coalition for (mostly) neo-liberal reform in Japan. In Kenji E. Kushida, Kay Shimizu and Jean C. Oi (eds) *Syncretization: The politics of corporate Restructuring and System Reform in Japan.* Stanford: Stanford University Asia-Pacific Research Center, 115–145.

Noble, Gregory W. (2014b). Too little, too late? raising the consumption tax to shore up Japanese finances. *The Japanese Political Economy* 40(2): 48–75.

Noguchi, Yukio and Takashi Mikuriya (2015). Kōdo seichō no gensō o abaku" [Exposing the illusion of rapid growth]. *Shūkan Tōyō Keizai* 6750 (January 17): 70–73.

OECD (Organisation for Economic Co-operation and Development) (2014). Household savings rates. *Economic Outlook* 96 (November). http://stats.oecd.org/Index.aspx?QueryId=51648#, accessed February 26, 2015.

Pekkanen, Robert, Steven R. Reed and Ethan Scheiner (eds) (2013). *Japan decides 2012: The Japanese general election.* Houndmills, Basingstoke, Hampshire: Palgrave Macmillan.

PFG (The Party for Future Generations) (2014). *Jisedai ga kibō o moteru Nippon o: Seisaku shū* ([Let's create] a Japan in which future generations can have hope: policy compilation). http://jisedai.jp/cp-bin/wordpress/wp-content/uploads/2014/11/ (政策集) 次世代が誇りを持てる日本を.pdf, accessed January 25, 2014.

Reed, Steven R., Ethan Scheiner and Michael F. Thies (2012). The end of LDP dominance and the rise of party-oriented politics in Japan. *The Journal of Japanese Studies* 38(2): 353–376.

Scheiner, Ethan (2006). *Democracy without competition in Japan: Opposition failure in a one-party dominant state*. Cambridge: Cambridge University Press.

Schoppa, Leonard J. (ed.) (2011). *The evolution of Japan's party system: Politics and policy in an era of institutional change*. Toronto: University of Toronto Press.

SDP (Social Democratic Party) (2014). *Heiwa to fukushi wa yappari Shamintō: Shūgiin senkyo kōyaku 2014* [Yep, for peace and social welfare the SDP is it: Electoral manifesto for the 2014 House of Representatives election]. http://www.sdp.or.jp/policy/policy/election/2014/commitment.htm, accessed January 27, 2015.

Suzuki, Akihiko (2015). *2015 nen no nihon keizai o tenbō suru – abenomikusu o koete seichō suru nihon keizai* [Assessing prospects for the Japanese economy in 2015 – Japanese economy going beyond Abenomics and growing]. Mitsubishi-UFJ Research and Consulting, *Kikan Seisaku, Keiei Kenkyū*. 1: 81–97. http://www.murc.jp/thinktank/rc/quarterly/quarterly_detail/201501_81, accessed February 23, 2015.

Tsutsumi, Gyō (2015). *Zaimushō o kanpai saseta Abe Shinzō shushō no senryaku* [The strategy of Prime Minister Abe Shinzo, who caused the Ministry of Finance to suffer a complete defeat]. *Liberaru Taimu* 15(2): 40–42.

Waseda RIM (Research Institute of Manifesto) (2014). *Shūinsen 2014 manifesuto (seiken kōyaku) no dekibae chekku hyō [shūinsen 2012 to no hikaku]* (Performance check list for the electoral manifestos for the 2014 House of Representatives election [comparison with the 2012 House of Representatives election]). http://www.maniken.jp/pdf/2014sosenkyo_dekibae_hikaku.pdf, accessed January 25, 2015.

14

The Kantei vs the LDP: Agricultural Reform, the Organized Vote, and the 2014 Election

Patricia L. Maclachlan and Kay Shimizu

At first glance, agricultural reform was a nonissue in Japan's 2014 lower house election. Neither the ruling Liberal Democratic Party (LDP) nor the opposition Democratic Party of Japan (DPJ) paid more than perfunctory attention to the issue in their election manifestos; nor did individual candidates, most of whom went out of their way to avoid talking about it on the stump. Given the centrality of agriculture to the third arrow – or "structural reform" component – of Abenomics, as well as Prime Minister Shinzo Abe's proclamation that the November 21 Diet dissolution would be the "Abenomics Dissolution" (*Asahi shimbun*, November 22, 2014), this glaring omission may strike some readers as surprising.

Upon closer scrutiny, however, it is clear that the 2014 election mattered deeply for agricultural reform. For no sooner were the ballots counted than the Abe government announced that it would press forward on shelved proposals to overhaul Japan Agriculture's (JA) national and prefectural organizations (*The Japan AgriNews*, December 17, 2014). In an illustrative example of what the editors of this volume have termed "bait-and-switch" tactics (Pekkanen, Reed and Scheiner, "Conclusion," this volume), Abe "punted" agriculture in order to win an election that he could then use as a mandate to forge ahead on farm reform.

This chapter analyzes the significance of the 2014 election for politics and policymaking in the agricultural realm. Our primary objective is to assess how the election and its aftermath reflected two inter-connected sets of conflicts that have influenced recent agricultural politics and Japanese politics more generally: independent voters vs the organized vote, and, more prominently, the Kantei vs the LDP.[1] We illustrate, for example, how the Abe Kantei ultimately addressed agricultural reform and issues of rural revitalization (*chihō sōsei*) during the election campaign in ways that appealed simultaneously to independent voters and the organized farm vote, as represented by JA. With the election behind it, the victorious Kantei then turned the tables on the party by moving quickly on proposals to weaken JA as an economic and political actor. The ultimate purpose of this two-step strategy, we argue, was to further empower the Abe Kantei in agricultural policymaking.

The farm vote and Abe's agricultural reform agenda

For decades after its establishment in 1955, the LDP's electoral support base was firmly rooted in the farm population. Buoyed by shared conservative values, the malapportionment of rural electoral districts, and a supportive Ministry of Agriculture, Forestry and Fisheries (MAFF), the two sides developed an exchange relationship in which JA delivered votes and other electoral resources to the LDP in return for particularistic policy favors. The arrangement proved mutually beneficial; while JA's electoral support helped compensate the LDP for its narrow membership base (see Endo and Pekkanen, this volume), weak organizational roots in the countryside, and low appeal in the cities, farm household incomes increased via generous government subsidies, tax breaks, and market protectionism.

Since the early 1990s, however, the power and legitimacy of that exchange relationship has weakened in the context of sluggish GDP growth rates, mounting pressures for trade liberalization, a shrinking farm vote caused by rural population decline and electoral reform, and the increasing influence of reformist politicians in the LDP (see George Mulgan, 2005; Maclachlan 2014). Meanwhile, vested interests like JA have been challenged by a shift in the center of policymaking gravity away from LDP politicians and bureaucrats and toward the Kantei – a shift that was facilitated by Prime Minister Ryutaro Hashimoto's (1996–1998) institutional reforms and then accelerated under Jun'ichiro Koizumi (2001–2006). By the time Prime Minister Abe returned to power in late 2012, the farm vote still mattered in electoral politics, but far less so than before.

Soon after the 2012 lower house election, Abe elevated agricultural reform onto the governmental agenda in response to mounting evidence of a deepening crisis in the farm sector: Japan's rapidly aging farmers face an acute shortage of successors (*kōkeisha*) as rural populations decline; farm household incomes are shrinking as domestic demand and producer prices drop and the cost of inputs increases; and scarce farm-land is mismanaged to the point where an area roughly one-and-a-half times the size of Metropolitan Tokyo is now lying fallow. Solving such problems is essential to the long-term revitalization of rural areas (*chihō sōsei*), one of the Abe government's most important policy priorities. But to do so, the government must overcome stiff resistance from JA, which is unwilling to entertain changes that might further erode the foundations of its economic and political leverage (*Asahi shimbun*, July 9, 2014).

Addressing Japan's farm woes has also been motivated by Trans-Pacific Partnership (TPP) negotiations, which are rooted in the principle of trade liberalization across *all* sectors, including agriculture. Abe recognizes in the proposed trade pact an opportunity for Japanese manufacturing and services to gain broader access to international markets. And although he has refrained from openly linking TPP to his reformist agenda and pledges to shield "5 sacred items" (rice, wheat, dairy, beef and pork, and sugar) from detariffication (see Katada and Wilbur, this volume), he appears to regard agricultural reform in general as an important step toward ensuring a more competitive farm sector in an increasingly globalized market.[2] Needless to say, JA is staunchly opposed to TPP as well.

JA is a vast organizational network that includes 694 local cooperatives and four national peak organizations and their prefectural chapters. Of particular importance for our purposes are Zenchū, the network's "control tower" (*shireitō*) that supervises local coops and represents them within the policy sphere, and Zennō, the national organ that sells fertilizers, pesticides, and other farm inputs to farmers and purchases and distributes their output. Zenchū has been heavily criticized for exercising excessive control over local coops and extracting tax-exempt levies (*fukakin*) from them that it uses for lobbying and other political purposes,[3] and Zennō for dominating the market for and raising the prices of farm inputs.

The reforms introduced or proposed since 2012 by the Abe Kantei under the banner of promoting more "aggressive agriculture" (*seme no nōgyō*) are designed in part to weaken Zenchū's and Zennō's influence. They include efforts to expand farm size through the establishment of prefectural land consolidation banks, the promotion of incorporated full-time family farms and non-farm corporate participation in the agricultural sector, and the abolition of *gentan*, a program introduced in 1970 to reduce rice output and stabilize producer prices by subsidizing rice farmers to cut back on their production. These and related measures should help reduce the number of inefficient part-time farmers who constitute the vast majority of JA's dues-paying and service-purchasing farmer-members. Even more ominously for JA, in May 2014 the Council on Regulatory Reform (*Kisei kaikaku kaigi*, CRR) proposed a string of reforms that included stripping Zenchū of its authority to audit and extract levies from local coops and converting Zennō from an agricultural cooperative, with its accompanying Anti-Monopoly Law exemptions, into a joint stock company. JA reform is designed to free up local coops and farmers to cut costs, pursue product development, and even increase exports.

Many of these reform proposals are riddled with weaknesses and loopholes that in some ways can be read as concessions to JA. Nevertheless, Abe has done more than any other reformist prime minister to tackle the thorny question of agricultural reform. Indeed, he appears poised to do to farming what Koizumi did to the post office: weaken the economic and political powers of its representative organizations by exposing the sector to freer market forces.

The art of the election manifesto and the 2014 campaign

But the similarities with Koizumi stop there. While Abe's former mentor made postal privatization the centerpiece of the 2005 election, Abe put the specifics of agricultural reform on the backburner during the 2014 election campaign.

Agriculture's "low posture" during the election is evident in the campaign manifestos of some – if not all – of the political parties. The manifestos can be divided into three groups. At one extreme stood the Japan Communist Party (JCP), which had very little to say about farm-related issues aside from criticizing Abenomics for negatively impacting rural Japan and demanding that Japan withdraw from TPP negotiations (*Nikkei*, November 28, 2014). At the other extreme was the Japan Innovation Party (JIP), which advocated strongly for TPP and other trade pacts and proposed a neoliberal roster of reforms that made Abe's accomplishments look relatively tame by comparison – a "textbook prescription for agricultural reform," as George Mulgan (2014a) put it (see also Noble, this volume).

The LDP and DPJ manifestos occupied the middle ground between these two extremes. The LDP manifesto stressed the party's longstanding commitment to strengthening agriculture and reminded voters of some of the measures already introduced by the Abe Kantei to achieve that goal, such as efforts to increase the self-sufficiency rate in food production and agricultural exports. Also noteworthy for our purposes was a lengthy section on "regional revitalization" (*chihō sōsei*), an extensive grab bag of proposals for boosting living standards in small cities, towns, and villages that reflects, among other things, the diversifying interests and rapid aging of the countryside (see Shimizu, *JD 2012*). On the hot button issue of JA reform, the manifesto simply noted the need to "promote and deepen discussions" (*Nikkei*, December 16, 2014); it made no mention of the specifics of reform, let alone the CRR's radical recommendations of May 2014, although Abe did state in a campaign speech that the party would "build on the internal investigations of agricultural organizations" (*Nihon nōgyō shimbun*, December 24, 2014). On TPP, the party reiterated its commitment to the negotiations while stressing its determination to respect the Diet resolutions regarding those "5 sacred items." Finally, the manifesto pledged to introduce measures to counter rapidly falling rice prices, a promise that the government partially fulfilled by subsequently announcing measures to provide stricken rice farmers with temporary subsidies.

In the DPJ manifesto (see Ikeda and Reed; Noble, this volume), which was framed in part as a statement against Abenomics and its alleged disregard for the livelihoods of ordinary Japanese, agriculture ranked 8th in a list of 10 policy priorities and was discussed under the politically innocuous heading of "Food Safety and Security." Like the LDP, the DPJ offered platitudes about the need to revive Japanese agriculture, defend food security, and raise farm household incomes, and it pledged its support for TPP in principle while acknowledging the importance of those "5 sacred items." Unlike the LDP, however, the party pledged to reinstate a system of individual household income subsidies, which the Abe Kantei was reducing in conjunction with its efforts to phase out *gentan*, and to entrench those subsidies in legislation. It also called for greater transparency in TPP negotiations.[4] The DPJ made no clear reference to JA reform.

The LDP and DPJ manifestos mirrored the realities and complexities of the intersection between farm politics and electoral politics more generally. First, they were examples of "killing two birds with one stone" (Mori, 2008) – of a "hybridized election campaign" (Koellner, 2009) that addressed two important but otherwise incompatible constituencies: the floating vote and the organized vote. Issues like regional revitalization, increasing farm household incomes, food safety and security, and expanding agricultural exports are issues that resonate not only with farmers but also with Japan's steadily growing cohort of nonaligned voters. Supporting TPP also appeals to floating voters, more and more of which now appear to endorse the pact as an antidote to the country's economic malaise (see *Tokyo yomiuri shimbun*, July 14, 2014; Katada and Wilbur, this volume). By contrast, pledging to protect those "5 sacred items," to boost subsidies – either temporarily or permanently – and to heed JA's input during future reform efforts represented nods to the particularistic wishes of JA.

Second, the LDP manifesto reflected the growing rift between the Abe Kantei and the party on agricultural issues. While Abe and his government champion agricultural reform, the party has been deeply ambivalent about the issue, with some lawmakers supporting radical change and others, particularly those representing rural areas, opposing it (*Yomiuri shimbun*, February 19, 2014). The party's manifesto represents compromise between these positions. During the drafting process, Abe purportedly urged the party to endorse the government's various farm-related objectives, including JA reform, but was ultimately overruled by the party's Policy Affairs Research Council (*Seimu chōsakai*, PARC), which was in charge of drawing up the campaign pledges. Pressured by council members who believed the party could never win an election on a platform of radical agricultural change, the council opted for vague wording on the issue. Only then, council chairwoman and reform advocate Tomomi Inada reasoned, could internal dissent be quelled (*Nikkei*, November 26, 2014).

Third, mixing a small number of concessions to JA and vulnerable farmers with vague pronouncements about the need for major changes in the countryside that would benefit *all* residents helped LDP candidates from rural SMDs secure electoral endorsements from prefectural agricultural political leagues (*nōseiren*), the electoral arms of prefectural JA organizations. These endorsements have long been important for candidates running in rural districts. Under the pre-1994 multi-member district system, it was not uncommon for a rural candidate to win a seat simply on the basis of that endorsement, given the JA network's formidable organizational capacity to mobilize large numbers of votes. The endorsement is not nearly so important in today's "winner-takes-all" single member districts (SMD), since candidates must appeal to a much broader spectrum of voters and interests in order to clinch a seat. What is more, there are now far fewer farmers to mobilize than there were under the old electoral system, thanks to rapid rural depopulation. But for two reasons, rural SMD candidates are still loath to ignore JA endorsements. First, the number of farmer-voters remains just large enough to conceivably make or break a candidate in a first-past-the-post race. Second, LDP candidates who run simultaneously in their single-member and PR districts covet the endorsements because their position on the PR list is ultimately determined by the size of the popular vote secured in the SMD race (the so-called "best loser" system; see Krauss and Pekkanen, 2010). Although we will never know exactly how many votes JA musters in any given election, the fact that 162 (84%) of 194 LDP Diet members elected in the 2012 general election had prefectural league endorsements underscores just how seriously the party continues to take them (*Asahi shimbun*, July 11, 2014).

JA also valorizes candidate endorsements. Although JA is all too aware of its declining clout in national elections, it also knows that endorsing winning candidates can mean leverage – however minor – over the policy process. To wit, JA representatives will frequently pressure lawmakers who had received their electoral backing to make good on their electoral promises during Diet deliberations (*Nihon nōgyō shimbun*, December 24, 2014). Ideally, JA would like those lawmakers to hail from the ruling party.

Securing JA's electoral endorsements can be tricky. In the past, the agricultural political leagues usually backed LDP candidates on the basis of their party label, although they would occasionally endorse opposition party candidates, particularly after a perceived betrayal by the ruling party. In the context of increasing two-party competition after the Koizumi era, JA and its affiliates began to spread their electoral wings. By 2009 and 2010, JA was actively reaching out to the now ruling DPJ, which was delivering on its promise to introduce income subsidies for farm households (see Maclachlan, 2014). But in the 2012 election, JA all but abandoned the DPJ for its former patron, the LDP, which seemed far more willing to offer concessions to farmers on TPP (George Mulgan, *JD 2012*). And it remained in the LDP camp in 2014, granting fully 89% of its endorsements to LDP candidates (George Mulgan, 2014b). This is not to suggest that JA was no longer susceptible to inter-party competition; while many coop leaders were clearly fed up with the DPJ in 2014, some were attracted to the party's promise to reintroduce household income supports in the context of plummeting rice prices (*Niigata nippō*, November 29, 2014).

Complicating the endorsement process was the fact that the two main parties were now internally split on questions of reform. To get around that challenge, the prefectural agricultural political leagues extended their endorsements on the basis not of a candidate's party label but rather his or her individual policy preferences. In 2014, the leagues had candidates fill out a public questionnaire and offered their official backing only to those who indicated support for the "self-reform" of JA and the sanctity of the "5 sacred items" in TPP negotiations. The LDP's (and DPJ's) vague and seemingly contradictory pronouncements on TPP and JA reform helped willing candidates clinch these endorsements without turning their backs on free trade, a balancing act that can be gleaned from the words of DPJ candidate Hidetoshi Murao while campaigning in his Miyazaki district: "Free trade is important. On the other hand, there are industries that must be protected. I would like to think we have the option of withdrawing from [TPP] negotiations if [the interests] of local economies are not taken into consideration" (*Tokyo yomiuri shimbun*, December 11, 2014).

And so, while the agricultural political leagues offered the vast majority of their endorsements to LDP candidates, some of them included opposition party members in the mix. In other instances, the leagues had so much trouble deciding among the candidates that they opted for a "free vote" (*jiyū tōhyō*), a tactic that had gained traction in the 2009 lower house and 2010 upper house elections when two-party competition was at its height, and also during the 2012 election (see George Mulgan, *JD 2012*). The tactic is likely to continue in the near future with the DPJ in internal disarray and the LDP ambivalent about reform.

Put simply, in 2012 the LDP may have entered into a "second honeymoon" of sorts with JA, but its stature with the organized farm vote was by no means secure. The 2014 election results underscore this point.

The 2014 election returns

In absolute terms, the LDP "won big" in 2014 in the countryside. The party won 45, or 79%, of 59 rural SMD seats, while the DPJ secured just five seats; other seats went to Independents (five), the Party for Future Generations (two), the People's Life Party (one), and the JIP (one) (George Mulgan, 2014b).

Other data suggest that the LDP had good reason to look over its shoulder during the election. The results of a *Nihon nōgyō shimbun* (*The Japan AgriNews*) exit poll of 458 subscribers, for example, offer some insights into the deepening complexities of farmer-voter preferences.[5] On one level, the numbers reveal an absolute lead for the LDP over the DPJ; 55% of the respondents leaned LDP in SMD districts and 43% at the PR level. Corresponding figures for the DPJ were 22% and 23%, respectively. But the gap between the LDP and the DPJ had narrowed since 2012; while the LDP scored one percentage point higher in the SMDs and five points higher at the PR level than in 2012, the DPJ gained five percentage points in the SMDs and 10 points in the PR districts. What is more, support for the LDP in the PR districts decreased 12% over levels recorded by comparable surveys of PR districts in the 2013 upper house election; the DPJ, for its own part, gained four percentage points. Some voters, moreover, engaged in strategic voting in 2014; of those who supported LDP candidates at the SMD level, just 75% voted LDP at the PR level. Finally, in a sign of deepening rural disillusion with *both* the main parties, 11% of respondents supported the JCP at the PR level in 2014 – an increase of four percentage points over both 2012 and 2013 (*Nihon nōgyō shimbun*, December 15, 2014; see also George Mulgan, 2014b).[6]

The LDP's narrowing lead over DPJ candidates is further corroborated by anecdotal evidence of very tight races in a number of single-member districts. In Hokkaido District 7, a struggling dairy region where many producers have given up farming in recent years, the DPJ candidate lost by only 225 votes to the LDP candidate, but then gained a seat in his PR district. In Hokkaido District 6, Takahiro Sasaki, a DPJ candidate who had served in several high level positions in the MAFF when his party was in power, regained his seat after losing it in 2012. And perhaps most dramatically of all, in Tochigi District 2, then-LDP Minister of Agriculture, Forestry, and Fisheries Koya Nishikawa lost his seat to the DPJ candidate by a mere 199 votes. Nishikawa retained a seat in the Diet through his PR district (*The Japan AgriNews*, December 16, 2014). Nishikawa's loss is a stark indicator of dissatisfaction among many rural voters with the government's agricultural agenda.

At a December 25 joint meeting of the LDP's agricultural committees, several politicians from rice growing regions spoke up about their "uphill battle" (*kusen*) during the election. Many had faced stiff criticisms of their party's allegedly insufficient responses to the devastating effects of plummeting rice prices on many farmers. One went so far as to speculate that the LDP's share of the popular vote was lower in districts where rice was the sole agricultural commodity than in other agricultural districts (*Nihon nōgyō shimbun*, December 26, 2014). As the next section illustrates, this trend does not bode well for the LDP in upcoming local elections.

The road to agricultural reform and the future of the farm vote

Prime Minister Abe proclaimed his party's electoral victory on December 14 as a strong show of public support for Abenomics and immediately pushed forward on his reformist agenda. The day after the election, he announced that his government was taking action on regulatory reform, including in the agricultural sector. On December 16, Minister of Agriculture, Forestry, and Fisheries Nishikawa outlined his government's plan to begin drafting a bill to amend the Agricultural Cooperative Society Law, which would be submitted during the upcoming regular Diet session. That same day, Haruko Arimura, minister of state for regulatory reform, revealed that the government was dissatisfied with JA's attempts at "self-reform," and the CRR reiterated its determination to strip Zenchū and Zennō of several of their powers (*The Japan AgriNews*, December 17, 2014). Meanwhile, the government looked ahead to TPP negotiations, which were expected to increase momentum following the (pro-free trade) Republican Party's sweep of the 2014 mid-term elections in the United States (see Katada and Wilbur, this volume).

The Abe Kantei's efforts to jumpstart coop reform after a nearly seven-month hiatus suffered a setback on January 11, 2015, when voters in Saga Prefecture, a predominantly agricultural area, went to the polls to elect a new governor. To the LDP's dismay, its candidate of choice, Keisuke Hiwatashi, lost by a wide margin of about 40,000 votes to independent candidate Yoshinori Yamaguchi, a former official of the Ministry of Internal Affairs and Communications. Yamaguchi had received the endorsement of both a coalition of local mayors and LDP assembly members and the prefecture's agricultural political league. Hiwatashi's failure to secure JA's backing and his ultimate defeat were interpreted as statements of farmer and voter opposition to the government's stance on coop reform and TPP, both of which had figured prominently during the election campaign (*Nikkei*, January 21, 2015).

The Saga results do not mean that farmers are uniformly opposed to reform. As we discovered for ourselves while interviewing farmers in mid-2014, while part-time farmers, who outnumber their full-time counterparts by more than two to one, tend to feel threatened by many of the reforms, many large-scale, full-time producers enthusiastically support them. A good number of these full-time farmers have quit the coop system and established independent channels for accessing necessary inputs and marketing their products, in some instances in cooperation with non-farm corporations. These and other large-scale farmers favor measures to promote land consolidation, freer trade, and other policies that would help them expand the scope of their operations and access to international markets. Abe no doubt hopes that their numbers will swell as a result of JA and other reforms, thus broadening the pool of rural voters whose economic interests mesh more closely with those of LDP reformers.

Nor should the Saga results suggest that that JA's influence is on an upward trajectory. At the national level, JA's electoral powers are decreasing and will continue to do so unless it discovers a way to reinvent itself – by appealing, for instance, to the needs of the rural population, which is aging at a rate much faster than that of urban Japan (see Shimizu, *JD 2012*). What the results do reveal are variations in JA's influence across prefectures. In Saga, that influence is significant – so significant, observed a leading representative of the prefecture's agricultural political league, that JA may have set a record in January 2015 for the number of votes gathered (*Mainichi shimbun*, January 12, 2015). But in other prefectures, JA's backing is far less consequential. In Yamagata during the 2013 upper house election campaign, for example, the LDP candidate lost the agricultural political league's endorsement to a candidate backed by the tiny Midori no Kai; the slight was deemed significant enough for LDP General Secretary Shigeru Ishiba to appeal to prefectural JA authorities himself. But the LDP candidate won his seat anyway, which suggests that JA lacked the capacity to make or break the race in that prefecture.

However inconsistent the JA's prefectural influence may be, ignoring it makes many LDP Diet members nervous. In July 2014, as the dust began to settle after the government's foray into JA reform, a lawmaker in the LDP's "farm tribe" (*nōrin zoku*) predicted disaster for the party in the unified local elections scheduled for April 2015. If the government were to persist in its crusade to weaken JA, he predicted, prefectural assembly members would surely protest. After all, "it is the agricultural political league's recommendation, and not the endorsement of the LDP, that will generate reliable (*kakujitsuna*) votes" (*Asahi shimbun*, July 11, 2014).

Fears about the LDP's prospects in the upcoming local elections are galvanizing pockets of resistance in the LDP to the Abe Kantei's agenda for JA reform, as illustrated by intra-party deliberations on the topic in January 2015 (*Nikkei*, January 25, 2015). Attended each day by as many as 140 lawmakers, the contentious discussions centered on proposed amendments to the Agricultural Cooperative Society Law to remove Zenchū's authority to audit local coops and convert Zennō into a joint stock company (*kabushiki gaisha*). Proponents of both sides of the debate framed their arguments in the virtually incontrovertible language of regional revitalization (*chihō sōsei*). PARC chairperson Tomomi Inada, a leading member of the party's "promotion faction" (*suishin ha*), helped set the tone by acknowledging that the coops were "pillars of regional revitalization" (*Nikkei*, January 21, 2015). Her allies took the argument a step further by reiterating the government's position that regional revitalization could only be achieved by weakening JA's national and prefectural powers. Zennō head Nakano Yoshimi disagreed, arguing that converting his organization into a joint stock company would wreak havoc on both local coops and individual farmers (*Sankei shimbun*, January 24, 2015). He and other JA representatives were backed by law-makers in the "cautious camp" (*shinchō ha*), most of whom, predictably, hailed from rural districts; any reform that risked casting local coops adrift or reducing the number of services available to farmers, the group argued, would be tantamount to *abandoning* rural areas. But when all was said and done, what really mattered to rural lawmakers was the impact of JA reform on their electoral prospects. In the words of one veteran lawmaker, "We don't want to turn [JA], with its vote gathering power, into an enemy" (*Asahi shimbun*, January 21, 2015).

And so the tug-of-war continues, with the reformist Abe Kantei bat-tling its opponents in the party for more control over the future of agriculture. The Kantei envisions a future in which farmers are bigger, more politically independent and efficient, and more internationally competitive. Many in the party want to shield vulnerable farmers from freer market forces and preserve what remains of the rural organized vote. One side believes that its objectives can only be achieved by weakening JA, the other side by preserving it.

The Abe Kantei already had a significant edge over the party on the eve of the 2014 election, as evidenced by its success in putting one of the most taboo subjects in Japanese politics – JA reform – on the government agenda. Abe's electoral victory in 2014 helped widen that lead. As of this writing, JA reform is almost a done deal; on February 8, 2015, Zenchū head Akira Banzai formally conceded to the Kantei's proposal to reform JA. What remains to be fully determined is the *scope* of reform, which in turn depends on the prime minister's leadership. If Abe acts quickly and boldly, he could very well achieve his goals; if he drags his feet, the specter of the 2016 upper house election could force him to compromise his reformist ambitions for the sake of remaining in power.

Notes

1. We use the term Kantei – lit., the prime minister's official residence and support staff – in the figurative sense to connote prime ministerial leader-ship. Although the term has been used in the past with reference to policy-making struggles between the prime minister and bureaucrats, our analysis focuses primarily on prime ministerial leadership vis-à-vis party politicians. Note that the "Kantei vs. LDP" relationship is also addressed by George Mulgan (2014a).

2. Interview, Yamashita Kazuhito, Canon Institute for Global Studies, Tokyo, January 5, 2015.
3. According to one estimate, Zenchū will extract a total of 8 billion yen in levies in FY 2014. *Nikkei*, January 4, 2015.
4. See "The DPJ Manifesto 2014", http://www.dpj.or.jp/news/files/2014DPJ.Manifesto.pdf.
5. As George Mulgan notes (2014b), subscribers to the *Nihon nōgyō shimbun* are believed to be mostly farmers.
6. The Komeito and JIP scored 7% and 6%, respectively, in the PR district, which represented a one point gain for each over the 2012 election.

Works Cited

George Mulgan, Aurelia (2005). Where tradition meets change: Japan's agricultural politics in transition. *Journal of Japanese Studies* 31(2): 261–298.

George Mulgan, Aurelia (2013). Farmers, agricultural policies, and the election. In Robert Pekkanen, Steven R. Reed and Ethan Scheiner (eds) *Japan Decides 2012: The Japanese General Election*. pp. 213–224. New York: Palgrave Macmillan.

George Mulgan, Aurelia (2014a). An election manifesto for the status quo on Japan agriculture (December 11). *East Asia Forum*. http://www.eastasia forum.org/2014/12/11/an-election-manifesto-for-the-status-quo-on-japanese-agriculture

George Mulgan, Aurelia. (2014b). The Japanese election and the farm vote. *The Diplomat* (December 31). http://thediplomat.com/2014/12/the-japanese-election-and-the-farm-vote/

Koellner, Patrick (2009). Japanese lower house campaigns in transition: Manifest changes or fleeting fads? *Journal of East Asian Studies* 9: 121–149.

Krauss, Ellis S. and Robert J. Pekkanen (2010). *The rise and fall of Japan's LDP: Political party organizations as historical institutions*. Ithaca: Cornell University Press.

Maclachlan, Patricia L. (2014). The electoral power of Japanese interest groups: An organizational perspective. *Journal of East Asian Studies* 14(3): 429–458.

Mori, Hiroki (2008). Senkyo katei ni okeru rieki dantai no dōkō [Interest group trends in the electoral process]. *Dōshisha hōgaku* 330: 45–77.

Shimizu, Kay. (2013). What the 2012 lower house election has to say about Japan's urban-rural divide. In Robert Pekkanen, Steven R. Reed and Ethan Scheiner (eds) *Japan Decides 2012: The Japanese General Election*. pp. 148–153. New York: Palgrave Macmillan.

15
Regional Inequality in 2014: Urgent Issue, Tepid Election

Ken V.L. Hijino

Introduction

In a statement made directly after dissolving the lower house, Prime Minister Shinzo Abe acknowledged criticisms of "Abenomics" as expanding inequalities between urban and rural areas (Noble, this volume). "Abenomics," the PM said, "will only be completed when the winds of economic recovery reach the struggling regions." Referring to a new program of "regional vitalization" (*chihō sōsei*) aimed to halt rural depopulation and stagnation, Abe promised to bring prosperity into "every bay and harbour" across Japan. The 2014 lower house election campaign thus began with a conscious effort by the ruling party to demonstrate its commitment to Japan's regions.[1]

The Abe government's initiative on regional development was in response to numerous signs of softening support in rural areas leading up the elections. Since the start of the Abe administration, cabinet approval has been falling faster in rural areas beyond the big cities (see Endo and Pekkanen, in this volume). Voters in agricultural areas continued to be distrustful of the LDP government's equivocating stance on TPP negotiations (see Maclachlan and Shimizu; Katada and Wilbur, this volume). Polls revealed that an increasing number of voters felt that regional inequality was worsening. The LDP also suffered a number of local electoral setbacks in the latter half of 2014, with losses in Shiga and Okinawa gubernatorial elections. LDP party executives stated that their new program for regional development would determine their success in major local elections in April of 2015 (*Nikkei*, September 24, 2014).

Faced with these challenges, the LDP actively sought to shore up support through new pledges of regional development. The 2014 election could therefore have played out as one focusing on the problems of regional development, yet electoral attention on regional issues during the campaign remained tepid.

This chapter investigates why this was the case. It asks how important regional issues were for voters and the media in the 2014 elections and how the parties competed on the question of dealing with the socio-economic and demographic crisis in Japan's regions. Before delving into the campaign itself, the chapter traces the evolution of regional policy in Japan over the last two decades. This is followed by an analysis of manifesto promises on regional issues for the major parties in recent national elections up to 2014.

The positions of the LDP and DPJ are shown to have largely converged to vague promises in recent years, while drifting away from promoting political and administrative decentralization as a solution. This lack of competing alternatives among the major parties is suggested as one reason why regional issues in the 2014 election gained little public traction. Like many other issues, regional policy generated no clear partisan divide between the DPJ and LDP, causing it to be a submerged topic in the electoral contest.

The context of regional development policy

The question of urban–rural inequality has played a salient role in Japanese post-war politics. As Japan's industrial economy expanded rapidly in industrial belts and urban centers during its high-growth era (1955–1973), the socio-economic gap between these areas and rural regions broadened. Successive LDP administrations promoted regional policies to ensure a "balanced development" of the nation, beginning with a series of national development plans in 1962. The ruling party campaigned on these policy programs, promising to redistribute concentrations of wealth and population from urban areas to depressed rural areas. Among the more famous regional development slogans have been the "remodeling of the Japanese archipelago" (1972) under Kakuei Tanaka and "creative development of hometowns" (1989–1990) under Noboru Takeshita. The Abe administration's latest "regional vitalization" initiative thus follows a long lineage of LDP programs, and attendant rhetoric, for regions.

Such emphasis on promoting regional economic growth naturally had an electoral rationale. The LDP, although developing into a catch-all party with support of certain urban clienteles such as small shop keepers, remained strongly rural in character during its dominant period (1955–1993). The LDP maintained its electoral dominance by channeling pork in the form of various agricultural subsidies and public works projects to rural areas, securing stable support from rural famers and construction workers (Rosenbluth and Thies, 2010; Saito, 2010), In the meantime, opposition parties – including the socialists, communists, and Komeito – were primarily urban parties, unable to make inroads into the LDP's rural strongholds. This led to a so-called "parallel party system" in which the LDP was one-party dominant in rural areas, while opposition parties were more competitive in urban areas (Scheiner, 2006).

This linkage of the LDP to rural interests has gradually unraveled in the last two decades. This has come about as the LDP's commitment to rural areas through center-led redistribution has eroded during this period due to a combination of factors: an ongoing decline in the rural population (particularly the active farming population); electoral reforms that have lessened the importance of the rural vote (Rosenbluth and Thies, 2010); and fiscal constraints forcing national governments to reduce spending on regions, including public works spending (Noble, 2010).

The LDP also undertook a number of whole scale administrative and fiscal decentralization reforms, begun in 1995 and accelerated under the Koizumi administration. Together with municipal mergers (1999–2005), which nearly halved the number of municipalities in Japan, these decentralization measures sought greater administrative efficiency and virtuous competition among local governments. A set of local government fiscal reforms (2002–2006) was implemented under the Koizumi administration. These so-called "Holy Trinity reforms" involved the reform of local government subsidies, general grants, and the transferring of tax bases to local governments (Ikawa, 2008). As a result, general grants, earmarked subsidies, and overall public works spending in the regions fell sharply. Between 2000 and 2006 general grants (Local Allocation Taxes) fell by 28% to 15 trillion yen, while public works spending has fallen by 26% to 6 trillion yen.[2]

Although decentralization reforms resulted in local governments gaining greater discretion from central funding and administrative control, the process also delinked the ruling party from local communities. Moreover, municipal mergers led to a sharp decline in the number of local politicians (who were largely affiliated to the LDP in rural areas). This is believed to have further distanced the LDP headquarters from rural branches and interests, while resulting in negative national-level electoral consequences for the party (Hijino, 2013; Shimizu, *JD 2012*).

These changes in the first half of 2000s triggered strong opposition from rural communities and politicians, including those from within the LDP, which cried out that such reforms exacerbated regional inequalities and hurt the weakest rural communities. Along with decentralization, the Koizumi administration pursued a host of controversial structural reforms including the privatization of highways, abolishing revenues earmarked for road construction, and privatization of postal services. These were all seen to negatively affect rural areas disproportionately as they reduced public works related employment in these areas. In response, local LDP legislators across the country passed resolutions in local assemblies criticizing and opposing these policies, even backing LDP rebel parliamentarians opposing these top-down policies in 2005 (Hijino, 2015).

This period of structural reforms was accompanied by growing regional inequalities as measured by a wide range of indicators. Tachibanaki and Urakawa (2012) have found evidence of growing regional inequality in per capita income, GDP growth, poverty levels, access and costs of public services (such as health care, education, and nurseries). Regional income inequality as measured by the Gini coefficient of per capita prefectural income has fallen throughout the post-war era after peaking in 1959. But the trend reversed itself in 2001, with inequality increasing until 2005. Although regional income disparities have fallen from 2006–2010, latest data points to a slight increase in 2011.[3] In another indication of growing income inequality, the ratio between the average income of households in the Tokyo area and non-Tokyo areas has increased between 2001 and 2008.[4] Fiscal decentralization measures under the Koiuzmi administration (2003–2006) have also led to a widening gulf in the strength of local government finances.

Even more relevant for electoral competition is how the public perceived of these changes in regional inequality. Annual cabinet office surveys illustrate increasing respondents agreeing to the statement that "regional inequality is worsening" during this period, peaking at 33% in 2008 and picking up again in 2014. At the same time, fewer and fewer respondents have agreed with the statement that "regional inequality has been improving since 2000" (Figure 15.1).

Expanding regional inequalities had electoral consequences for both the LDP and DPJ. The upper house elections as well as local elections in 2007 saw the LDP suffer significant losses as rural voters distanced itself from the LDP which was perceived to have "abandoned the regions" (*chihō kirisute*) under Koizumi (Chiavacci, 2010). The DPJ which had been primarily urban in character until then targeted and captured the dissatisfaction of rural voters. It gained significantly in rural districts

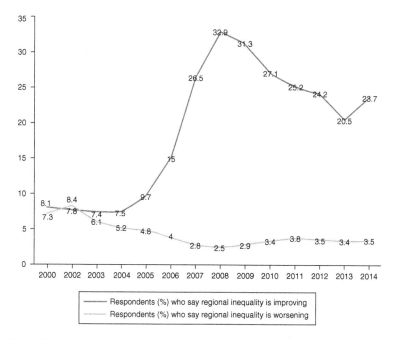

Figure 15.1   Perceptions on regional inequality
Source: Compiled by author from cabinet office survey: *Shakai ishiki ni kansuru seron chōsa,* January 2014.

both in the 2007 and 2009 elections campaigning on a program to lessen the "pain" of LDP neo-liberal reforms and support livelihoods of rural communities and those working in agriculture, forestry, and fishing industries (Hasunuma, 2012: 274). By these two elections, it was clear that, at least for national-level elections, the LDP no longer held an unshakeable grip over rural districts. Faced with a backlash on regional inequality, both the LDP and DPJ have toned down emphasis on decentralization reforms and reverted to court rural votes through centrally driven redistribution since 2007.

In contrast, local and Third Force parties emerged around this time calling for more aggressive decentralization (Hijino, 2013). These include Your Party, founded in 2010, and the Japan Restoration Party, started by Osaka Mayor Tōru Hashimoto and Tokyo Governor Shintaro Ishihara in 2012 (Reed, *JD 2012*). These new parties were primarily urban in their support base, areas that could become potential beneficiaries of decentralization. They thus pushed for drastic "regionalization," merging prefectures into several regions (called *dōshusei* in Japanese).

During the 2012 and 2013 national elections, Hashimoto used his considerable popularity and momentum at the time to demand the LDP and DPJ commit to local government reform (*Asahi*, February 13, 2013; *Yomiuri*, November 23, 2012). Despite these pressures from Hashimoto, the Abe administration has largely failed to move forward with local government reforms in its first two years. Faced with strong opposition from within the LDP as well as local governors and mayor associations, the Abe administration has had to delay the submission of a promised bill on the regionalization in both 2013 and 2014.

Abe's first two years in office focused on national-level macroeconomic, fiscal and security matters, and by and large paid relatively little attention to regional issues. Instead, Abe's initial regional policy was a narrow focus on reviving traditional public works spending. In the 2012 campaign, the LDP called for spending up to Y200 trillion yen over the next ten years to strengthen Japan's resilience toward natural disasters. The LDP has expanded public works for the 2013 and 2014 budgets, reversing a general downward trend. These increases in public works, although still far below peak levels in 1998, have been criticized as a return to the old LDP of wasteful and ineffective pump-priming measures (*Asahi*, January 1, 2013). Moreover, the sudden surge of public works spending has resulted in a shortage of construction laborers and rise in construction material costs, with record levels of unused budgets and uncompleted construction orders (*Asahi*, September 18, 2014).

Thus the LDP was blocked on two fronts. Further decentralization had largely been discredited in rural areas as a policy of abandoning regions, while traditional pump-priming measures ran into fiscal constraints, broader media criticism, and lack of industry capacity to absorb construction orders. The LDP was in search of a new approach to regional issues. The publication of a high profile article – the so-called "Masuda report"[5] – in May of 2014 on rural depopulation provided a cue.

In the article, Masuda and his research team recalculated future demographic predictions based on the assumption that the population inflow from rural to major urban areas would continue. Under this scenario, half of Japan's municipalities would see the portion of their 20–39 year old women (child-bearing population) fall below half of current levels by 2040. These 896 municipalities were deemed to become potentially "extinct,"[6] while 523 of them under a population of 10,000 were deemed to have a very high likelihood to become extinct. The predictions estimate that 80% of municipalities in Hokkaido, Aomori, Iwate, Akita, Yamagata, and Shimane – including larger cities such as Akita,

Aomori, and Hakodate – were at risk of becoming extinct due to a shortage of childbearing women (Masuda, 2014: 30).

The article also linked the mechanism of this depopulation to over-concentration in the metropolitan regions. Tokyo, with the lowest fertility rate of all prefectures (1.13 compared to national average of 1.41), was sucking in younger generations like a demographic "black hole" who on arrival were not bearing children, resulting in a demographic "polar society."[7] Compared to other developed economies, Japan was exceedingly concentrated in Tokyo: 30% of its population was living in the capital region, compared to between 5 and 15% for Paris, London, New York, Rome, and Berlin (Masuda, 2014). This trend has continued, with Japan's population declining for the 5th straight year while Tokyo's population has increased and 39 of Japan's prefectures have declined in 2014 (*Japan Times*, November 24, 2014).

By publicizing a list of municipalities at risk of extinction, and applying the dramatic term "extinction" (*shōmetsu*) in contrast to past terms of "marginalizing" (*genkai*) or "depopulating" (*kaso*) for rural municipalities, the report triggered a flurry of news reports, editorials, and television documentaries. Soon after publication, local assemblies deliberated the matter in their assembly sessions, while the Governors Association responded to the article by declaring a state of emergency concerning depopulation.

To reverse regional depopulation, the Masuda report recommended the creation of compact and core cities in regions to act as "dams" to stop the outflow of young people from rural to urban areas. These ideas have been linked to proposals from the Ministry of Internal Affairs and Communications and the Ministry of Land, Infrastructure and Transport to select and focus administrative resources on select cities (with proposals including the creation of 60 or so core designated cities) as well as promote municipal coalitions. The Masuda report, however, was explicit in arguing that counter-depopulation policies should not rely on decentralization, which could potentially weaken regions and accelerate the population shift to Tokyo (Masuda, 2014: 38).

The Abe administration's regional policies quickly coalesced around the report's new theme combining depopulation and regional development. In 15th May, the 31st Local Government System Research Council was established to deliberate on depopulation and local governance. In June, the Council on Economic and Fiscal Policy (CEFP) announced a long-term goal to maintain Japan's population at around 100 million 50 years later. One of the sub-committees of the CEFP recommended to raise the total fertility rate to 2.07 by 2030, making it the first time a fertility target has been set by the government (*Nikkei*, May 13, 2015). In September 2014, a Cabinet council on depopulation and local economy[8] was established with former LDP chairman Shigeru Ishiba as special minister in charge.

Prior to the dissolution of the lower house, the ruling party passed a bill for regional development. Although specific details of the regional development program were not available prior to the election, proposals floated to the press including dispatching central ministry bureaucrats to local governments, the creation of special deregulatory zones, and providing new block grants to fund proposals from local communities. In general, however, these were criticized as a rehash of past policies and leading to uncoordinated distribution of subsidies. Editorials and analytical pieces doubted whether the measures could generate enough employment in rural communities to stem the continued population exodus to the cities (*Yomiuri*, October 14, 2014; *Nikkei*, December 11, 2014).

The 2014 campaign and regional development

Considering the context described above, regional issues linking the major issues of economic recovery, depopulation, and socio-economic inequality could have become a focal point of the 2014 election. Yet this appears not to be the case.

Newspaper editorials on the 2014 election have largely bemoaned a lack of clear electoral issues and have not given much space to discuss regional policy or decentralization. And where regional policy was discussed, the policies promoted by the LDP were criticized as lacking in substance and novelty (*Mainichi*, December 6, 2014; *Asahi*, December 13). In the pre-election coverage, major media outlets provided comparative charts of party programs. Yet most of these did not include a separate rubric for comparing the parties' regional policies or decentralization plans (*Asahi*, December 3, 2014; *Nikkei*, December 1, 2014; *Jiji News*, December 12, 2014 web).

In polls asking voters what policy issues they were interested in, most newspapers have not included regional development or decentralization, instead they are subsumed under the broader option of "Abenomics" or "economy." One exception was a national poll conducted by Yomiuri (*Yomiuri*, November 23, 2014), where respondents were given the choice of "regional vitalization" as one of nine electoral issues that they may consider important when casting their vote. Here, interestingly, "regional vitalization" (56%) was second only after

Table 15.1   Reporting frequency on regional issues in general elections

Election Year	Articles including the following terms (in Asahi Shimbun)				
	Decentralization	Regional Inequality	Regional Vitalization	Doshusei	Combined total
2000	149	6	16	23	194
2003	134	3	18	29	184
2005	129	10	18	36	193
2009	145	23	58	74	300
2012	84	9	34	91	218
2014	35	3	43	30	111

Source: Compiled by author. Number of articles in *Asahi Shimbun* referring to regional issues in past general election periods (12-day electoral period).

"economy and employment" (70%) in importance to voters. Despite this single Yomiuri poll results suggesting interest in regional issues, the overall tone of media reporting did not present rural depopulation and regional inequality as an important electoral theme. Media reports on regional issues were markedly fewer than in recent past general elections (Table 15.1). Where separate editorials or analysis was given, the tone tended to be skeptical and tepid.

This lack of enthusiasm may reflect, in part, the continued convergence and increasingly vague policy promises given by parties. Looking at the election manifestos of the LDP and DPJ, there is increasingly less focus on concrete decentralization measures and local government reform, compared to the past two general elections.

The LDP's 2014 manifesto re-iterates Abe's dissolution speech, which frames the election as promoting Abenomics to ensure economic benefits are felt across Japan. The manifesto pamphlet promises to: "accelerate economic recovery to ensure that it reaches the regions" in very large font on the second page. Four main policy planks are listed on page four in the following order – "economic recovery," "regional vitalization," "women participation," and "fiscal reconstruction." Regional development promises come in second, but there are no specific measures, only a pledge to "create attractive and unique regions." This is in contrast to more specific measures for the other planks provided on the same page, including numerical targets for fiscal reconstruction.

In the more detailed LDP policy bank section appended to the main text of the manifesto, policies to strengthen regions are presented jointly under policies to promote "womenomics." The promise to further decentralization appears early on, but these are paired with promises to secure stable financial resources for the regions. Many policies are listed under the rubric of "creating attractive and unique communities" but these are largely focused on providing central government support through personnel and funds for local communities in agriculture, ICT, education, transport, among other areas. The 2014 LDP manifesto contains no promises concerning specific transfers of powers from central ministries to regions – although there is a call for selectively establishing local deregulatory zones for "local governments who are determined and wish to make a difference." Regionalization is mentioned only briefly in a section on administrative reform, stating the LDP will promote and seek a national consensus on administrative reform with no policy deadlines.

Thus the 2014 manifesto reflects a broader shift in LDP's commitment to decentralization over the past few years. In the party's general election manifesto five years ago, decentralization was promoted as part of its main plank of structural reforms, under the phrase "forward with decentralization. Create a vigorous team (Japan) where all the members (regions) are lively." The 2009 manifesto also criticized excessive centralization, stating the need to "break up the current situation in which the central government is constraining the regions." The LDP at the time specifically called for abolishing the regional branches of central ministries, revising subsidy and tax distribution to local governments, establishing a dispute resolution commission between the country and regions, plus promises to implement regionalization by 2017.

By 2012, the LDP manifesto no longer uses the term decentralization. The campaign theme of "regaining" various things that have been lost in Japan de-emphasizes structural reform, including decentralization. The more nostalgic and emotive term "hometowns" (*furusato*) is used here, rather than "regions" (*chihō*). There is no longer a deadline for regionalization, but a promise to implement a basic law promoting it in response to pressures from Third Force parties led by Hashimoto to include this clause. Although the 2012 document calls for "reviving and emphasizing the regions," it does so without promises to transfer central government powers to local governments.

The opposition DPJ has also changed its tone on decentralization during the same period, from an emphasis on virtuous competition to one of a need to combine decentralization with greater support for weaker regions. The DPJ repackaged decentralization under the new term "regional sovereignty reforms" in its 2009 manifesto. Nevertheless, the DPJ allotted a full page to decentralization in its manifesto pamphlet and considerable detail in its appendix. These included a combination of promises for greater fiscal support to regions (increasing local government tax revenue, provide income support for farmers, reverse postal privatization) together with structural reforms to "fundamentally alter the centralized regime that had continued since Meiji period." This in practice meant drastic reforms of the central ministries including abolishing ministry regional branches and their earmarked subsidies, while expanding general block grants.

By 2012, however, the DPJ mentions decentralization only very briefly in its manifesto main text (giving it one sentence) under the rubric of continuing administrative reform. In its more detailed policy list, decentralization appears only in two sentences. There is no longer talk of abolishing excessive centralization or a "large-scale" transfer of responsibilities to local governments" as in 2009. The DPJ promises reforms of the administrative system for large cities (relating to Osaka) and mentions looking into regionalization in the long term (also a response to possible pressures from JRP).

The DPJ continues with this reticent tone on decentralization in 2014 – mentioning it only in three sentences – twice under the rubric of economic reform and once under the rubric of administrative reform. Although the DPJ pamphlet calls for "listening to the voice of regions and reviving hometowns" there are a few promises relating to devolution or challenging centralization. Any mention of regionalization is dropped. Overall, it is a far more restrained document, focusing on criticizing the outcomes of LDP macro-economic policies rather than proposing alternatives to the LDP's regional policy or promoting fundamental structural changes. Much of the policies are universal social-democratic measures – expanding regional healthcare/nursing care, expanding education and child-care – rather than initiatives specific to rural areas.

The convergence away from decentralization by the two major parties contrasts with the more aggressive structural reforms promoted by the Third Force parties, YP and JRP, in the 2012 and 2014 elections. Although here, too, the merger between the two parties and weakening of the regional party contingent led by Hashimoto has reduced the urgency of decentralization in the JRP's manifesto.

In the 2012 manifesto, YP claimed that, "excessive centralization and top-down standardization by bureaucrats ignored the diversity of regions and caused continued atrophy of regions." Regionalization would provide a "new shape for the country" and is "necessary to make vitalize regions" (YP, 2012). The JRP pushed similar themes in 2012, although the language is more drastic. In its preamble, the party argues that "the old Japanese model" is "paralyzed by centralization and complex regulations." The way to overcome the "oppressive mood weighing down on Japan and restore the hope of the public" is to encourage "local and private ingenuity." In its eight policy goals, JRP emphasized "independence," "responsibility," and "virtuous competition" of local governments, noting in particular the need for fiscal responsibility of local governments. It proposed a system in which local governments "bear the risk of bankruptcy," separating national from local administrations, and with "regionalization being the ultimate goal" (JRP, 2012).

By 2014, the two Third Force parties merged and became the third-largest party in the lower house (see Pekkanen and Reed, this volume). Becoming a larger party has apparently resulted in a dilution in focus on decentralization reforms, which was at the heart of the JRP's formation as an Osaka-based regional party. Unlike 2012, where the JRP had placed decentralization front and center of its reform packages, the 2014 JRP manifesto focused on criticizing the limitations of Abe's policies in 2014. JRP also tried to co-opt LDP terminology by calling for "regional vitalization" while criticizing the ruling party's tendency to make "indiscriminate handouts" to regions.

The JCP and Komeito, two other prominent parties in the 2014 election, did not differentiate itself from the major parties in terms of regional policy. The Komeito placed regional development as a central policy in its manifesto, providing detailed measures of expanding welfare programs and labor policies in the regions without resorting to decentralization (see Klein, this volume). The JCP, traditionally opposed to decentralization, did not mention regional policies in its election pamphlet either. Instead the communists focused on macro-national issues of consumption tax, Abenomics, collective security/constitutional reform, nuclear power, and US bases in Okinawa.

Conclusion

It should be noted that regional policy and decentralization has traditionally not been high on the agenda for most voters. Polls indicate that voter interest in policies to develop regions receive middling interest (around 15–25%), whereas decentralization rests lower (around 8–15%) in the past 15 years.[9] These levels of interest are far lower than the 40–70% of voters who seek government action on pensions/medical care, aging, employment, and economic recovery. In polls conducted by The Association for Promoting Fair Elections for the past four general elections before 2014, popular interest in decentralization as an electoral issue has hovered between 4 (2005) and 14% (2009).[10]

Media reporting on the campaign also suggests regional issues did not become a focal point for this election, in fact becoming less so than past general elections (Table 15.1). This is in spite of the fact that during the election year, a widely-debated report had dramatically combined some of the most crucial structural challenges facing Japan today – depopulation, "womenomics," casualization of labor, socio-economic inequality, and sustainable economic recovery – under the theme of reviving rural areas. Faced with local elections in 2015, the ruling party and its coalition partner also had strong reason to promote regional issues as a key electoral issue. Nevertheless, the 2014 election was certainly not one focused on regional development or rural-urban cleavages.

There are two potential explanations for this situation of tepid interest. One is that of policy convergence. No clear alternatives have emerged in terms of regional policy between the LDP and DPJ. Both the two main parties have de-emphasized decentralization and other structural reforms in the past two elections, converging on a "softer" approach of providing support to struggling regions. At the same time, the Third Force parties, which have been most aggressive in pushing for drastic decentralization reforms to kick-start local economies, have diluted their positions. With the weakening of their electoral threat and declining popularity of Hashimoto, who spearheaded debate about regionalization, the third parties have lost ability to steer debate toward decentralization. Instead, the LDP and DPJ have resorted to vague promises of supporting regions in the campaign.

Recent studies have noted this convergence of the two parties in other policy areas (Scheiner, 2012). This chapter indicates that such convergence applies to decentralization as well. Faced with largely undifferentiated positions on local government reform from the two major parties, interest may have been muted.

The second reason, linked to the first, is what appears to be a kind of voter distrust toward any policy promise related to reversing the continued stagnation of regions. Both before and after the election campaign, the LDP's new flagship program of "regional vitalization" has triggered knee-jerk reactions in the public discourse claiming that the latest campaign was merely empty rhetoric. Editorials in national media have decried the package as potentially rife with wasteful handouts to the regions, with calls for both LDP and opposition parties to provide more concrete measures to combat rural depopulation (*Nikkei*, December 11,

2014; *Jiji News*, December 8, 2014 web). Regional newspapers too have pointedly declared that voters in the regions do not have any illusions about Abe's regional development plans. These initiatives were described as merely the latest in a series of "rose-colored policy phrases without substance" from Tokyo (*Kōchi Shimbun*, December 12, 2014).

The LDP, of course, is aware of these criticisms and have made effort to promote the policies as something new: neither wasteful handouts nor heartless decentralization of abandoning the regions.[11] Yet the long lineage of failed and frayed regional policy packages appears to weigh heavily on the credibility of the ruling party. For now, the lack of an alternative program promoted by a viable opposition party has allowed the LDP to secure victories in rural electoral districts. But how the party will be able to reverse, let alone halt, the deepening existential crisis in rural areas remains unclear. Until an answer is found, regional issues – though submerged in the 2014 campaign – will potentially be Achilles' heel in the LDP's precarious electoral dominance.

Notes

1. The term *chihō*, strictly speaking, include all geographical subdivisions of Japan, including metropolitan Tokyo. But in common parlance it refers to all regions except the Tokyo area or rural areas in general.
2. Compiled from Ministry of Land, Infrastructure, and Transport and Ministry of Internal Affairs and Communications data on LAT and public works spending.
3. Data after 2011 are not yet available. Latest data taken from *Naikakufu keizai shakai sōgō kenkyujo* report in July 2014, *Heisei 23 nendo kenmin keizai keisan ni tsuite*.
4. Tachibanaki and Urakawa (2012) also provide data demonstrating an exceedingly high concentration of business, cultural, and educational assets in Tokyo compared to other developed democracies even after the period of decentralization reform.
5. The article, published in in *Chuō kōron* magazine, was authored by Hiroya Masuda, former Minister of Home Affairs and Communications, and researchers at the Japan Policy Council. It was entitled "Stop the rapid depopulation society: realizing the people's desired fertility rate and creation of core regional cities" and later published in book form (Masuda 2014).
6. The term *shōmetsu jichitai* is used originally, directly translating to "municipalities that become extinct."
7. Tokyo, in turn, was also facing a demographic crisis of its own, as its population ages rapidly. Currently, new nurse homes are being built around Tokyo which are drawing in nursing care-workers from rural areas (in effect depopulating rural areas for which there exist few other job opportunities

for young women). Eventually, however, this pool of younger female workers from rural areas will also be depleted, leaving Tokyo with a host of old people unable to receive old-age care (Masuda 2014).
8. Council on Overcoming Population Decline and Vitalizing Local Economy in Japan.
9. Cabinet Office survey, *Kokumin seikatsu ni kansuru seron chōsa* for June 2014.
10. *Dai 46kai shugiin sōsenkyo zenkoku ishiki chōsa:chōsa kekka no gaiyō* pg 56.
11. See, for example, Shigeru Ishiba's comments in *Chihō sōsei datsu baramaki sengen* [Declaration to avoid indiscriminate handouts in regional vitalization] in *Chuō kōron* magazine December 2014.

References

Chiavacci, David (2010). Divided society model and social cleavages in Japanese politics: No alignment by social class, but de-alignment of rural-urban division. *Contemporary Japan* 22(1–2): 47–74.
Hasunuma, Linda (2012). Decentralization and the democratic party of Japan. In K. Kushida and P. Lipscy (eds.) *Japan Under the DPJ*. Stanford: Walter H. Shorenstein Asia-Pacific Research Center: 281–304.
Hijino, V. L. Ken (2013). Delinking national and local party systems: New parties in Japanese local elections. *Journal of East Asian Studies* 13(1): 107–135.
Hijino, V. L. Ken (2015). Campaigning against Tokyo: Multi-level intra-party policy conflicts in the LDP. Paper presented at the Association of Asian Studies Conference, Chicago, March 30, 2015.
Ikawa, Hiroshi (2008). Years of decentralization reform in Japan. *Council of Local Authorities for International Relations*, http://www.clair.or.jp/j/forum/honyaku/hikaku/pdf/up-to-date_en4.pdf.
Masuda, Hiroya (2014). *Chihō shōmetsu Tokyo ikkyoku shuchu ga maneku jinkō kyugen* [Vanishing regions: How concentration in Tokyo brings rapid depopulation]. Chukō Shinsho.
Noble, Gregory W. (2010). The decline of particularism in Japanese politics. *Journal of East Asian Studies* 10(2): 239–273.
Reed, Steven R. (2013). Challenging the two-party system: Third force parties in the 2012 elections. In Robert Pekkanen, Steven R. Reed and Ethan Scheiner (eds) *Japan Decides 2012: The Japanese General Election*, pp. 72–83. New York: Palgrave Macmillan.
Rosenbluth, M. Frances and Michael F. Thies (2010). *Japan transformed: Political change and economic restructuring*. Princeton: Princeton University Press.
Saito Jun (2010). *Jimintō chōki seiken no seijigaku: Rieki yudo seiji no jiko mujun* [The political economy of LDP dominance: Contradictions of particularist politics]. Keisō shobō.
Scheiner, Ethan (2006). *Democracy without competition in Japan: Opposition failure in a one-party dominant state*. Cambridge: Cambridge University Press.
Scheiner, Ethan (2012). The electoral system and Japan's partial transformation: Party system consolidation without policy realignment. *Journal of East Asian Studies* 12(3): 351–379.
Shimizu, Kay (2013). What the 2012 lower house elections have to say about Japan's urban-rural divide. In Robert Pekkanen, Steven R. Reed and Ethan

Scheiner (eds) *Japan Decides 2012: The Japanese General Election.* pp. 148–153. New York: Palgrave Macmillan.

Tachibanaki Toshiaki and Urakawa Kunio (2012). *Nihon no chiiki kakusa: Tokyo Ikkyokushuchuugata kara yatsugatake hōshiki e* [Japan's regional disparities. From centralization in Tokyo to Yatsugatake model] Nihon hyōronsha

16
Abenomics and Japan's Energy Conundrum

Llewelyn Hughes

Introduction

Energy policy shifted to the margins of the 2014 House of Representatives (HR) election. This is remarkable given the importance of energy within the national political debate since the disaster of March 11, 2011. In addition to compensating those suffering from the lingering effects of the disaster, and managing the thorny problem of decommissioning the damaged nuclear site and removing spent fuel rods, a core issue has focused on whether to restart the Japan's idled nuclear reactors. Given these difficult issues, why did energy issues play a less significant role in the electoral debate during the 2014 House of Representatives election?

In this chapter I suggest the relegation of energy to another "dog that did not bark," to repeat the phrase used elsewhere in this volume, partly reflects strategic choices made by political actors. Just as the Fukushima disaster was a "man-made disaster" (Fukushima Nuclear Accident Independent Investigation Commission, 2011: 16) caused not only by the natural disaster at Fukushima-Daiichi nuclear power plant but also by organizational failures prior to and after the event, so the defusing of energy policy as a political issue in the 2014 election reflected a successful effort to insulate the government against its possible reignition as an electoral issue.

Most basically, the power companies, with the support of the government, have succeeded in avoiding unplanned blackouts, which could have had a political impact. Beyond this, however, the government minimized the differences between itself and the major opposition Democratic Party of Japan (DPJ) in electorally relevant time-scales, and sought to shift responsibility for nuclear restarts to the newly established Nuclear Regulation Authority (NRA). While this has slowed the process of restarting nuclear plants, it has also transformed the question of how to position nuclear power into a technocratic rather than a political issue. Third, the government has forged ahead with power market liberalization, reversing the approach it adopted more than a decade earlier. This means it has avoided public anger over protecting the Tokyo Electric Power Company (TEPCO) or other power utilities, which continue to be unpopular in the public eye.

I proceed in three sections. In the first section I briefly describe the challenges Japanese energy policymaking has faced since the disaster of March 11, 2011, and the role it played in the 2012 House of Representatives and 2013 House of Councillors elections. In the second section I contrast this with the 2014 House of Representatives election, using the electoral manifestos as evidence.

Nuclear power in Japan's energy policy

Nuclear power has historically been positioned by the government as the fuel most suitable to meeting the energy security, environmental, and economic public policy goals identified by Japan's postwar administrations. This does not mean it dominates Japan's fuel mix. The most important fuel in Japan's national energy mix remains oil, primarily because of the lack of substitutes for gasoline, diesel, and jet fuel for use in the transport sector available at competitive prices. The installed capacity of nuclear power nevertheless continued to grow prior to 2011, and the government sought to continue increasing its share of nuclear generating capacity. Since the passing of the Basic Energy Law (BEL) in 2001, the Japanese cabinet is required to agree to a comprehensive plan for energy supply and demand every three years. The plan passed by the government in 2010 established a target of 50% of power to be generated using nuclear power by 2030, up from 20% in fiscal year 2007. Matching this expectation, three nuclear units (4,141 megawatts) were under construction (excluding the "Monju" fast-breeder reactor), with eight units in the planning stages (11,147 megawatts) (Japan Atomic Industrial Forum, 2014).

The decision to idle all Japan's nuclear units until it could be demonstrated they met safety standards thus had important implications for Japan's power generation mix, implying that a large share of Japan's electricity would need to be generated by non-nuclear sources of power in the short-term, assuming constant demand. It also had enormous implications for Japan's power utilities. The Japanese power system continues to be dominated by ten electric power companies (EPCOs), of which the Tokyo Electric Power Company (TEPCO) is the largest. Despite limited reductions in the regulatory barriers to market entry in the 2000s, these firms remain utterly dominant in their service areas and remain unthreatened by new market entrants.[1] Importantly, other than the Okinawa Electric Power Company, all the utilities generate a portion of the their electricity from nuclear fuel, although the share of nuclear power within total generating capacity varies by firm.

For the power utilities, the disaster thus had implications beyond TEPCO, which was the owner and operator of the Fukushima Daiichi nuclear plant. Instead, its effects extended to the other utilities because of the decision to shut-down Japan's nuclear facilities until they were deemed safe. Consistent with this challenge, each has posted financial losses following the disaster as they struggled with idled assets, as well as problems such as reduced demand and the need to purchase increased volumes of fossil fuels to make up for the loss of nuclear power by increasing the burning of coal, natural gas, oil, and other fuels used in power generation. TEPCO accepted partial nationalization through an injection of funds from the government in return for preferred shares that gave the latter a controlling stake in the firm, suggesting that – like the financial sector – the government judgment the systemic risk associated with allowing the largest of Japan's quasi-monopoly power utilities to fail was too great.

Japan's energy policy and the 2014 election

The Abe government thus faced a thorny set of issues related to energy policy. Public opinion polling prior to the July 21 House of Councillors election of 2013 suggests the public had mixed opinion toward the approach the government was taking toward Japan's energy policy dilemmas. At the beginning of 2013, 75% of respondents stated they were in favor of reducing Japan's reliance on nuclear power. On the specific question of a nuclear restart of the Oi reactor in Fukui Prefecture – the first proposed restart following the nuclear disaster – 49% of respondents opposed this, while 35% supported the change, suggesting that the general preference for less nuclear power was moderated when the question of specific restarts was asked.[2]

In a poll fielded on July 6 and 7, 2013 – just two weeks before the 2013 election – nuclear power and energy policy was identified as the third most important issue by respondents when asked which issues they would like to see more debate on, with 30% of respondents recording in the affirmative – similar to the consumption tax at 29% – but behind the economy and social security. In another measure of the relative importance of energy policy in the election, 70% responded the nuclear power plant issue would greatly or somewhat affect their vote, while 27% responded that it would "not really" affect their vote, or not affect their vote at all. On nuclear power plant restarts, once again a plurality recorded their opposition at 48%, but with 34% in support. This suggests that energy policy remained important by late-2013, approaching three years since the Fukushima disaster.

Testing the counterfactual question of how the results of the 2013 upper house election might have changed if the Abe government's approach to energy policy had been different is challenging empirically. One possibility is that while many voters may not have supported restarting nuclear plants, they may not have been willing to punish the government for supporting retaining nuclear power within Japan's generation mix. This is consistent with Lipscy and Scheiner (2012), who note that changes in Japan's electoral system have not lead to deep programmatic competition between the two parties, and that voters have responded by increasingly voting according to non-policy issues such as general impressions of party competence. Certainly the appearance of the Prime Minister Abe at the leaders' debate at the Japan National Press Club suggested his calculation that the LDP would not lose substantial votes through adopting this position; at the debate Abe recorded his support for nuclear restarts, and justified this choice using the government's responsibility to ensure a stable supply of power. This matched the 2013 electoral manifesto released by the party, which also noted the party's support for restarting nuclear facilities while framing it within a broad reconsideration of the energy strategy Japan adopted to date.[3]

The Abe government's willingness to support retaining nuclear power within Japan's energy mix in its 2014 House of Representatives election manifesto may thus be partly the result of experience. Polling prior to the 2014 election did not differ substantially from that of the previous' years election. In poll results released on March 18, 2014, respondents remained unhappy with the approach the Abe government was taking toward nuclear power, with 53% of respondents not supporting their approach, against 25% in support. In terms of nuclear restarts, 59% of respondents opposed restarting the plants, against 28% in support, and a larger number (77%) favored gradually reducing the number of nuclear power plants over time.[4] In a poll by the Asahi Shimbun fielded on July 29, 2014 – less than five months before the election – respondents continued to express skepticism regarding the approach taken by the Abe government toward nuclear energy. When asked whether they favored restarting the Sendai nuclear plant in Kyushu Electric Power Company's supply area, 59% of respondents answered in the negative, with 23% answering positive.

Against this, an increased number of respondents believed that nuclear power plant restarts had important implications for the economy, with 42% answering in the affirmative when asked whether the Japanese economy was likely to be damaged if they were not restarted. Importantly, regardless of the potential repercussions for the economy of nuclear restarts, or respondents' views on nuclear power plant safety, a large plurality of respondents did not trust the Abe cabinet's handling of the problem: 61% of respondents replied that they did not think Prime Minister Abe's government set nuclear policies by applying the lessons of the Fukushima Nuclear Power Plant disaster.[5]

The fact that energy was not a centerpiece of the election may thus be attributable to the fact that voters had already demonstrated they were not willing to punish the government even though it publicly stated its willingness to restart Japan's nuclear units. It is possible to identify a series of strategic choices made by the Abe government prior to election, however, that may have helped insulate it from the potential for energy policy to be an election-defining public policy issue. Three choices, in particular, appear important: (i) lack of differentiation between the government and major opposition parties on the role of nuclear energy within electorally relevant time scales; (ii) shifting of responsibility for decisions about the safety of nuclear restarts to the newly created Nuclear Regulation Authority (NRA); (iii) distancing politically from the power utilities by continuing with power market liberalization. Below I discuss each of these in turn.

Reducing the gap with the opposition on nuclear energy

One strategy the Abe Administration adopted during the electoral campaign was to reduce the differences between it and the opposition in relation to energy policy, including both nuclear power and renewable energy. Indeed, evidence gleaned from the electoral manifestos suggests there was little difference between the Liberal Democratic Party and the major opposition DPJ on the role of nuclear power within electorally relevant time-scales. In this sense voters may not have seen a large difference between the parties, despite differences in rhetoric.

The manifestos that have become a central part of party efforts to woo voters offer one source of data for determining the position the political parties took toward the nuclear power, and energy policy more generally, during the campaign. The most important difference between the major government and opposition parties within energy policy focused, unsurprisingly, on the appropriate long-term role for nuclear power. The implications of the differences the parties adopted on the role for nuclear power in the short- to medium-term, however, was insignificant. The Abe government went into the election arguing that its goal – should it be reelected – was to set an appropriate fuel mix for the economy in order to meet Japan's long-standing public policy objectives of enhancing energy security, environmental stewardship, and economic efficiency. With regard to nuclear power, the LDP argued that it would respect the judgment of the NRA on whether the established nuclear plants were able to be safely restarted, and would seek to persuade localities of the merits of restarting plants where it was determined they met newly outlined safety regulations.

The broad direction for the energy mix outlined in the LDP manifesto pointed toward a reduced role for nuclear power however. The manifesto noted that nuclear power would be reduced "as much as possible," through increasing the deployment of renewable energy, the use of demand management, and the increased use of thermal power.[6] In doing so, the LDP adopted a stance that was not far from the position expressed collectively by voters in public opinion polling. In doing so it demonstrated that the party was capable of practicing "creative conservatism," in Pempel's apt phrase, in the energy sector by jettisoning its long-standing position of actively promoting the growth in nuclear power when this may have emerged as an electoral liability (Pempel, 1982).

The position adopted by the Abe government was also consistent with the Basic Energy Plan agreed to in cabinet in April 2014. The Plan noted that nuclear power, thermal coal, geothermal, and hydropower could be considered "baseload" power because they are capable of generating continuously at comparatively low cost (Government of Japan 2014: 19). It also eschewed naming targets for future mix of fuels used in the economy, instead noting that the energy mix should be decided after taking into consideration the situation regarding nuclear restarts, the state of deployment of renewable energy sources through the Feed-In-Tariff system, and the status of international negotiations over climate change mitigation (Government of Japan, 2014: 26–27). This position recognized the role of the NRA in determining the pace of nuclear restarts, but also avoided the potentially controversial task of naming a target for nuclear power relative to other sources of fuel.

At first glance, the major opposition DPJ broke from the position of the LDP in proposing that Japan, like Germany, should shut down all nuclear power within the country. The DPJ, in contrast to the Abe Cabinet, proposed in its Manifesto that all of Japan's nuclear units should be decommissioned after 40 years of use, and that there should be no new plants built and also no increase in generating capacity allowed for existing units. This position guaranteed that the share of nuclear power within the generation mix would fall over time until replaced by other fuel sources.

This contrasted with the Abe Cabinet's naming of nuclear power as a continued stable source of power. The target identified in the DPJ's electoral manifesto for completely removing nuclear power from the generation mix was 2030, and the DPJ, like the LDP, stated in its manifesto that it would allow for nuclear restarts for those units that pass the safety regulations established by the NRA. For voters considering which party they would prefer to see elected for the next three years the short to medium term difference in terms of the role of nuclear power was thus not significant.

This does not mean there were no differences between the LDP and the DPJ. One point of contrast between the two parties was with regard to the role of renewable energy, and the relationship with the localities. The DPJ was far more bullish on the merits of renewable energy, proposing a *Fundamental Law on the Promotion of Distributed Energy* designed to promote local economic revitalization and employment opportunities in the regions through the deployment of distributed energy. The LDP, by contrast, was less enthusiastic, arguing for the promotion of renewable energy, but also pointing to the constraints on the promotion of renewable energy such as the higher power prices implied by the Feed-In-Tariff, and the need to ensure "sustainable" growth in renewable energy deployment, which suggested they emphasized intermittency of supply and other limitations of renewable energy, in addition to potential capacity constraints in the transmission grid.

Indeed, the most significant difference between the major parties may not have been between the LDP and the DPJ, but rather in the approaches adopted by these two parties and the LDP coalition partner Komeito. Where the former two parties focused on supply-side issues centered on the appropriate role for nuclear power, how to increase the share of renewable energy sources within the grid, and whether to reorganize the utilities, the Komeito focused almost wholly on the implications of energy policies for the costs borne by household consumers of electricity and small business.

Political utility of the nuclear regulation authority

An important change to the nuclear planning process in the wake of the March 11 disaster was the creation of the Nuclear Regulation Agency (NRA). The NRA was created following a decision by the former DPJ government to separate the institutional locus of s nuclear safety regulation from policymaking (Cabinet Secretariat, 2011). Both were previously located within the Ministry of Economy, Trade, and Industry, which was thus positioned both as promoting the deployment of nuclear power in Japan, while also regulating its safety. The Fukushima Nuclear Accident Independent Investigation Commission, established by the Diet to review the causes of the Fukushima nuclear accident, identified insularity between firms and regulators as a core problem in the industry.

An important response to this was the passing into law of The Law Establishing the Nuclear Regulation Authority, which was passed through the House of Councillors, entering into law on June 20, 2012. The new organization began functioning on September 18, 2012, a little more than 18 months since the disaster of March 11, 2011. Once it developed new safety requirements for existing reactors, the NRA created a process for accepting applications from the operators of nuclear power plants and determining whether they meet these newly established safety requirements. On July 8, 2013, the power utilities began utilizing the new process by submitting applications to restart a total of 10 nuclear power generating units located at five nuclear plants. The power utilities continued to submit plants for consideration for nuclear restarts.[7]

The establishment of a new regulatory authority located in the Ministry for the Environment, and development of a new process for examining the safety of Japan's existing nuclear plants, did not wholly resolve the status of nuclear energy within Japanese nuclear energy mix: in addition to the formal process involving the NRA, the support of local government increased in importance. From the perspective of national electoral politics, however, the political problems associated with gaining the support of local governments differs from the larger question of whether to retain nuclear power within Japan's energy landscape, as the former primarily involves relations between the government and local administrations, and may have been less of an electoral threat at the national level.

Regardless, the Abe government consistently stated that nuclear restarts require both the agreement of the NRA, and the support of local communities hosting the units, prior to restarts. The LDP manifesto stated, for example, that the restart of nuclear facilities would only be considered once the NRA determined the plant for which the application was made met the new nuclear safety regulations. It also stated that the national government would actively seek the understanding and cooperation of the localities in supporting the restart of the nuclear facility (LDP 2014: 12). This was repeated by Chief Cabinet Secretary Suga following the agreement of the mayor of Satsumasendai City to the request from Kyushu Electric to restart units one and two of the Sendai nuclear power plant located in Kagoshima Prefecture in the southern island of Kyushu.

Power market liberalization

The third strategy adopted by the Abe-led LDP government in relation to the energy sector was to commit to continuing with reforms to the power sector. While the effects of this reform remain to be seen, the willingness to continue with reforms that weaken the market position of the power utilities made it more difficult to claim that the LDP was behaving in ways consistent with TEPCO and other power utilities.

The initial wave of legislation sought to deal with one problem identified with the structure of Japan's electricity market in the wake of the disaster of March 11, 2011: the lack of sufficient transmission capacity between the service areas of the vertically-integrated regional power utilities, a problem compounded by the split in the transmission network between 50Hz and 60Hz service areas. A plausible response to this dilemma was to establish incentives designed to increase investment in transmission lines crossing the regional utilities' service areas, thus enabling power to flow to areas in which there were more limited supplies in the event of an emergency. The initial reforms enacted by the Abe cabinet aimed to manage this problem by establishing an Organization for Cross-regional Coordination of Transmission Operators (OCCTO). The organization began operating on April 1, 2015, with an organizational mission including overseeing improvements in the interregional transmission system and monitoring market competition.

The Abe government went further than this, however, supporting a three stage process that revisits proposals for reorganizing the power market discussed 15 years earlier. These were opposed by the power utilities at the time, and ultimately rejected by the government, and included committing to full liberalization of the retail power market, and reducing the barriers to entry by new companies into the power market by separating the functions of power generation and electricity sales from the operation of the transmission grid.

The electoral commitment to push ahead with these changes in the industrial organization of Japan's power market thus marked an important change. Legal reforms designed to dismantle the barriers to market entry within the domestic oil market were introduced beginning in 1986 (Hughes, 2014). These were then extended into the markets for natural gas and power beginning in 1995. In the case of power market reform, however, they produced only limited results, if understood by the market share gained by new entrants into the power market.

In the case of the three-stage reforms supported by the Abe government, the extent to which they achieve the stated goals of improving the effectiveness of the power system to distribute power nationally in emergencies, increasing consumer choice at the retail level, promoting energy efficiency and the deployment of renewable energy, and reducing retail prices, remains to be seen. As an electoral strategy, however, it represents an important break from the past. The last time the LDP government sought to enact reforms to the power sector it did not to reorganize the industrial organization of the power utilities themselves. Instead the government preferred to leave them intact as vertically-integrated companies incorporating power generation, transmission and distribution, and sales within the same firm. The willingness of the Abe administration to pass legislation mandating the separation of these functions is thus an important change. Politically, it plausibly distanced the LDP from the utilities, which remain unpopular.

Conclusion

There are a number of possible explanations for why energy policy did not play a defining role in the House of Representatives election of 2014: the snap election may not have given opposition parties sufficient time to develop a cogent criticism of the Abe governments approach to nuclear power, and to energy market reform more generally. Energy issues may not have resonated with voters as memories of the March 11, 2011, disaster became more distant. More generally, electoral system changes are reducing programmatic differences between the parties, leading voters to focus more on general impressions of party competence and other non-policy related issues.

In this chapter I have suggested, however, that in addition to these factors, the Abe government adopted a strategy designed to minimize the potential of energy policy as an election defining issue. It did so through a threefold strategy focused on minimizing differences between itself and the major opposition party DPJ over electorally-relevant time scales, shifting responsibility over nuclear restarts to the newly established Nuclear Regulation Authority and thus depoliticizing that choice, and finally signaling its distance from the power utilities by pushing ahead with plans to reform Japan's electricity market in ways that were inimical to the firms.

Notes

1. For a summary of these barriers to market entry see Hughes (Forthcoming). For a description of Japanese power sector in historical perspective, see Scalise (2009).
2. It may also suggest the politics of NIMBY ("Not In My Backyard"), where respondents were more willing to consider the idea of restarts when it was clear they would not be nearby. Data from Asahi Poll of January 22, 2013. Poll fielded by telephone on January 19 and 20, 2014, with 1703 valid responses. On NIMBY politics in the energy sector in Japan see Aldrich (2008).
3. A number of conclusions can plausibly explain this relationship. It is possible, for example, that voters opposed government policy but did not rate its importance highly in determining their vote. It is also possible that candidates did less well than they otherwise would have with a different position toward nuclear power, but they still retained sufficient support to be reelected. Finally, it is possible that the LDP victory would have been larger if it adopted a different policy in the area of nuclear power.
4. Data from Asahi Poll of March 18, 2014. Poll fielded by telephone on March 15 and 16, 2014, with 1721 valid responses.
5. Data from Asahi Poll of July 29, 2014. Poll fielded by telephone on July 26 and 27, 2014, with 1590 valid responses. On public opinion after the March 11, 2011, disaster also see Midford (2014).
6. "Genpatsu izondo ni tsuite ha, tettei shita shō enerugii to saisei kanō enerugii no saidaigen no dōnyō, karyoku hatsuden no kōritsuka ni yori, kanō na kagiri teigen sasemasu [We will reduce the reliance on nuclear power generation as much as possible through a thorough deployment of energy efficiency and renewable energy deployment, and increased efficiency in thermal power generation.]" (LDP, 2014: 11).
7. Applications were made for Hokkaido Electric Power Company, Kansai Electric Power Company, Shikoku Electric Power Company, and Kyushu Electric Power Company For details of the order of application for idled nuclear power units see Nuclear Regulation Authority (2013: 51).

Works cited

Aldrich, Daniel P. (2008). *Site fights: Divisive facilities and civil society in Japan and the West.* Ithaca: Cornell University Press.
Cabinet Secretariat (2011). Genshiryoku Anzen Kisei ni Kan suru Soshiki no Minaoshi [On Organizational Reform of Nuclear Power Safety Regulations].

(August). Available at: http://www.cas.go.jp/jp/genpatsujiko/info/kakugi_1108 15.html

Fukushima Nuclear Accident Independent Investigation Commission (2011). *The official report of the Fukushima nuclear accident independent investigation commission.* Tokyo: National Diet of Japan.

Government of Japan (2014). *Enerugī Kihon Keikaku [Basic Energy Plan].*

Hughes, Llewelyn (2014). *Globalizing oil: Firms and oil market governance in France, Japan, and the United States.* Cambridge, UK: Cambridge University Press.

Hughes, Llewelyn (Forthcoming). Renegotiating Japan's energy compact. In Carol Hager and Cristoph Stefes (eds) *Green Pioneers: Germany's Energy Transition in Comparative Perspective.* London: Palgrave.

Japan Atomic Industrial Forum (2014). *Nihon no Genshiryoku Hatsuden no Gaiyo [An Outline of Japan's Nuclear Power Generation],* May 27.

Liberal Democratic Party (2014). *Jūten Seisakushū 2014 [Major Policies 2014].*

Lipscy, Phillip Y. and Scheiner, Ethan (2012). Japan under the DPJ: The paradox of political change without policy change. *Journal of East Asian Studies* 12: 311–322.

Midford, Paul (2014). The Impact of 3–11 on Japanese public opinion and policy toward energy security. In Espen Moe and Paul Midford (eds) *The Political Economic of Renewable Energy and Energy Security.* pp. 67–96. London: Palgrave.

Nuclear Regulation Authority (2013). *Annual Report FY 2013 (Provisional English Translation).*

Pempel, T. J. (1982). *Policy and politics in Japan: Creative conservatism.* Philadelphia: Temple University Press.

Scalise, Paul J. 2009. "The Politics of Restructuring: Agendas and Uncertainty in Japan's Electricity Deregulation", D. Phil. Doctoral Dissertation. University of Oxford.

17
Nationalism and the 2014 Snap Election: The Abe Conundrum

Jeff Kingston

The Abe conundrum refers to the resilient popularity of Prime Minister Shinzo Abe despite strong opposition to virtually all of his signature policies on security and energy, and very little enthusiasm for Abenomics, constitutional revision, or his controversial views on history. Examining party pledges, manifestoes, debates, and campaign speeches, it would seem that nationalism was not a significant factor in Japan's 2014 lower house elections, or at least not embraced as a winning strategy to woo voters. Although nationalism is the talismanic calling card of the Liberal Democratic Party (LDP), and would be inscribed on its coat of arms if it had one, in campaign 2014 it steered clear of nationalist issues like a minefield and won what the media called a "landslide" victory even though it lost four seats and voter turnout was a record low (see Endo and Pekkanen, this volume). Post-election polls showed little enthusiasm for the LDP or Abe's plans for constitutional revision or security, but that did not stop him from claiming a mandate for this nationalist agenda (*Asahi*, December 18, 2014; on this bait-and-switch strategy, see Pekkanen, Reed, Scheiner, "Conclusion," this volume). Here I argue that understanding the role of nationalism in campaign 2014 depends on examining the wider context leading up to the elections that put wind in Abe's sails (see Pekkanen, Reed, and Smith, this volume, for this context).

When Abe announced the snap poll, the public reaction was negative, with most asking why he was dissolving the Diet when there was much urgent business at hand that would be delayed by elections. Given that Abe's coalition already enjoyed a two-thirds majority and he was elected to promote reforms and revive the economy, voters criticized the elections as a waste of time and money, especially since he had not delivered either growth or reforms. In the end, nearly half of eligible voters stayed away from the polls, showing that the LDP's campaign strategy of sidestepping nationalist issues was a "success"; low voter turnout helped the LDP, relying as it does on a loyal core constituency of about one quarter of voters. A key factor in the LDP's victory was winning 21.5% of unaffiliated voters in a campaign marked by an overall lack of voter enthusiasm (*Asahi*, December 18, 2014); attracting these fence-sitters meant not taking inflammatory stands on hot-button nationalist issues, but instead offering "safe-hands."

Campaign strategies

Team Abe features a dedicated group of PR professionals who approach politics in terms of marketing and branding, focusing on the optics while cultivating favorable media coverage and keeping everyone, especially their boss, on message (see also Pekkanen and Pekkanen, 2015). Thus, no improvised, extemporaneous comments, or other risky exposure that might lead to the gaffes that were the undoing of Abe I (2006–2007). They know that nationalism and ideology are toxic to mainstream voters but crucial to important rightwing organizations and thus position, segment, and sell their man accordingly. Paradoxically, even though Prime Minister Shinzo Abe is the most ideological post-World War II political leader since his grandfather Nobusuke Kishi, he framed the election as a referendum on Abenomics and remained silent about the nationalist issues that he really cares about, such as constitutional revision, collective self-defense, and revisionist history. This appears to have been a deliberate strategy of downplaying Abe's nationalist passions because party loyalists will vote for him anyway and there is no reason to arouse opponents. Just as in 2012, Abe campaigned on economic policies and the promise of better days ahead, the so-called "good Abe," while giving the nationalist "bad Abe" a campaign holiday.

The Japan Innovation Party's (the party formed by merging Toru Hashimoto's Japan Restoration Party (JRP) with refugees from the Your Party) campaign also veered away from the more ardent nationalist stances of the JRP wing under the relatively bland leadership of policy wonk and ex-bureaucrat Kenji Eda while keeping the mercurial and often petulant Hashimoto under wraps (on this so-called Third Force, see Pekkanen and Reed, this volume). Pundits predicted disaster for the party, with some forecasting a loss of more than half its seats, but JIP managed to hold its own, dropping only one seat to 41 based on a relatively strong showing in the proportional representation (PR) vote. Hashimoto termed the outcome a disastrous showing while the party is relieved that it held on to so many seats; Eda's strategy of repositioning the party away from the Hashimoto's strident nationalist persona and radical policy reforms paid off. The party's poor performance in single-seat elections and strong showing in the PR vote suggests that voters are less interested in Hashimoto's agenda, hence his disappointment, than in putting a tether on the LDP by backing an opposition to one-party rule.

In terms of advocating a nationalist agenda on security, immigration and traditional values, only The Party for Future Generations took a strong stance and it was decimated at the polls, dropping from 19 seats to 2. Voters rejected two of its highest profile nationalist candidates; former Tokyo governor Shintaro Ishihara lost his seat while former Air Self-Defense Chief Toshio Tamogami was smoked in his first bid for a Diet seat. Clearly, staking out a rightwing stance and forthrightly embracing nationalist issues did not resonate with voters, although one could argue that it may have been a case of rejecting the messengers rather than the message as the PFG never overcame its image as a motley crew of geriatrics representing the past rather than blazing a trail toward the future.

So the leading parties of the right, the LDP and JIP, that are closely associated with nationalist policies seem to understand that these don't resonate with voters. This doesn't mean they are not nationalistic, but does mean that crafting winning campaigns depends on not alienating voters by emphasizing a nationalist agenda. The rightwing conservative leadership that has dominated Japanese politics in the 2000s is much more nationalistic than ordinary citizens and wins elections by not trumpeting nationalistic stances and convincing voters to elect them based on other merits and policies. In this sense, nationalism sneaks in the backdoor, "hidden" in plain sight, but it remains an unappealing siren song for voters. Prime Minister Abe's first stint at premier in 2006–2007 imploded in part because he showed his true colors on constitutional revision, patriotic education, and historical revisionism. In doing so he trampled on post-WWII norms and values that he wants to recalibrate. In the 2007 upper house elections, the LDP was routed and Abe ousted soon thereafter, signaling the dangers of both nationalist posturing and demonstrating insouciance about lost pension records in an aging society where the elderly have a voting participation rate about double that of younger voters. Prior to the 2012 elections, the LDP did table a draft revised constitution and bitterly criticized the DPJ's Noda Cabinet for its mishandling of the Senkaku territorial dispute with China, but campaigned almost exclusively on Abenomics and the promise of economic recovery because the economy remains voter's bottom line. In 2014 it stuck to that winning strategy.

Top down ideological shift

Christian Winkler has conducted a cross-national analysis of party manifestos and finds that the LDP is less nationalistic than other conservative parties in western democracies and it has not moved significantly rightward in the 2000s (Winkler, 2014). This finding may say more about the usefulness of focusing on what is promised in manifestos than what the government has been actually doing under Abe's leadership. In the preceding volume in this series covering the 2012 Diet elections, Winkler points out that Koizumi won a landslide in 2005 more due to his charisma and reform agenda than ideology (Winkler, *JD 2012*). Winkler notes, however, that the LDP has became more ideological and that rightwing groups in the Diet that espouse nationalistic positions helped Abe to victory in the 2012 LDP party presidential elections.

There are competing views as to why the LDP has become more rightwing and nationalistic, but the 21st century LDP is undeniably less ideologically diverse than the 20th century version. The moderate mainstream leadership has faded away and the 1994 electoral reforms that introduced "first past the post" (FPTP) single seat constituencies have also played a role, transforming what was a broad church into a more fundamentalist party with stronger ties to right wing organizations like Nippon Kaigi that was established in 1997 and the Association of Shinto Shrines. As Koichi Nakano, a political scientist at Sophia University, explains, "FPTP destroyed the inner (factional) pluralism that used to exist in the LDP. In the old system, as LDP candidates competed against each other, they had incentives to distinguish themselves not just in pork barrel they can bring home, but also in ideological tendencies. That's why it used to be a broach church" (email February 12, 2015). The need for funds and grassroots mobilization also propelled the LDP rightward, as Nakano points out that, "In 1994, state finance of political parties was also enacted alongside FPTP. The LDP became increasingly reliant on that since it has much less to spend on public works projects and subsidies [down in 2014 about 1/3 from the 1998 peak]. Right wing organizations including Nippon Kaigi, became more and more important for grassroots mobilization, together with Soka Gakkai from the 2000s (Koizumi onwards). Thus, the party that once used to be the political arm of Keidanren and Nokyo became the party of right wing organizations that is subsidized by the state." Moreover, the 2007 and 2009 electoral debacles left the LDP a downsized party, one with fewer moderates as ideologues with backing from rightwing organizations gained strength and repositioned the party by catering to these core constituencies, a shift driven by internal dynamics in response to crisis. The rise of China as a more threatening regional presence may also be a factor in the LDP's rightward shift, representing a nationalistic backlash. Regarding the more ideologically resolute and uniform LDP, Winkler concludes, "Therefore, it would be hard to argue that the ideological movement we can observe was the result of electoral choices. The rise of the right is no function of electoral outcomes, but party internal changes, specifically the decline of the conservative mainstream and the liberal elements within it" (Winkler, *JD 2012*: 211). Hironori Sasada argues that the LDP leadership contests are a significant factor in this rightward shift as presidential candidates seek local support by staking out more nationalistic positions, knowing this appeals to party members (Sasada, 2010). But winning over voters in national elections means striking a balance between stroking the base and seducing the increasingly unaffiliated mainstream, something Team Abe proved adept at in campaign 2014.

Barking dog?

The electoral rise of the right has happened despite, not because of, its nationalistic agenda (see Conclusion, this volume, by Pekkanen, Reed, and Scheiner). An intriguing aspect of the Abe conundrum is how an ardent nationalist may well become Japan's longest serving postwar premier in a nation where nationalistic sentiments are relatively tepid. The nationalist pit bull didn't bark in campaign 2014 because this would scare off many voters, but its fur bristled and it growled just enough to convince loyalists that it would fight their fight. Nationalism thus played a role in the campaign, but not as a banner boldly brandished, but more subtly as patriotic mood music (see Krauss for a similar view on foreign policy). I argue that nationalism mattered in the LDP–Komeito coalition victory in several ways: (1) campaigning on Abenomics diverted attention from unpopular nationalist policies; (2) culture wars waged during Abe's tenure established his nationalist credentials and aroused his base; (3) tensions with China and South Korea, and the menace of North Korea created a favorable context for the LDP; (4) the Japan Communist Party's remarkable showing; and, (5) Okinawans' repudiation of the LDP.

Three Arrow Monty

The "Abe conundrum" refers to Abe's resilient popularity despite strong public opposition to his signature policies on state secrecy, arms exports, patriotic education, collective self-defense, and nuclear reactor restarts – coupled with widespread perceptions that "Abenomics" is floundering (Kingston, 2014 c.f). He is a polarizing figure, lauded as the resolute leader Japan needs to revive its flagging fortunes and slammed for mishandling history controversies in ways that undermine national interests. Curiously, his advocacy of hot-button nationalist issues appeals to a limited, but activist constituency, while not really hurting him with the vast majority of voters who are disinterested or oppose this agenda. How does an unapologetic nationalist prevail given little popular support for his nationalist agenda? Packaging and positioning the brand helps, but Abe's ace up his sleeves in 2014 was a pathetic opposition in disarray and on the ropes.

In campaign 2014 the political opposition was divided and lacked a coherent campaign strategy, never figuring out how to exploit Abe's vulnerabilities and failing to offer voters a credible alternative (Asahi, December 18, 2014). The snap election was thus a savvy strategy of tapping the advantages of incumbency and catching the opposition off-guard and poorly prepared. Making it into a referendum on Abenomics and postponement of a second tax increase nobody wanted (except for the Ministry of Finance) was also inspired electioneering, shifting attention away from Abe's unpopular nationalist initiatives and gestures and putting pragmatic bread-and-butter issues center stage. Even if the LDP had touted its nationalist stripes it probably would not have mattered, but nobody wanted to take a chance that the public might get motivated if Abe got too annoying about the constitution, security, and history. And in case the media had ideas, the LDP warned journalists to provide fair and balanced coverage, mindful of the media hammering in 2009 that swayed voters in favor of the DPJ. Understanding the theater of politics, throughout campaign 2014 Abe played the "good Abe," maestro of the three arrows, lulling voters into the safe zone of complacency and/or resignation, while the nationalist "bad Abe" played hooky, a diverting scam that gave Abe a two year extension to get on with his ideological agenda.

Culture wars

The culture wars in the Abe era deliver red meat for rightwing organizations like Nippon Kaigi, the Association of Shinto Shrines,

Nippon Izokukai (War Bereaved Veteran's Family Association) and others of their ilk that constitute Abe's base, arousing the membership and mobilizing them in support of the LDP. Having demonstrated where he stands during his nearly two years in office, Abe could campaign on less controversial economic policies and downplay his nationalist agenda. He and the LDP need not tout their nationalist credentials in manifestos or on the hustings precisely because they have nothing to prove and conservative voters implicitly trust them as champions of this agenda. Why wouldn't they?

Abe has delivered. He visited Yasukuni Shrine, stood by as his colleagues in the Diet repeatedly smeared the 1993 Kono Statement, has promoted patriotic education, lead a banzai cheer for a bemused Emperor Akihito on Sovereignty Day 2013, talked tough and put some swagger into Japan's presence on the international stage and is making headway on constitutional revision while gutting Article 9. Moreover, almost all of his cabinet ministers in his two 2012–2014 cabinets were affiliated with the Association of Shinto Shrines (ASS) and 84% were members of Nippon Kaigi (Reuters, December 11, 2014). ASS advocates patriotic education, rewriting the constitution to remove both the pacifist shackles of Article 9 and the separation of state and religion in Article 20.

For reactionary conservatives and these rightwing groups, it can't get much better. Abe is their man and they didn't need any reassurances or promises. So the pledges in party manifestoes may make the LDP look relatively bland, but that is because politics are being waged elsewhere in terms of actual policies, initiatives, and gestures. Abe is the most ideological premier since his grandfather Nobusuke Kishi, and draws inspiration from him. What he has learned is that the general public is unenthusiastic about the very issues that fire him and his base up so has learned to project a more soothing and appealing image of a man focused on economic revival; the nationalist ideologue in a monetarist cloak looking for redemption.

Abe repeatedly calls for overturning the postwar order that he feels is humiliating for Japan and keeps it subjugated. His main bête noire are wartime history and the US written constitution and this is the terrain where the culture wars have been waged most stridently from his victory in 2012 until the 2014 campaign (Kingston, 2014a, 2014b). Japan's 21st century culture wars reflect concerted efforts by conservative nationalists to downplay Japan's wartime misdeeds in order to promote a history that can better nurture pride in nation. They denounce what is termed "masochistic" history that they think shames the nation and stifles nationalistic impulses among Japan's youth.

Japan has experienced a recrudescent nationalism since Abe came into office in 2012, a time when reactionaries, jingoists, and ultra-nationalists have become emboldened, notably targeting the large ethnic Korean minority with hate speech and orchestrating attacks on liberals and liberal institutions (Kingston 2014d). Abe's government has averted its eyes from these disturbing developments while he became cheerleader in chief for the anti-Asahi campaign, actually voicing support for the sustained bashing by the Sankei and Yomiuri newspapers and various pundits and politicians that were settling scores with a liberal newspaper that over the years often made conservatives squirm (Kingston, 2014d). The anti-Asahi campaign is part of a larger battle regarding revisionists' efforts to rewrite the history of the comfort women and downplay the extent and nature of this wartime system of sexual slavery. These reactionaries pounced on the Asahi's admission in August 2014 that it relied on one soldier's testimony regarding forced recruitment of comfort women long after he was discredited. They kept harping on a handful of articles published two decades ago to undermine the Asahi's overall credibility and to sow doubts in the court of public opinion about the comfort women system. In doing so, they are mining a rich vein of perpetrator's fatigue among Japanese who feel beleaguered by China and South Korea relentlessly hammering Japan on the anvil of history. The discredited soldier's testimony is tangential to the mounds of evidence regarding this sordid chapter in Japan's wartime history, but hyping his unreliability is aimed at making people wonder if all the accusations about the comfort women are wrong, and part of an orchestrated campaign designed to tarnish Japan's dignity. This saga is after all more about politics and rehabilitating Japan's shabby wartime past than journalistic standards. Abe's victory in 2014 didn't depend on his nationalist skewering of the liberal causes and institutions his supporters love to hate, but helped mobilize the base.

Prime Minister Abe's various moves to overturn the postwar order, and recalibrate the nation's norms and values is driven by his nationalist agenda and the yearnings of this base. Earlier in 2014 Abe stood by as Diet colleagues mounted an investigation into the 1993 Kono Statement acknowledging responsibility and apologizing for the wartime comfort women system, and the evidence given by former comfort women about their forcible recruitment and horrific experiences. The point of this hit-and-run initiative was to discredit the Kono Statement and encourage skepticism about the damning narrative of the comfort women system. Moreover, at the outset of 2014 the Ministry of Education issued new teaching guidelines pressuring textbook publishers to portray controversial issues like the comfort women in accordance with government positions and Supreme Court rulings. This follows Abe's 2013 termination of the "neighboring nations" policy adopted in 1982 that committed Japan to portraying the shared history with East Asia in textbooks in ways that would be mutually acceptable, or at least, not offensive to China and South Korea. Battles over revisionist history are not new, but they are being waged more vigorously as the history wars have heated up with China and South Korea. It is a nationalistic backlash orchestrated by Japan's conservative elite against Seoul and Beijing playing the history card, especially President Park Geun-hye's repeated insistence that Abe needs to embrace a "correct history as a condition for a summit.

On Abe's watch popular media discourse has also become quite nationalistic and xenophobic. Sophia University's Koichi Nakano told me that he feels "intellectually groped" on the trains by the ubiquitous weekly magazine ads hyping anti-Korean or anti-Chinese stories. Editors privately acknowledge that this has more to do with boosting sales than principled jingoism, but the tenor of angry and aggrieved nationalism has intensified. The results can be seen in public opinion polls conducted by the Cabinet Office at the end of 2014 that reveal that 83% of Japanese have negative attitudes toward China while two thirds are anti-Korean, both figures rising from 2013 (JT, December 20, 2014). It seems that rising tensions over territorial disputes and history controversies are taking their toll on public perceptions and this helps the LDP.

Security threats

It has long been troubling to Japanese conservatives that in various opinion surveys young Japanese are much less willing to die for their country than counterparts elsewhere around the world and are less nationalistic than youth in China and South Korea (Linley, 2015). Conservative nationalists advocate Japan assuming a greater security role in the context of a rising and more assertive China, and thus seek revision of the US written constitution to remove existing restrictions on Japan's military forces (see Krauss chapter, this volume). Yet Japan's hawkish nationalists find that their constitutional revision and security agenda does not resonate with the public. An Asahi poll conducted just after the election found that only 3% prioritized constitutional revision, one of Abe's pet nationalist projects (Asahi, December 18, 2014). Moreover, it appears that this project is losing momentum in terms of voter attitudes.

The Yomiuri newspaper has conducted polls on public opinion about Article 9 since 2002, finding increased opposition to revision since then: "Respondents seeking to amend Article 9 declined from a peak of 44.4% in 2004 to 30% last February, while those opposing revision rose to 60% from 46.7% in the same period" (JT, January 2, 2015)

Yet regional tensions did create a favorable context for the LDP because like the Likud in Israel, it has a lock on the security issue. This was evident in the 2012 campaign when former Tokyo Governor Ishihara did the LDP an enormous favor by instigating an imbroglio with China over the Senkaku islands also claimed by Beijing as the Diaoyu. His intention to purchase some of the islands from the private Japanese owner panicked the central government into preemptively purchasing, and effectively nationalizing, the islands despite warnings from Japan's ambassador to China that this would be a serious mistake.

In 2010 the DPJ mismanaged the territorial dispute, sparking anti-Japanese protests in China when then Transport Minister Seiji Maehara authorized the arrest of a Japanese trawler crew rather than defusing the situation by returning them to China. This was the modus vivendi the LDP had worked out with Beijing. Noda's 2012 gambit, however, was a far more serious breach of an informal bilateral accord to shelve the territorial sovereignty issue reached in the 1970s (Drifte, 2014). In this context, purchasing and nationalizing the islands were needlessly provocative and the negative repercussions of this initiative still persist. Noda succeeded in destroying the DPJ's credibility on security issues and, by exacerbating tensions with China, made voters more concerned about national security. Surely there are many other reasons why the DPJ was decimated at the 2012 polls, but this was a significant factor exposing the DPJ's incompetence, an image that it still has not shaken off despite a leadership change (NHK 7PM News, February 9, 2015).

Thus, the deterioration of Sino-Japanese relations during Abe's post-2012 tenure created a favorable context for the LDP in 2014 because it's the only party voters really trust to cope with the threat, and that also involves effective US alliance management. Japan under the hapless Yukio Hatoyama (2009–2010), the DPJ's first of three premiers, experienced a sharp deterioration of relations with Washington that amplified the vulnerabilities of worsening relations with Beijing. Washington's hand in Hatoyama's downfall also underscored the risks of testing the limits of what is expected of a client state and left voters disillusioned about the DPJ (Murphy, 2015).

Security issues may not be high on voter's priorities, but do get a lot of media coverage that influences public attitudes. In September 2014 the NPO Genron released the results of its annual survey indicating that 93% of Japanese have an unfavorable impression of China, with two thirds saying their impression has worsened over the past year. When Prime Minister Koizumi stepped down in 2006 at a time when he antagonized China with six visits to Yasukuni Shrine, only 36.4% of Japanese had an unfavorable impression of China, spiraling upward to 66.3% by the time Prime Minister Abe left office in 2007 and exceeding 90% for the first time in 2013. The LDP is positioned to reap the rewards of such negative sentiments toward the region's aspiring hegemon.

On the eve of and throughout campaign 2014, there was extensive television coverage of dozens of Chinese trawlers poaching red coral in the waters surrounding the Ogasawara Islands 1,000 km south of Tokyo. Japanese reacted angrily to these images of a fleet of rust buckets dredging the sea bottom for red coral that is used in expensive jewelry. The Ogasawara Islands are a UNESCO World Heritage site prized for pristine waters and unspoiled natural environment so this Chinese poaching was seen as a hostile act of desecration. Aside from being environmentally irresponsible, the massive fleet of Chinese boats reinforced concerns about China's grandiose ambitions and rapacious inclinations. There is no overstating how angry these news reports made many Japanese feel judging from an unrepresentative sample of Tokyoites.[1] This resentment translates into "someone has to stand up to them" and who better than the LDP?

Tensions with South Korea over history issues also angered the Japanese public, and even if most deplore the hate speech directed at zainichi, many also resent President Park's repeated criticism of Abe over history. This doesn't mean the public buys into revisionist history, but many are weary of South Korean leaders repeatedly playing the history card. North Korea's nuclear weapons program and missile tests make it a credible security threat, again playing to the LDP's advantage. Moreover, Abe is strongly associated with the *rachimondai*, the kidnapping of dozens of Japanese citizens by North Korean agents in the 1970s and 1980s. Abe has been a stalwart advocate for the families of the abductees and continues to press Pyongyang for a full accounting of their fate. This has not been forthcoming, but yet again Abe is seen to be standing up for the national interest and "owns" this nationalist issue.

The security threats may not be top on voters' priorities, but to the extent that these weigh on their minds the LDP benefits because it is seen to be better at managing the US alliance and more steadfast on national security.

Rising reds?

It was left to the JCP to remind voters about Abe's nationalistic initiatives on security and constitutional revision, tapping into voter concerns that Abe was steering the nation rightward and into dangerous waters. Doing so paid off for the JCP as it increased its total seats in the lower house from 8–21. It was not that suddenly voters discovered the magic of Marxism, but rather anti-Abe voters were looking for a home and only the JCP seemed credible in taking the prime minister to task on his signature policies. It mainly pilloried Abenomics for accentuating disparities and promoting welfare for the wealthy, a refrain echoed by the DPJ that rode this issue to power in 2009. In 2014, however, the DPJ flailed about under the ineffectual leadership of Banri Kaeda and lingering doubts among voters about whether it was capable of governing based on its lackluster record 2009–2012. Moreover, due to internal fractiousness the party was unable to offer a convincing alternative vision to the LDP and failed to take the premier to task for his revisionist views on history and lifting constitutional curbs on Japan's military forces. Problematically, the DPJ is something of a rainbow party representing views across the ideological spectrum and its more rightwing members agree with the LDP on security issues. The JCP doesn't, warning voters that Abe was leading them down a slippery slope of militarism. Thus anti-Abe voters leery of Japan becoming America's deputy sheriff registered their protest by rallying to the JCP.

Okinawa repudiates

Okinawa voters exemplify what Ramachandra Guha (2012) terms the "little nationalisms." This concept refers to the identity politics of minority groups that are marginalized, find ambitions thwarted, feel they are treated unfairly or endure the indignities of discrimination. It is fair to say that Okinawans can check off all those boxes. Identity politics among Okinawans target the extensive presence of the US military bases on their islands and resentment toward Tokyo for foisting this on them (McCormack and Norimatsu, 2012). Grievances feed on the disproportionate basing burden as 75% of US military forces stationed in Japan occupy 18% of the island's territory while crimes committed by American servicemen rankle. Furthermore, there is considerable lingering resentment about Okinawa being used by Tokyo as a sacrificial pawn at the end of WWII to buy time for strengthening the "inner" island defenses even though the outcome of the war was already clear; over 100,000 civilians lost their lives in the Battle of Okinawa, constituting as much as one-third of the population. In 2007, Prime Minister Abe ignited a firestorm among islanders when his Ministry of Education instructed textbook publishers to reword sections referring to Japanese troops complicity in instigating group suicides by Okinawans. Abe and other revisionists have objected to this depiction even though it is based on Okinawan eyewitness testimony. This whitewashing of history sparked one of the largest rallies ever in Okinawa, estimated at some 100,000 in the capital of Naha. Subsequently the Japanese courts ruled in favor of the Okinawan plaintiffs, but the experience rubbed salt in the wounds of the collective psyche. The little nationalism simmering in the westernmost fringe of Japanese territory has been expressed consistently at the ballot box as Okinawans in local, prefectural, and national level elections support anti-base candidates, with the 2014 lower house elections being no exception to this prevailing pattern. No LDP candidate running in Okinawa won a Diet seat in 2014 because islanders oppose Prime Minister Abe's plans to build a replacement facility in Henoko for the US Marine Airbase Futenma. Many are incensed that Abe offered an extravagant "bribe" of central government subsidies and public works exceeding $20 billion over eight years to convince former Governor Hirokazu Nakaima to approve work on the Henoko project. He was ousted in the gubernatorial race only a few weeks before the 2014 Diet elections because of his apostasy on the base relocation issue, an unforgivable act of betrayal in the eyes of islanders (Kingston, 2014e). They know more than they would like to about betrayal over the US bases as in 2009 the DPJ's Hatoyama pledged in his campaign that the Futenma base would be relocated outside Okinawa, not Henoko, raising hopes with a promise he failed to keep.

Conclusion

In conclusion, nationalism was not a decisive factor in campaign 2014, but it was a key element in the positive context facilitating the LDP's unsurprising victory. Overall, nationalism was tangential to the LDP–Komeito coalition retaining its two-thirds majority, and mostly implicit since Prime Minister Abe campaigned on Abenomics rather than his nationalist agenda (Kingston, 2014f). As Pekkanen, Reed, and Scheiner argue in the conclusion to this volume, Abe relied on a "bait-and-switch" strategy of running on the economy and then claiming a broader mandate encompassing his unpopular agenda on security and the constitution, a ploy that goes a long way in explaining the Abe conundrum.

Nationalism mattered, however, because the culture wars waged in Abe's Japan, driven by nationalist issues, aroused and pleased his base constituencies. So the dog didn't have to bark in the campaign because it had been a prominent and menacing presence beforehand, reassuring rightwing organizations about where Abe stands on the issues that matter to them most and they delivered the vote accordingly. Contextualizing the appeal of the LDP from a longer and broader perspective helps to highlight the role nationalism played in reinforcing the party's dominance of Japanese politics. While analysis of campaign rhetoric or party pledges and manifestoes might lead one to dismiss the importance of rightwing ideology or nationalism in campaign 2014, if one looks in the right places where politics is happening, policies are enacted and gestures made, then it seems clear that Abe's nationalist riffs put conservative voters in the mood.

To the limited extent nationalism was embraced and expressed in the campaign in terms of typical issues such as constitutional revision, security policy, immigration, history, values, and identity, the results were mixed. The PFG presented a forthright rightwing nationalist alternative to the LDP and JIP; other parties usually associated with conservative nationalism, and found little support, retaining only 2 of its 19 seats. The JCP staked out a leftwing critical stance toward the LDP's economic and security policies and did remarkably well, nearly tripling its seats. To some extent this success can be attributed to voters' anxiety about the LDP's rightwing nationalist agenda, but anti-Abe sentiments also drew on concerns about the neo-liberal economic policies of Abenomics and perceptions of widening disparities and rising risk at a time when the economy still appeared to be sputtering.

Finally, Okinawan voters yet again repudiated Tokyo's continued insistence that their islands remain the epicenter of the US–Japan alliance. The little nationalism smoldering in the Ryukyu archipelago represents a backlash against Tokyo foisting a disproportionate base-hosting burden on this southwestern periphery, in addition to lingering wartime grievances. The clash of Japanese and Chinese nationalisms, and territorial dispute between Beijing and Tokyo in Okinawa's vicinity, has ominously upped the ante, heightening anxieties in a community that draws on the shared trauma of being caught in between as part of its collective identity.

Note

The author is grateful for the helpful comments from fellow contributors Robert Pekkanen, Ellis Kraus, Axel Klein, Ethan Scheiner, Dan Smith, and Michael Thies.

1. I was unprepared for the visceral expressions of anger about the Chinese poaching in the Ogasawara waters while conducting impromptu "fieldwork" at Izakaya in Tokyo during such coverage and chats with fellow dog walkers in my local park. Now alcohol consumption may have influenced the Izakaya focus groups intemperate comments, but I regularly meet the dog walkers, a staid group that almost never wants to talk politics or foreign affairs.

References

Drifte, Reinhard (2014). The Japan-China confrontation over the Senkaku/Diaoyu Islands – between "shelving" and "dispute escalation". *The Asia-Pacific Journal* 12(30): 28. http://japanfocus.org/-Reinhard-Drifte/4154

Guha, Ramachandra (2012). *Patriots and partisans*. New Delhi: Allen Lane.

Kingston, Jeff (2014a). Abe's culture wars boomerang against Japan. *Japan Times*, February 22.

Kingston, Jeff (2014b). Reactionaries waging culture war. *Japan Times*. March 1.

Kingston, Jeff (2014c). The abe conundrum and pitfalls ahead. *Japan Times*. October 18.

Kingston, Jeff (2014d). Right-wing witch hunt signals dark days for Japan. *Japan Times*. November 8.

Kingston, Jeff (2014e). Okinawans reject Abe's base deal, but he won't listen. *Japan Times*. November 22.

Kingston, Jeff (2014f). Abe seeks mandate for floundering abenomics. *Japan Times*. November 29.

Linley, Matthew (2015). Nationalist attitudes among mass publics in Asia. In Jeff Kingston (ed.) *Asian Nationalism Reconsidered*. Routledge forthcoming.

McCormack, Gavan and Satoko Oka Norimatsu (2012). *Resistant islands: Okinawa confronts Japan and the United States*. Rowman and Littlefield: Boulder, CO.

Murphy, R. Taggart (2014). *Japan and the shackles of the past*. Oxford University Press: New York.

Pekkanen, R. J. and S. M. Pekkanen (2015). Japan in 2014: All about Abe. *Asian Survey* 55(1) January–February.

Sasada, Hironori (2010). The electoral origin of Japan's nationalistic leadership: Primaries in the LDP presidential election and the pull effect. *Journal of East Asian Studies* 10: 1–30.

Winkler, Christian (2013). Right rising? Ideology and the 2012 House of representatives election. In Robert Pekkanen, Steven Reed and Ethan Scheiner (eds) *The Japanese General Election*, pp. 201–212. London: Palgrave Macmillan.

Winkler, Christian (2014). Getting the right drift: Japanese elites' move to the right: Fact or fiction? Paper presented at AAS-in-Asia Conference (Singapore) July.

18
Unraveling the Abe Conundrum in Foreign Policy: The Mystery of the "the Dog That Didn't Bark"

Ellis S. Krauss

When it comes to foreign and defense policy and the 2014 election, there is a mystery at the heart of the subject, similar to the old mystery of why didn't the dog bark in the night? Jeff Kingston poses the apt conundrum about Abe: why does he remain popular and win elections despite most Japanese disagreeing with almost all of his policies (see Kingston, this volume, and his article in *JT* October 25, 2014, web)? Nowhere is this question more relevant than in foreign and defense policy in the 2014 election. Polls reveal deep divisions among the Japanese public on Abe's foreign policy these last two years, with significant portions of the population avidly disagreeing with his unprecedented moves in the areas of defense and historical memories[1]; and yet once again Abe and the LDP won a landslide election in 2014.

This is not an easy mystery to unravel because the answers to it are multi-dimensional. They involve a complex, intertwined string of explanations, ranging from the motivations of voters regarding specific issues; Abe's shrewd focus on the issues where he is stronger and the failure of the main opposition party to craft a viable alternative policy on foreign and defense policy issues; voters' ambivalent and contradictory attitudes on key foreign affairs issues today intensified by changing perceptions of Japan's vulnerability and situation in its East Asian neighborhood; the understandable but non-strategic voting behavior of the most alienated and opposing voters.

Background: Japan's divisions over foreign policy

Ever since WWII, Japan has been irrevocably divided over foreign policy issues, most especially the issues of military defense and the US–Japan alliance, in the context of its "peace constitution" (Article 9) given Japan by the US Occupation that literally forbids Japan from going to war or maintaining armed forces. The onset of the Cold War and China falling to the Communists resulted in the American Occupation and subsequent Japanese governments reinterpreting Article 9 to mean the Constitution could only proscribe aggressive war because all nations retained the "inherent right of self-defense." This change has always permanently divided Japan.

Japan's conservative prime minister (three times) in the latter part of the Occupation, Shigeru Yoshida, saw that the United States would insist that the price of restoring Japan's independence and sovereignty was rearmament; but he also understood that full rearmament would dangerously divide the public and alienate even further Japan's neighbors that had suffered its aggression. Instead he came up with a skillful compromise to satisfy the Americans without total rearmament: Japan would only partially rearm and maintain Article 9 but instead its main military contribution would be the provision of many US bases in Japan through the signing of a US–Japan Mutual Security Treaty (signed in 1951). This became known as the "Yoshida Doctrine." It was to become the framework for Japanese foreign policy until at least the late 1990s. Yoshida's moves also divided the conservatives into those who supported Yoshida's minimalist defense strategy versus some conservatives who wanted to restore Japan as a "normal nation" someday. The left, on the other hand, clung to the original, literal interpretation of Article 9 and opposed any moves for rearmament of any kind

One of the first LDP prime ministers after that party was formed in 1955 was Nobusuke Kishi who had been in Tojo's cabinet and was an unindicted Class A war criminal under the Occupation. Kishi, who rose to become prime minister in 1957, opposed Yoshida's low profile foreign policy on defense. As Samuels (2001) describes him: "He worked relentlessly to gain political support for revision so that Japan could rearm, become an equal security partner of the United States, and enjoy an autonomous foreign policy."

When, after he negotiated a revision of the 1952 security treaty with the US on more equal terms in 1960 and then forced it through the National Diet despite great opposition from the left, he was ousted as PM. After this crisis, the LDP then reverted for the next 40 years to the tenets of the Yoshida Doctrine in foreign policy. Abe is Kishi's grandson who supposedly revers his grandfather and his beliefs (see Kingston, this volume).

Abe's foreign and defense policies

Abe's interests are like his grandfather's: shore up the US–Japan alliance but with Japan playing a greater role in defense and becoming a more equal partner. In his first, failed, stint as prime minister (2006–2007) he concentrated on this dimension and quickly became unpopular, in part because he gave the public the impression he wasn't interested in their domestic issue concerns. After taking power this time Abe seemed to have learned his lesson and quickly made "Abenomics" and the revival of the Japanese economic growth the focal point of his goals (see Noble, this volume, and Pekkanen and Pekkanen, 2015), including supporting the TPP even in the face of intra-party and interest group opposition (see Katada and Wilbur, this volume). Yet neither did he at all neglect his revisionist foreign policy goal. Pekkanen, Reed, and Smith (this volume) indicate several of the steps he took to buttress Japan's military preparedness and counter the rise of a more powerful China, defend against North Korea, reassert Japan's rights in territorial disputes, and revise perceptions of Japan's role in Pacific War history.

As if these weren't enough, the Abe's government's other initiatives prior to the 2014 election also included: the LDP's publication of a "draft reform proposal" in 2012 on revising the constitution that included severe reinterpretations of rights and giving the prime minister new powers in an emergency (Repeta, 2013); establishment a new National Security Council to advise the prime minister; publicly announced that he wished to revise the Constitution including Article 9 (Japan Today online, January 1, 2014); intended but failed to revise Article 96 of the constitution to allow only a majority of the Diet to pass a constitutional amendment instead of the current two-thirds and thus make it easier to revise Article 9 (NewsOnJapan, AFP, January 31, 2014); for the first time brought space and cyberspace into an interim report of the US–Japan defense guidelines; threatened to shoot down any N. Korean missile that would land in Japanese territory (Reuters, April 5, 2014); allowed the SDF to provide refueling and medical aid to UN-sanctioned multinational military operations even in previously forbidden combat zones (NewsOnJapan, Kyodo, May 8, 2014); met with President Xi of China for the first time since 2012 (because of strained relations over their islands dispute) and while neither altered their countries' stances on the territorial dispute, did agree to try to establish conflict management mechanisms to avoid dangerous escalation of a such disputes (JT online, November 10, 2014).

On historical memories issues, he also visited Yasukuni shrine for first time in person in December 2013 and then sent an offering to Yasukuni Shrine in both August and October 2014, angering China and South Korea; shelved any plans to revise the Kono statement of remorse about comfort women issued in 1993 (Asahi Shimbun online February 1, 2013) but said in Diet testimony that accusations that Japan used state coercion in this system were false and brought defamation on Japan globally (YS, Japan News online, October 3, 2014), a statement refuted by American experts (WSJ online, October 7, 2014).

None of these extensive Abe government's changes and proposed changes would alter Japan's defense only policies, or mean Japan was going to become a constitutionally unrestrained military power, and critics have exaggerated the extent of change involved (see Green and Hornung, 2014). This record nonetheless represent an unprecedented postwar foreign policy revisionism in Japan's defense posture, interpretation of constitutional limits, and perceptions of Japan's wartime role and its remorse over its actions. In their entirety, it is clear that Abe wishes to overtly end belief in the Yoshida Doctrine once and for all, closely align Japan with the United States and other democratic allies militarily to counter China, but expand Japan's autonomous foreign policy options and assert its own interpretations of history. It is also clear that Abe wishes to have it both ways: do all this but maintain good political and economic relations with his Asian neighbors, even though his historical memories revisionism and their perception of his military changes may well prevent this.

The public's views

What is equally clear is that the public in general does not much agree with Abe's foreign policies: public opinion polls show that his policies do not obtain majority support on almost any single defense dimension except their fear and dislike of China, and was fairly divided on historical memories issues.

Probably the most comprehensive single survey on defense and constitutional foreign policy issues is a special public opinion poll conducted by the AS newspaper in February 2014 (Maureen and Mike Mansfield Foundation, 2014).[2] This survey found 64% were against amending Article 9 (with 49% of these opposing because they supported the renunciation of war and military forces and another 15% because it might cause instability in East Asia); 68% were against transforming the character of the SDF to make it more of an official army by amending Article 9; 77% against the expansion of arms exports to a foreign country; only 17% supported the refueling and provision of military equipment for the United States; 63% were in favor of Japan not exercising collective defense and 67% did not think that if the prohibition against collective defense remained it would weaken the US–Japan alliance; 52% were greatly concerned and another 36% partially concerned that if collective defense were authorized it might involve Japan in war; 60% thought the cabinet's authorization of collective defense under certain conditions would have a negative effect on stability and prosperity in Asia.

Other polls varied from these results a bit.[3] Thus for example, about the same time (March, 2014) as the comprehensive AS survey, the more conservative and LDP-supporting YS found a very even split (42% vs. 41%) among supporters and opponents of constitutional revision, but those who supported it had dropped 9% from a similar survey the year before and only 30% supported revising Article 9 itself; reinterpretation of collective defense showed the public divided (YS online, March 15, 2014) while still other polls showed at least a majority opposed its use (Richards, 2014). Even Abe himself admitted in an understatement in a NKS interview cited in the NYT (Inoue and Gough, 2014) that "Unfortunately, we cannot say that public is fully supportive," when it came to reinterpreting collective defense.

On historical memories issues, according to the comprehensive Asahi survey, the public was equally divided but slightly more conservatively inclined than on the constitutional and defense issues. Thus they are almost exactly polarized whether these issues had been settled or not (48% vs. 47%); 53% disagreed that history education was masochistic (a conservative claim) because its views deny the past war that Japan experienced; 47% think Abe's visit to Yasukuni was not preferable (41% that it was), many (64%) because it is merely a place to mourn the war dead rather than as a symbol of militarism, and 63% believe there is no need for official compensation of comfort women.

At most a majority and at least, a substantial minority or near majority, oppose Abe's defense and constitutional revision and reinterpretation policies, and are fairly divided on his historical memories interpretations. While Abe is busy trying to wean Japan away from its foreign policy posture under the Yoshida Doctrine, a majority of the Japanese public seems still to be firmly wedded to it.[4] Yet, none of these divisions or opposition seems to have been reflected in the 2014 election results.

Why the dog didn't bark

Several complex and related variables explain why defense and foreign policy issues, so salient in the Abe administration's policies, failed to resonate with most voters when they went to the polls. These reasons I discuss below closely match the findings of political scientists about the conditions under which foreign policy may matter (or not) to voters in an election: even if voters have coherent views on foreign policy, they must be able to "access" those attitudes – that is their view on issues must be salient to them – and the major candidates must give them alternatives to be able to choose. (Aldrich et al., 1989; Aldrich et al., 2006). As we will see, partly because of the strategies of Abe and the LDP in the election, these conditions were not particularly met.

Another factor in the context of this election was the specific characteristics of the electoral system (see Scheiner, Thies, and Smith, this volume). Japan's Mixed Member Majoritarian (MMM) system, with its two separate SSD and PR tiers in which voters choose individual candidates in the former and parties in the latter allows almost encourages some split-ticket voting. This is because it provides incentives to choose between the two dominant parties in the plurality SSD tier (because otherwise they are "wasting" their vote smaller parties have little chance of gaining seats given the plurality rule in these type of systems) but "voting their conscience" for the party – even a small party– closer to their beliefs and views on salient issues to them because such a party can still gain seats in a PR system. We will also see this factor at work, intertwined with the conditions for foreign policy mattering, in our explanations below.

Elections may not be mandates on specific issues

Political scientists have long known that specific elections may not predict voters' issue choices (Gopoian, 1982). Although in a polarized party context, specific issues creating that polarization can influence voting, when parties converge ideologically, as the LDP and DPJ have done (Lipscy and Scheiner, 2012), voter perceptions of the competence of the party matter more to voters in casting their ballots (Green and Hobolt, 2008).[5] Another intervening factor between support of issues and vote choice is the salience of the issue to voters: parties' positions on particular issues may only be important in their voting if that issue is a particular priority to them (Belanger and Meguid, 2008).

The context of the 2014 election in Japan confirms the importance of these factors of party ideological convergence and issue salience to voters in explaining the results. After the electoral reform of 1994, as political scientists would have predicted, increasingly the number of seats in the HR came to be monopolized by the two largest parties, the LDP and DPJ. By 2009 this reached 95% of the seats. Although in the 2012 election the rise of several smaller parties cut into this figure, in 2014 these smaller parties did not fare as well and the two major parties still managed to retain 74% of the seats. With the LDP's coalition partner, the CGP, this figure rises to 84% (see the seat figures in the Pekkanen, Reed, Smith, this volume). The CGP retains some differences on defense in private, and may restrain some of Abe's defense preferences in the future, but has moderated those publicly to avoid conflict with its coalition partner and did not discuss these issues in this election (Klein, this volume).

The DPJ's position on foreign policy issues, especially defense, is not terribly different than the LDP's, even though there are some differences in emphasis due to internal party disagreement on these issues. As the DPJ's seat numbers increased in the 2000s, the number of its representatives who came from either the LDP or Socialists proportionately declined to be replaced by "pure" DPJ members, many of whom were moderate or center-right who had never been affiliated with any other party. But especially when Ozawa's Liberal Party merged with the DPJ, the party's overall posture on defense moved rightward (Miura, et al., 2005). Indeed, some of its representatives are as conservative on defense or more so than some LDP representatives and some of what it wanted to achieve but couldn't realize was similar to the LDP's defense program (Delamotte 2011: 100; on the DPJ also see Kushida and Lipscy, 2013). Although it wanted to improve relations with China and rebalance some of the US–Japan alliance elements,[6] it could hardly offer a strong alternative to the LDP's program under these circumstances. Additionally, its former leftist members were more highly represented among its leadership when it was in power 2009–2012 than among its general representatives (Smith et al., 2013) so its foreign policies undoubtedly caused some internal friction that could only be resolved by downplaying these issues publicly.

Thus with the main opposition party not even discussing foreign policy much in the campaign, voters were confronted with a choice, especially in the SSD tier, of no real alternatives at all on foreign and defense policy. Thus their only choice was which of the two main parties would at least be more competent about handling these issues in power. After the DPJ's debacle on its handling of both US alliance and China relations when in power previously, this too favored the LDP.

This interpretation of competence mattering more than issue positions is reinforced by the results of a post-election YS poll (December 16, 2014) which found that 65% of respondents thought that the major reason for the overwhelming victory of the LDP was that it was better than the other parties but that 61% thought that the reason the DPJ did not increase more was that it had not been able to revive trust [in it]. Thus the two major government and chief opposition partners are not that ideologically polarized on foreign policy, shifting a substantial number of voters' attention to the issue of the better party to govern as well as to other, more domestic, issues. An AS survey found about the time of the start of the campaign that even though those opposed to Abe's collective defense policies outnumbered those who supported it by 50% to 32%, a fifth of even those who opposed it were planning to vote LDP (AS online December 1, 2015). Clearly voters had other priorities in making their decisions at the ballot box.

This also can be seen in how salient many voters perceived the most crucial foreign policy issues in the whole panoply of issues in this election. A YS survey just about three weeks before the election found when giving respondents multiple choices among 9 issues would most influence their voting in the forthcoming election, that only 29% of the voters chose constitutional revision and 51% foreign relations and security. This compared to 70% choosing employment and economic conditions, 56% revitalizing locales, and 54% recovering from the Great East Japan disasters. The percentage of those choosing the raising of the consumption tax (47%), energy policy and money and politics (46% each) was nearly as great as those choosing foreign relations and security (YS online, November 25, 2014). In short, voters' attention was focused greatly on the domestic issues facing Japan and not its foreign and defense issues.

Japan's conflicted voters

One possible motivation for voters to generally ignore foreign and defense policy issues is that many voters are conflicted and hold contradictory attitudes about some of these issues. Although a substantial number (as described above) oppose Abe's initiatives to change the status quo, they are also increasingly afraid of and hostile to a militarily rising China and the unpredictable nearby North Korea.

In recent years with China's rise as an economic and especially military power, and its conflicts with Japan over the Senkaku/Diaoyu Islands that Japan owns but China claims, and the historical memory issues, perceptions of the other have turned toxic. 63% of the public see territorial issues, 48% see China's military power, and 38% the Korean peninsula as causing them the most concern to threaten the peace in East Asia, and 55% see China as the greatest threat to Japan, with North Korea following at 29%, by far the most perceived dangers to the country. Only 4% have a positive feeling toward China, but 53% have a negative feeling, with the remainder neither one nor the other. Half of them believe that the history issues between Japan and China and Japan and Korea have not been settled yet (Maureen and Mike Mansfield Foundation, 2014). Other polls show an even worse image: 91% of Japanese have an unfavorable view of China and only 6% have confidence in President Xi according to the Pew Research Center (2014).

Thus, the Japanese voter seems to hold contradictory and somewhat conflicting attitudes, feeling extreme threat and fear and hostility to a militarily rising China with which Japan has deep territorial and memory issues yet trusting to the traditional postwar policies of the Yoshida Doctrine and the United States to protect it rather than Abe's new defense policies. Influenced in both directions simultaneously, many probably prefer not to confront either the issue or the contradiction.

Abe's skillful focus on other issues leading up to the election and the DPJ's playing into his hands

Another main reason for voters downplaying foreign policy issues in casting their ballots is that is essentially the way that the LDP and even most opposition parties defined the election for them. One of the greatest postwar political scientists, E.E. Schattschneider (1960, 1964), once defined power in terms of who defines the issues in political competition and therefore how they divide the voters:

> The definition of the alternatives is the supreme instrument of power.... He who determines what politics is runs the country, because the definition of alternatives is the choice of conflicts, and the choice of conflicts allocates power.

Abe skillfully exemplified Schattschneider's principle in this election. As noted above Abe failed in his first term in office (2006–2007) because he ignored domestic politics to concentrate on foreign policy, but did not make that mistake after his 2012 election. In the 2014 election as well he continued to push the domestic issues as the heart of his campaign, the one issue the public is least polarized about (Horiuchi et al., 2014). In a press conference after dissolving the Diet, Abe defined this election as "the Abenomics dissolution," and the "To advance

Abenomics ahead? Or to try and stop it? That is the question of this election." A source close to the prime minister stated that this was an explicit attempt to narrow the election issue down to Abenomics, much as Prime Minister Koizumi successfully did with postal reform in the 2005 election (YS online, December 1, 2014).

Abe's hammering on his domestic and economic policies as the focus of this election continued through the campaign (see Noble, this volume). In the first weekend after dissolution, the Secretary-General of the LDP emphasized the accomplishments of Abenomics (*YS*, November 23, 2014). In this he was backed by his party's candidates in the election. Among the coalition's candidates in this election between 96% and 99% of the LDP and CGP evaluated Abenomics highly (YS online, December 5, 2014). Abe reiterated the focus on his economic policy rather than his foreign relations when he even implied during the campaign that pushing economic recovery was the only way to enhance Japan's position in the world again: "I promise to win this election, push through the recovery efforts, return the economy to a strong state and put this region and Japan back at the glowing centre of the world" (BBC News Asia online, December 4, 2014).

The major opposition party, the DPJ, unintentionally aided Abe in making this election about Abenomics instead of the prime minister's foreign and security policies (where they might have gotten more traction among more voters), by in the first part of the campaign focusing their critical attention on it as well, for the reasons discussed above. When polls showed this wasn't working, they switched their priority campaign theme, not to foreign affairs but to the dangers of a large majority for the LDP/CGP coalition (News on Japan online, December 8; see also Ikeda and Reed, this volume). It's not that there was huge support for Abenomics but rather that voters preferred the LDP anyway even if they weren't convinced that Abe's economic policies were working (AS online December 1, 2014).

Protest voting over strategic voting

Surprisingly, the Social Democratic Party that has always been in the forefront of opposition to constitutional revision and any changes in defense policy did not take up Abe's foreign and defense policy issues as a central part of its campaign. It neither gained nor lost any seats from its irrelevant two prior to the election. The only party to take on these issues frontally in their campaign was the JCP (Fukushima, 2015; WJS online December 11, 2014), historically a strong opponent of the US–Japan alliance. Its unique stance of making foreign policy and anti-nuclear energy central themes in the campaign paid off: it gained 13 seats to raise its total to 21. For example, many voters who opposed Abe's policies to restart nuclear reactors also said they would vote for the JCP (AS online December 1, 2014). Those most opposed to Abe's foreign and defense policies too would have found the JCP a target for their protest vote.

Political scientists would argue that this was not a "rational voting strategy" because had these votes gone to the DPJ, the major opposition party, in the local districts where only the two larger parties had much chance of winning seats, even had it not prevented an LDP majority it would have cut its size and given the main opposition party the ability to claim some degree of victory and increase its influence in the Diet. However, from the perspective of the voters opposed to Abe's foreign and defense policies, there was probably a different logic at work here in the MMM electoral system. Because the DPJ did not take an opposing stand to these policies and make the issues salient in the campaign, what was the incentive for these voters to cast their ballots for the DPJ even in the local districts? From their viewpoint, since these issues were so important to them, they probably either voted with their feet and stayed home (thus increasing the abstention rate) or cast their ballots for the JCP in the PR tier and "wasted" their vote by also casting it for the JCP (note that the JCP nearly doubled their vote compared to the previous election in both the SSD and PR tiers) or some other small party in the local districts. Protest voting, rather than strategic voting, was such deeply opposed citizens' only real choice.

The one exception that proves the rule

There is one significant exception to the generalization that foreign and defense policy were not salient issues in this campaign: voting in Okinawa Prefecture. The continuing conflict between many Okinawans and the central LDP government over the many American bases on the island and particularly over the attempt by the United States and Japan to move the Futenma Air Base in populous southern Okinawa to the Nago peninsula and the town of Henoko in less crowded northern Okinawa was an important issue in that Prefecture's 2014 HR election. Although this move represents an improvement to southern Okinawans' conditions of the kind Okinawans have been demanding, in recent years many Okinawans have come to want many of the bases completely off-island, a demand very difficult for either Japan or the United States to satisfy.[7] Negotiations between the two countries continue, but so does opposition to the move to Henoko (*JT*, August 23, 2014 for example; see Kagotani, this volume).

In the year before the HR election the anti-base movement won two big local election victories, re-electing an anti-move Mayor in Henoko (*JT*, 14 January 2014) and an anti-move Governor for the whole prefecture who defeated the incumbent that had approved a landfill permit to start construction on the base (*NYT*, November 16, 2014). The anti-base movement continued its electoral success in the HR election, winning all four seats in the prefecture by defeating LDP candidates. These electoral results will provide more confidence and impetus to the anti-base movement there, probably making the movement of the base even more difficult to realize for the two countries (Fukushima, 2015).

Concluding comments

Like the dog that didn't bark in the night, the most significant impact of Abe's specific foreign and defense policies in this election is that despite their deviation from postwar traditional policies, they seem to have little impact in this election, but for complicated reasons. Some might argue that this is due to the fact that all voting publics are primarily domestic issue-oriented, and in fact this may usually particularly be the case with Japanese voters suffering from a 20-year recession and slow or no economic growth.

There is partial truth to this. But given the unprecedented initiatives by Abe that bode to at least partially change Japan's foreign and defense policies and practices of at least the past 60 years, and the Japanese public's perceptions of the China and North Korean threats, on the surface it nonetheless appears at first surprising. The explanation for the "mystery" must lie in the specific dynamics of the campaign and the salience and consistency of voters' attitudes in response to it, and how their choices were structured by the current electoral system itself. Foreign and defense policy and Abe's changes to it mattered to many voters, if not all.

For those for whom it did, however, it was either not as salient as other issues because of Abe's and the LDP's skillful pre-electoral strategy of legitimizing nationalism (see Kingston, this volume) and their campaign strategy to ignore or denigrate them compared to other issues on which the LDP was stronger; their own conflicted views on the matter; or they were not offered a viable alternative choice by the some of the other parties, especially in the SSD tier. Clearly the dog that didn't bark in foreign policy fits the overall "bait and switch" strategy of Abe in this election (Pekkanen, Reed, and Scheiner's "Conclusion," this volume). For those that did want to express their adamant opposition they could only really do so through abstention, or to affect the results by voting for one of the few parties that did represent their foreign policy views, the JCP, but only in the PR tier. The dog may not have barked for these complicated and intertwined reasons, but under different conditions, presented alternatives and better opposition strategies, it may yet at least growl.

Notes

1. Because other chapters in this volume focus on foreign policy-related issues such as TPP (see Katada and Wilbur, this volume) and nationalism (Kingston, this volume) I focus more on issues related to Abe's specific defense policies and relationship with China, Korea, and the U.S.
2. Mail survey, 2045 respondents representing a 68% return rate. Of the sample, 52% supported the Abe cabinet, 39% did not; 38% supported the LDP, 41% supported no party.
3. Japanese newspaper polls' results often vary depending on their methodology and the political leanings of the newspaper (Yoshida, 2014).
4. For those curious, my own personal evaluation of the most rational foreign policies for Japan is between Abe's and the public's views. I think the Yoshida Doctrine effectively ceased to be very relevant in the 1990s with the end of the Cold War, the emergent threats from China and North Korea, and Japan becoming more economically integrated with East Asia. So Abe's moving closer militarily to the United States and some revision of Article 9 while maintaining the defense-only provisions may be rational in this context; however, his administration's positions and behavior on historical memories runs counter to Japan's national self-interests.
5. The theme of the LDP being identified with competent governing for much of the postwar period is found in (Krauss and Pekkanen, 2011) and was a major theme in the 2012 election as well (see *JD 2012*). See also (Schoppa, 2011; Reed et al., 2012; and Lipscy & Scheiner 2012)
6. Hughes (2012) has the best and most extensive discussion of the DPJ's foreign and defense policies.
7. Many of these higher expectations were stimulated by Prime Minister Hatoyama of the DPJ in the 2009 election campaign when he foolishly first raised Okinawans' hopes.

References

Aldrich, John H. (2011). *Why Parties? A second look.* Chicago: University of Chicago Press.

Aldrich, John H., John L. Sullivan and Eugene Borgida (1989). Foreign affairs and issue voting: Do presidential candidates waltz before a blind audience? *The American Political Science Review* 83(1): 123–141.

Aldrich, John H., Peter Feaver, Chris Gelpi, Jason Reifler, Kristin and Thompson Sharp (2006). Foreign policy and the electoral connection. *Annual Review of Political Science* 9: 477–502.

Belanger, Eric and Bonnie M. Meguid (2008). Issue salience, issue ownership, and issue-based vote choice. *Electoral Studies* 27: 477–491.

Cox, Gary W. and Frances Rosenbluth (1995). Anatomy of a split: The liberal democrats in Japan. *Electoral Studies* 14(4): 355–376.

Delamotte, Guibourg. (2011). Political constraints, legal devices and Japan's defense doctrine: A reassessment after the democratic party's victory. *Korean Review of International Studies (KRIS)*, April: 89–109.

Fukushima, Teruhiko. (2015). Japan: putting the December election in context. *The Strategist* –The Australian Strategic Policy Institute Blog online at http://www.aspistrategist.org.au (January 8).

Gopoian, J. David (1982). Issue preferences and candidate choice in presidential primaries. *American Journal of Political Science* 26(3): 523–546

Green, Michael and Jeffrey W. Hornung (2014). Ten myths about Japan's collective self-defense change: What the critics don't understand about Japan's constitutional reinterpretation. *The Diplomat*, July 10.

Green, Jane and Hobolt Sara (2008). Owning the issue agenda: party strategies and vote choices in British elections. *Electoral Studies* 27(3): 460–476.

Horiuchi, Yusaku, Daniel M. Smith, Teppei Yamamoto and Mayumi Fukushima (2014). Shuugiin senkyo, kinkyuu kaiseki! Deetaga akashita yuukensha no honnne. [Urgent analysis of the House of Representatives election! Data reveal the true preferences of voters]. *Nikkei Business Online*, December 18. URL: http://business.nikkeibp.co.jp/article/topics/20141218/275309.

Hughes, Christopher W. (2012). The democratic party of Japan's new (but failing) grand security strategy: From 'reluctant realism to resentful realism. *Journal of Japanese Studies*. 38(1): 109–139.

Inoue, Makiko and Neil Gough (2014). 'Polls slow Japan's plan to revise constitution.' *New York Times Online*, July 9.

Kushida, Kenji E. and Phillip Lipscy (eds). (2013). Japan under the DPJ: The politics of transition and governance. Walter H. Shorenstein Asia-Pacific Research Center, 2013.

Lipscy Phillip Y. and Ethan Scheiner (2012). Japan under the DPJ: The paradox of political change without policy change. *Journal of East Asian Studies* 12: 311–322.

Maureen and Mike Mansfield Foundation online (2014). Asahi Shimbun Special Public Opinion Poll.' Asahi Opinion Poll Database, 2014. http://mansfieldfdn.org/program/research-education-and-communication/asian-opinion-poll-database/asahi-shimbun-special-public-opinion-poll-040714/

Miura, Mari, Kap Yun Lee and Robert Weiner (2005). Who are the DPJ?: Policy positioning and recruitment strategy. *Asian Perspective* 29(1): 49–77.

Pew Research Center (2014). Global opposition to U.S. Surveillance and drones, but limited harm to America's image: Many in Asia worry about conflict with China, July 14 .

Pekkanen, Robert J. and Saadia M. Pekkanen (2015). All About Abe: Japan in 2014.' *Asian Survey* 551.

Pyle, Kenneth B. (1996). Japan's postwar national purpose. *Ch. 3* of his *The Japanese Question: Power and purpose in a new era*. Washington: AEI Press: 20–41.

Reed, Steven R., Ethan Scheiner and Michael F. Thies (2012). The end of LDP dominance and the rise of party-oriented politics in Japan. *Journal of Japanese Studies* 38: 2.

Repeta, Lawrence (2013). Japan's democracy at risk – the ldp's ten most dangerous proposals for constitutional change. *The Asia-Pacific Journal* 1128: 3.

Richards, Clint (2014). Polls Give Abe a Bump, But Not on Collective Self-Defense. *The Diplomat*, August 5.

Samuels, Richard J. (2001). Kishi and corruption: An anatomy of the 1955 system,' Japan Policy Research Institute Working Paper No: 83.

Schattschneider, Elmer E. (1960, 1964). *The semi-sovereign people: A realist's view of democracy in America*. New York: Holt, Rinehart, and Winston.

Scheiner, Ethan (2014). Review of the evolution of Japan's party system: Politics and policy in an era of institutional change. *The Journal of Japanese Studies* 40(1): 239–244.

Smith, Daniel M., Robert J. Pekkanen and Ellis S. Krauss (2013). Building a party: Candidate recruitment in the democratic party of Japan, 1996–2012. In Kenji E. Kushida and Phillip Lipscy (eds) *Japan under the DPJ: The Politics of Transition and Governance*. Stanford: Walter H. Shorenstein Asia-Pacific Research Center.

Yoshida, Reiji (2014). Polling shows voters unclear about Article 9 reinterpretation: Expert. *JT*, July 11, 2014.

19
The 2014 Election in Okinawa

Koji Kagotani

Elections in Okinawa differ from the rest of the country. The issue of US bases dominates all other considerations. Over 73% of the area for US bases in Japan is currently located in Okinawa.[1] Bases cause many problems for the local population, including the noise of planes taking off and landing, periodic accidents, and inter-cultural friction. However, bases also provide economic benefits. The Liberal Democratic Party (LDP) has long represented voters who see the benefits as outweighing the costs. Opposition to the bases has been represented by a variety of parties, including the Japanese Communist Party (JCP) and a local party, the Okinawa Social Mass Party, in which reformists honor Article 9 of the constitution and pursue pacifism. Whenever protests have threatened the bases, the LDP government has responded by supplementing the benefits, such as base-related subsidies to improve the quality of local life and mitigate problems (Calder, 2007: 130–139; Cooley and Martin, 2006). In the 1972–2006 gubernatorial elections, foreign threats also stimulated patriotism and the demand for national security, raising political support for the pro-base candidates (Kagotani and Yanai, 2014). Yet base opponents continue to win elections, especially local gubernatorial and mayoral elections and local referenda on the bases. Even in those races, however, material interests affect voting behavior (Eldridge, 1997).

Did compensation policy and foreign threats still matter in 2014? Okinawans supported the anti-base candidate even though they received more base-related subsidies and confronted China's territorial ambition for the Senkaku Islands, as well as North Korea's repeated missile experiments. I first describe and examine recent electoral results. Next, I present the basic background for the base issue. Finally, I report on an analysis of the 2014 gubernatorial election that suggests that the LDP lost because of its weaker party discipline and a split in the LDP–Komeito coalition and that base-related subsidies no longer have a significant impact on election outcomes.

Elections results

Okinawans indicate their support for or opposition to the current security policy of Japan through both national and local elections. Five lower house elections were held after redistricting the single-member districts (SMDs). Candidates competed against each other in four SMDs of Okinawa.

In the 2003 election, two LDP candidates and two opposition candidates (the Komeito and the Social Democratic Party (SDP)) were elected from the SMDs, and two opposition candidates won proportional representative (PR) seats. While the LDP-led ruling coalition formed the majority in the Diet, an anti-base mood prevailed among Okinawans. In the 2005 election, four SMD seats were split by two LDP candidates and two opposition candidates (an independent and the SDP). An LDP candidate and an opposition candidate (the JCP) won PR seats. Even though Prime Minister Junichiro Koizumi brought a landslide victory at the national level, Okinawans' opinions were balanced between the pro-base and the anti-base camps. In the 2009 election, all SMD seats went to four opposition candidates (two of the Democratic Party of Japan (DPJ), the People's New Party, and the SDP), and no candidate won a PR seat. As the DPJ prevailed throughout Japan, the LDP lost in every Okinawan district. In the 2012 election, three LDP candidates and an opposition candidate (the SDP) were elected from the SMDs. PR seats went to an LDP candidate and two opposition candidates (the JCP and the Tomorrow Party of Japan (TPJ)). As the DPJ lost public confidence in the nation, the LDP regained the public's trust. In the 2014 election, all SMD seats went to opposition candidates (an independent, the JCP, the People's Life First Party, and the SDP), but three LDP candidates and an opposition candidate (the Japan Restoration/Innovation Party) won PR seats. Even though the LDP received nationwide support, Okinawans indicated their mixed feelings because of the Futenma issue.

Except for the 2009 and 2012 general elections, the electoral results in Okinawa did not follow national trends and some Okinawans constantly opposed the LDP and the security policy of Japan. As for the Okinawa gubernatorial elections, the LDP won by supporting an independent candidate in 2002, 2006, and 2010, but lost in 2014. Only the 2002 and 2006 electoral results reflect the LDP's popularity at the national level. Thus, a series of electoral results shows that the LDP has been struggling for the consolidation of pro-base support.

The latest 2014 lower house election was held immediately after the LDP's defeat in the 2014 gubernatorial election. In such a tough situation, the LDP won three PR seats even though all four SMD seats went to anti-base candidates. How did the LDP manage to secure three PR seats? One year before the election, the LDP started strengthening its party discipline. Unless its Diet members from Okinawa had followed its stance of security policy, the LDP would have expelled them from the party membership (*Yomiuri*, November 27, 2013). The LDP forced the local LDP of Okinawa to back the proposed solution for the Futenma problem (*Yomiuri*, December 1, 2013). Finally, the LDP compelled Governor Nakaima to approve the relocation of the Futenma base to Cape Henoko (*Yomiuri*, December 27, 2013). The LDP argued that the relocation of the Futenma base to Cape Henoko was immediately required for removing the risk of plane accidents. In fact, 70,000 of Okinawans signed for indicating their support for its proposed relocation plan and more than 20,000 of them are residents in Ginowan city and Nago city (*Yomiuri*, November 25, 2013). These cities are the parties in interest. The LDP's clear policy stance was helpful for attracting its core supporters and securing PR seats in the 2014 general election.

At the same time, the LDP's stance also did not help enhance a coalition of the LDP and the Komeito. Although the Komeito endorsed the LDP candidates in the SMDs, it kept its policy stance by insisting that the Futenma base be relocated to other prefectures or overseas. Therefore, the LDP had difficulty mobilizing a broader political support in the 2014 lower house election as well as the 2014 gubernatorial election.

The Futenma issue

The Futenma base is located in the center of Ginowan city and residents are exposed to the risk of plane accidents. To remove such a risk, the United States and Japan agreed to relocate the Futenma base to Cape Henoko in 1997. One year and two months later, Governor Masahide Ota opposed this proposal and decreed that the Futenma base be relocated to other prefectures or overseas. An anti-base mood prevailing among Okinawans did not allow him to relocate the Futenma base to anywhere else within Okinawa (*Ryukyu Shimpo*, February 6, 1998).

The pro-base candidate Keiichi Inamine defeated the incumbent candidate Ota in the 1998 gubernatorial election, but Governor Inamine made little progress in implementing the relocation plan of the Futenma base during the subsequent eight years (Moriya 2010: 25–28). The DPJ moved toward opposition to the bases and defeated the LDP in the 2009 general election. Prime Minister Yukio Hatoyama promised, in effect, to relocate the Futenma base to other prefectures or overseas, thus raising Okinawans' expectations. However, Hatoyama failed to make progress in the relocation process, resigning in June 2010 (*Nikkei*, June 2, 2010, web). This DPJ policy failure devastated the party in Okinawa, as noted above.

The 2014 Okinawa gubernatorial election

The latest gubernatorial election was held on November 16, 2014, and it was a competition among four candidates; Takeshi Onaga, Hirokazu Nakaima, Mikio Shimoji, and Shokichi Kina received 360,820 votes, 261,076 votes, 69,447 votes, and 7,821 votes, respectively. The electoral result shows that the election was a two-horse race of Onaga and Nakaima. Both candidates came from the conservative camp, which is different from the previous elections in which a conservative often competed with a reformist. The incumbent, Nakaima, and the challenger, Onaga, addressed the relocation issue of the Futenma base in the electoral campaign. Nakaima accepted the proposed relocation of the Futenma base to Cape Henoko, while Onaga insisted that the base be relocated to other prefectures or overseas. The difference in their policy stances regarding national security policy determined the electoral outcome.

Nakaima's defeat can be explained to some degree by political reasons. First, LDP discipline was weak in the early stages. In June, 11 members of the LDP group, Shinpukai, in Naha city assembly asked Onaga to run for election (*Sankei*, June 6, 2014, web) and 320 executives in 100 Okinawan companies agreed to support Onaga (*Ryukyu Shimpo*, June 10, 2014, web). Later, 12 members of Shinpukai were expelled from the LDP of Okinawa (*Ryukyu Shimpo*, August 10, 2014, web). Nakaima accepted the request from the LDP of Okinawa and decided to run for election on July 26 (*Okinawa Times*, July 27, 2014, web).

Nakaima was not an ideal candidate for the LDP because the LDP's coalition partner the Komeito opposed the proposed relocation of the Futenma to Cape Henoko and would not support him (*Okinawa Times*, July 25, 2014, web). There was a gap between the LDP of Okinawa and the LDP. Nonetheless, Nakaima and the members of the LDP of Okinawa met Prime Minister Shinzo Abe to ask electoral support from the LDP (*Ryukyu Shimpo*, August 6, 2014, web). The LDP officially endorsed Nakaima for the next Okinawa governor on August 27 (*Sankei*, August 27, 2014, web). Nakaima ended up with no electoral cooperation from the Komeito (*Okinawa Times*, October 22, 2014, web).

In contrast, the five opposition groups in the Okinawa prefectural assembly, such as the SDP of Okinawa, the JCP of Okinawa, and the Okinawa Social Mass Party, formed the selection committee and quickly agreed to choose Onaga as the candidate for the next governor in the time (*Okinawa Times*, July 26, 2014). Onaga succeeded in forming a broader coalition across different ideologies. Therefore, Nakaima's position regarding the Futenma relocation issue split the coalition of the LDP and the Komeito and made him weaker in electoral campaign.

Finally, Nakaima failed to divert public attention to material benefits. To implement the transformation of US army, the central government started investigating the provision of more base-related subsidies to prefectures which host US troops (*Sankei*, July 22, 2014). The central government also intended to promote the development of the Okinawan economy to offset the loss from implementing the relocation of the Futenma base to Cape Henoko. Yoshihide Suga, the chief cabinet secretary, visited Okinawa to support Nakaima in the electoral campaign and announced that the central government would like to help to attract an entertainment park, Universal Studios, to Nago city (*Asahi*, November 8, 2014).

Even though the state of the Okinawan economy was not good, material benefits did not seem to influence voting behavior. Similarly, the central governments kept the amount of base-related subsidies even after the DPJ's victory of the 2009 general election, but the vote share of the pro-base candidate dropped from 2010–2014 in Okinawa municipalities overall. It appears that base-related subsidies no longer work as a policy instrument for consolidating pro-base support in the 2014 election.

Conclusions

Recent Okinawan electoral results suggest two political reasons for the LDP's defeat. The proposed relocation of the Futenma base to Cape Henoko made the LDP–Komeito coalition weaker and then the LDP had difficulty mobilizing a broader support. Opposition to US bases has grown to the point that the LDP tactic of supplementing benefits and ameliorating costs will no longer be as effective in maintaining local support for the bases.

Note

1. See the Ministry of Defense website: http://www.mod.go.jp/j/approach/zaibeigun/us_sisetsu/sennyousisetutodoufuken.html (date last accessed February 1, 2015).

Bibliography

Calder, Kent E. (2007). *Embattled garrisons: Comparative base politics and American globalism*. Princeton: Princeton University Press.

Cooley, Alexander and Kimberly Marten (2006). Base motives: The political economy of Okinawa's antimilitarism. *Armed Forces & Society* 32(4): 566–583.

Eldridge, Robert D. (1997). The 1996 Okinawa referendum on U.S. Base reductions: one question, several answers. *Asian Survey* 37(10): 879–904.

Kagotani, Koji, and Yuki Yanai (2014). External threats, US bases, and prudent voters in Okinawa. *International Relations of the Asia-Pacific* 14(1): 91–115.

Moriya, Takemasa (2010). Futenma' Kōshō Hiroku [The Futenma Chronicle: the Negotiations behind the Scenes]. Tokyo: Shinchōsya.

20

Japan's Stealth Decision 2014: The Trans-Pacific Partnership

Saori N. Katada and Scott Wilbur

The year 2014 appeared to be a decisive one for the Trans-Pacific Partnership (TPP) trade agreement. Despite numerous unmet predictions of the negotiations' impending completion and Tokyo's downplaying of much of the negotiations' progress on protecting certain "sacred areas" of the Japanese economy, Prime Minister Shinzo Abe's administration established a solid foundation to move forward on the TPP. We argue that 2014 was a crucial year for the TPP, despite its lack of tangible results, and that the December 2014 election was a key step for the Abe administration to hammer out Japan's negotiation stance on the TPP's most politically difficult aspect, namely its impact on Japan's agricultural sector. By keeping the TPP largely out of the electoral campaign, Abe's Liberal Democratic Party (LDP) was able to avoid significant controversy that might divide key party members and constituencies, which led to the party's smooth victory in the December 2014 election. This has, in turn, preserved support for the TPP at the highest levels of the Japanese government.

When the Abe administration initially took office in December 2012, Japanese public opinion was already generally in favor of the TPP, so Abe's challenge was not in convincing the majority of Japanese to support the agreement. Rather, the primary obstacle to Japan's involvement lay in Abe's own party, the LDP, where Abe had to contend with many politicians whose rural district backgrounds and close relationships with agriculture associations, above all Japan Agricultural Corporative (JA), led them to strongly oppose Japan's participation. As this chapter shows, the Abe administration was generally able to manage this intra-party opposition while designing limited tariff concessions that would still uphold Japan's fundamental interest in certain agricultural goods. Furthermore, Japanese farmers seemed to accept the general direction of the

Abe administration in pursuing the TPP, despite their concerns about the agreement. Hence, Abe's victory in the December 2014 election spelled out a much increased likelihood of Japan's ability to reach a settlement in the TPP and thereby bring the negotiations to completion.

Of course, seven years after the 2008 inception of the multimember TPP negotiations based on an earlier high-quality free trade agreement among Singapore, Chile, New Zealand, and Brunei, the ultimate conclusion of the TPP still depends on many other factors large and small. One key factor is the US position. The Obama administration needs to acquire trade promotion authority (TPA) to allow President Obama to determine the TPP negotiations' details and restrict Congress to a simple majority vote on whether to approve any final agreement without the possibility of amendments or filibusters, in order to accelerate the US ratification process before the next presidential and congressional electoral campaigns start in full force in fall 2015. The TPP's other ten negotiating members besides Japan and the United States must also sign on to many contentious issues of this "platinum standard" trade agreement ranging from intellectual property rights to service sector liberalization (Schott et al., 2013). Despite these remaining difficulties, however, a closer inspection of the TPP negotiations reveals that 2014 did in fact see notable progress toward the conclusion of the agreement, especially by Japan. While the year did not witness the ultimate completion of the negotiations, nor domestic ratification and enforcement by TPP member countries, considerable efforts and accomplishments were made that moved the agreement substantially nearer to consummation. On June 23, 2015, the US congress granted TPA to President Obama, which was a necessary step for the TPP's successful conclusion. Therefore, there is some reason to believe that a final agreement on the TPP might be possible in the near future, and at last bring to fruition a painstaking negotiation process that has taken the better part of the last decade.

This chapter covers the history of Japan's domestic politics regarding the TPP and analyzes why the 2014 election elevated the prospect of Japan to conclude the agreement. Following this introduction, we first discuss how the TPP was contentious prior to the 2012 LDP victory. The next section covers Abe's decision to join the TPP negotiations in March 2013 and how the TPP negotiations evolved over the remainder of the year. The third and fourth sections analyze the TPP negotiations' progress in 2014 and how the LDP made the TPP a stealth issue at the time of December 2014 election. The chapter concludes with an epilogue of what has happened since December 2014 and discusses the TPP's future likelihood given the LDP's solid electoral victory.

Japan in the TPP before Abe

Prior to the ascendancy of the Abe administration in December 2012, the two previous Democratic Party of Japan (DPJ) administrations led by Prime Ministers Naoto Kan and Yoshihiko Noda incrementally pushed Japan toward the TPP negotiations, though they were unsuccessful in getting Japan to join the negotiations before the DPJ fell from power. Prime Minister Kan in particular was responsible for launching Japan's pursuit of the agreement. On October 1, 2010, shortly after a DPJ intra-party election that saw him defeat Ichiro Ozawa for party presidency, Kan signaled his desire for Japan to consider joining the TPP negotiations in a major policy speech (Kan, 2010). Yet Kan's bold declaration was subsequently undercut by inconsistent assessments of the TPP's economic impact on Japan by ministries within his own government (Cabinet Secretariat, 2011), as well as fierce resistance from Japanese farmers, agricultural association members orchestrated by the JA, and many politicians inside the DPJ and LDP, then the opposition party. Given the political controversy surrounding the TPP and the DPJ's internal disunity, Kan was only able to tepidly announce at the November 2010 APEC summit in Yokohama that Japan would gather information on possibly joining the TPP negotiations. Kan hoped that Japan would eventually be able to decide on membership in the agreement by June 2011, but the "3.11" triple disaster in March 2011 effectively took the TPP question off the policy agenda and ultimately caused Kan to resign several months later in the face of mounting pressure over his administration's handling of the disaster recovery efforts.

Prime Minister Noda came to power in September 2011 with the ambition to advance Japan toward TPP membership, and he demonstrated this ambition by announcing that Japan would begin consultations on joining the TPP negotiations just prior to his departure for the November 2011 APEC summit in Honolulu. Noda's TPP aspiration was hampered by his inability to repair intra-party tensions and unify the DPJ behind the TPP, however. The opposition LDP was also unsupportive of Japan's participation in the TPP negotiations, which left Noda facing considerable political headwinds in moving Japan closer to the TPP. Noda's announcement at the 2011 APEC summit left observers with the impression that while Noda personally preferred participation in the

TPP, it would be a steep task for him to realize his TPP aspiration given Japan's domestic opposition. After committing Japan to start consultations on the TPP, Noda spent much of his political capital in early 2012 on convincing the DPJ's Lower House legislators to support a bill for doubling the consumption tax. To secure the bill's passage in the LDP-dominant upper house, Noda promised his partisan opponents that he would dissolve the lower house and hold a general election in exchange for their support of the tax increase. Though Noda did not immediately keep this promise after the tax-increase passed in August 2012, he eventually dissolved the Diet in November, setting up an election for the following month.

The TPP re-emerged in the December 2012 general election, though it was not a core campaign issue for either of the two main parties or the smaller parties like the Japan Restoration Party and Your Party that contested the election. Prime Minister Noda initially proposed to include TPP participation in the DPJ's manifesto. But internal disagreement within the DPJ dampened this possibility, and the party's actual manifesto only ambiguously professed to "advance negotiations" on the TPP along with the China–Japan–South Korea free trade agreement and the Regional Comprehensive Economic Partnership (RCEP) (DPJ, 2012).[1] The LDP's manifesto was similarly cautious toward the TPP, stating that Japan should not join the agreement without keeping protections on certain "sacred areas" (LDP, 2012). The two parties' hesitation on the TPP was probably not a decisive factor in the election's outcome, however. According to a poll by TV Asahi in late November 2012, Japan's participation in the TPP had the lowest level of respondents' concern among six policy issues for the election, behind economic policy, pensions and the social security system, maintaining the ban on nuclear power, diplomatic and security policy, the consumption tax increase, and revising bureaucrat-led politics (TV Asahi, 2012).

Japan joins the TPP negotiations: 2013

When Shinzo Abe was in opposition (2009–2012), he never publicly committed to bring Japan into the TPP negotiations. However, in his December 2012 election campaign, he did avow that the "LDP has sufficient power to break through tariff abolition without exceptions," indicating that he might in fact direct Japan to join the agreement if his party returned to power (Mulgan, 2013: 217). Indeed, within a few weeks after the LDP won a majority in the election, Abe initiated intra-party discussions to build consensus for eventual entry into the TPP and appointed Koya Nishikawa, a LDP politician with expertise on agricultural policy, to lead the LDP's TPP Affairs Committee and coordinate the party's position on the agreement (Mulgan, 2014). Nevertheless, Abe's most immediate policy goal was to maintain a stable political environment until the summer 2013 upper house election, which the LDP hoped to win and thereby guarantee party control over both houses of the Diet for the following three years. To this end, Abe did not aggressively pursue the TPP immediately after the LDP's 2012 election triumph, and instead advanced his "Abenomics" agenda, which emphasized lifting Japan's stagnant economy through the three "arrows" of (a) public spending; (b) loose monetary policy, including inflation-targeting by the Bank of Japan; and (c) Japan's economic structural reform (see Noble in this volume).

In early 2013, however, the Abe administration was faced with increasing urgency to commit Japan to the TPP, as President Obama became energized to conclude the TPP after his reelection and existing TPP member countries were quickly reaching a turning point in the negotiations. Facing mounting US pressure and the choice of either joining the TPP negotiations soon or losing the opportunity to be an original member country that could shape the agreement's character, Abe formulated a carefully worded statement on Japan's TPP policy which he jointly issued with President Obama following a summit meeting in Washington DC on February 22, 2013:

> Recognizing that both countries have bilateral trade sensitivities, such as certain agricultural products for Japan and certain manufactured products for the United States, the two governments confirm that, as the final outcome will be determined during the negotiations, it is not required to make a prior commitment to unilaterally eliminate all tariffs upon joining the TPP negotiations.
>
> (White House 2013)

With this discreetly phrased statement, Abe was able to keep the LDP's election pledge that Japan would avoid complete tariff abolition on certain "sacred areas," because full tariff elimination was never actually a precondition for joining the TPP negotiations and any tariff reductions would only be determined by member countries in the process of the negotiations. At the same time, the statement demonstrated Abe's view that Japan would be able to enter the TPP, since it suggested that Japan might still obtain protections on these areas within the negotiations. One month later, on March 15, Abe formally announced Japan's intention of joining the TPP negotiations. While Abe's decision was greeted excitedly by TPP supporters because Japan's inclusion effectively doubled the economic size of the agreement, trade officials and politicians in the United States were still concerned about Japan inadequately opening its domestic market and possibly delaying the agreement's completion beyond the 2013 APEC summit (FT, 12 April 2013, web). The decision also triggered protests by thousands of farmers in Tokyo and renewed criticism of the TPP by the Ministry of Agriculture, Forestry and Fisheries (MAFF) and JA, with the latter foreboding that after TPP membership, "We may no longer be able to eat the safe, secure domestic food that has nourished our lives" (FT, 18 March, 2013, web). On the other hand, a survey published by the Yomiuri Shimbun on March 18 recorded that 60 % of respondents supported Japan's TPP participation, suggesting that a majority of Japanese citizens were in favor of the agreement (Yomiuri, 18 March 2013, web) (Figure 20.1).

It took another four months for Japan to actually join the TPP negotiations, however. Internationally, Japan's involvement in the negotiations had to be accepted first by all TPP member countries. In the case of the United States, American trade negotiators obtained preliminary concessions such as increased car imports to Japan and an assurance that Japan would not enlarge a life insurance program operated by the state-owned Japan Post before the conclusion of the TPP negotiations, in exchange for US support of Japan's participation (FT, 12 April 2013, web).[2] Moreover, certain member countries like the United States also had to satisfy domestic laws for launching international trade negotiations, which required additional time to be met. Within Japan, the approaching date of the upper house elections in summer 2013 made Abe particularly reluctant to have the TPP emerge as a potentially negative campaign issue, which could threaten the LDP's chances of winning the election and securing a long-term majority with its junior coalition partner, the Komeito, in both houses of the Diet. In fact, Abe avoided any controversial developments about the TPP by sticking to his previous pledge to protect "sacred areas," which he enumerated in the campaign period as five particular categories of traded agricultural goods: rice, wheat, beef, dairy products, and sugar. With a promise to uphold tariffs on these select goods, which bolstered rural LDP legislators' electoral prospects in their home districts, Abe's party soundly defeated the DPJ and enabled the LDP–Komeito coalition to regain control of the upper house on July 21.

Japan officially joined the TPP negotiations on July 23, two days after the upper house election.[3] Japan's participation in the TPP negotiations

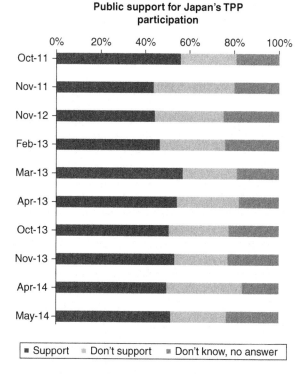

Figure 20.1 Public support for Japan's TPP participation (NTV, 2011–2014)
Source: Nippon Television Network Corporation, October 2011–May 2014. http://www.ntv. co.jp/yoron/..

under Abe's insistence on tariff exceptions and a weakened Japanese yen due to Abenomics ignited fierce criticism from more than 200 US House of Representatives members, who subsequently signed a letter to President Obama asking for currency manipulation to be taken up as a negotiating issue inside the TPP.[4] Many US lawmakers were also unsatisfied with the concessions on car imports acquired from approving Japan's TPP membership, especially within the left-wing of Obama's Democratic Party, and pressed Obama to extract greater opening of Japan's market in the negotiations. The US government could not assert heavier pressure on Japan in fall 2013 for two domestic political reasons, however. First, the Senate Finance Committee encountered trouble in producing a bill to grant TPA to President Obama, as the complexity of the TPP as a "21st century" trade agreement with more than 20 chapters covering unfamiliar and sensitive issues such as state-owned enterprises and intellectual property protections made drafting this legislation particularly onerous (FT, 8 August 2013, web). Second, the lack of political compromise between Obama and House Republicans over the federal budget precipitated a US government shutdown on October 1, causing Obama to miss the APEC Summit in Bali, which foreclosed the possibility of a decisive outcome for the TPP at the meeting.

In the relative absence of US pressure, Japan's progress in the TPP negotiations during this period was largely contingent on Abe's achievement of consensus building inside the LDP. Two especially contentious points for Abe were how to reform Japan's domestic agricultural sector, and how such reform might facilitate Japan's ability to accept lower tariffs on agricultural products under the TPP. In relation to these points, the Abe administration approved plans to end two major subsidies to rice farmers on November 26, 2013. One was the *gentan* subsidy that since 1970 had given direct payments to farmers to meet rice production quotas and sometimes shift to other crops; the other was a subsidy introduced by Prime Minister Yukio Hatoyama's DPJ administration in 2010 (FT, 26 November 2013, web). The proposed elimination of the *gentan* subsidy, which was to be halved in April 2014 and completely removed in 2019, was particularly significant because it heralded the decrease of Japan's numerous small farms that had been inefficient producers and dependent on financial supports from the government, and the increase of large-scale farms that would be internationally competitive and able to withstand sectoral liberalization through the TPP. Then, in early December, two agriculture reform bills passed in the Diet: one bill to lower the amount of idle land, promote farm consolidation and boost productivity; and another bill to provide credit insurance to Japanese farmers and thereby enable them to obtain loans from banks outside the JA-dominated network of agriculture finance institutions. The goal of this December legislation was to shift producers' efforts away from the shrinking domestic market, and toward overseas markets where high-quality, value-added Japanese goods like rice and beef had seen growing demand in recent years and were anticipated to be increasingly popular (Bloomberg, 12 December 2013, web). Together with the proposed *gentan* subsidy removal, these bills encouraged the formation of large farming operations and the corresponding decline of the small farms that resisted the TPP.

Despite these reform achievements, Japanese trade negotiators did not compromise on tariff eliminations at a December 2013 meeting of the TPP member countries' trade ministers.[5] Such stubborn insistence put a spotlight on Japan, as it was reported that other aspects of the negotiations had been successfully advanced and the talks were in their final stage. One senior official in the Singapore meeting said, "Japan is at the center of any of the market negotiations. For everyone it is the number one priority," indicating the Abe administration's unwillingness to decide on tariff reductions had become the major hurdle in reaching an agreement (FT, 9 December 2013, web).

Japan's stealth decision: 2014

At the start of 2014, the TPP negotiations' conclusion seemed more likely to happen than the Japan's lower house election that ultimately occurred in December. In January 2014, the US appeared to reenergize its TPP commitment as a bill to reestablish TPA was introduced by the Senate Finance Committee and House Means and Ways Committee, which has authority for trade agreements in the House of Representatives. President Obama also called for TPA in his January 29 State of the Union address. Although Obama's request was opposed by Harry Reid, the Senate majority leader for the Democratic Party, US Trade Representative Michael Froman continued to work toward ironing out the vast gap that existed between Japan and the US regarding market access. The US side believed that parallel Japan-US bilateral talks would be more effective in resolving this thorny issue, and several bilateral meetings were held in February and early March but did not produce many results. Consequently, the next hope for a TPP breakthrough was put on an Abe-Obama summit meeting during President Obama's visit to several countries in Asia in April. Even though the summit produced a joint statement that the Japan-US talks had reached a "key milestone in the TPP negotiations and will inject fresh momentum into the broader talks," it was unclear what specific progress had been made (FT, 25 April 2014, web). A further series of bilateral and multilateral negotiation meetings followed, but to the frustration of many TPP negotiators, Japan did not offer greater market opening toward agricultural imports. This triggered a New Zealand trade representative to reportedly propose that Japan be excused from the negotiations (Chicago Tribune, 12 July 2014, web). US frustration was also apparent in critical remarks made by USTR Froman in October:

> When Japan asked to join the TPP negotiations last year, it expressed a bold vision that matched the ambitions of the United States and its 10 other Asia-Pacific partners. Today, the world is still waiting for

that bold vision to be translated into forward-looking positions at the negotiating table … What's on the line is nothing less than the success of Japan's structural reform efforts, its capacity to pull itself out of two decades of stagnation and its ability to play a leadership role in the region and the global trading system.

(FT, 10 October 2014, web)

The Obama administration's desire to conclude the TPP negotiations and ratify an agreement before the 2016 presidential election campaign led US negotiators to redouble their efforts. As hope dwindled near the end of 2014 that the TPP negotiations would be concluded within the year, Obama received a paradoxical electoral blessing in the November 2014 midterm elections. Though Obama's Democratic Party was trounced, the Republican Party's triumph meant that a more pro-free trade party would control both the House and the Senate, increasing the prospect that Obama would gain TPA once the new Republican legislators began their work in January 2015.

In 2014, Prime Minister Abe and the LDP leadership balanced their commitments to the TPP and intra- and inter-party politics by insisting on five "sacred areas" of exemption on the one hand and soft-pedaling the TPP negotiations toward the Japanese public on the other. The Abe administration clearly wanted to make progress on the TPP negotiations on both domestic and foreign policy grounds. In the domestic realm, realizing the TPP would contribute to structural reform of Japan's economy, which was an essential part of Abenomics's third arrow. On foreign policy grounds, concluding the TPP would not only contribute to favorable US-Japan bilateral relations because of Japan's support of the Obama administration's Asia rebalancing strategy. It would also elevate Japan's importance in Asia in the face of China's economic rise, since Japan would be counteracting Beijing's active foreign policy under new leader Xi Jinping and showing initiative vis-à-vis the non-TPP negotiating country (see Krauss in this volume). The TPP negotiations' completion became increasingly important, particularly after Beijing started to push for an alternative Asia-Pacific FTA scheme in the form of the Free Trade of the Asia Pacific (FTAAP).[6]

The Japanese government demonstrated how far it was willing to compromise on agricultural liberalization by first signing a FTA with Australia on April 7, which had been under negotiation since 2007. Significantly, the agreement between Canberra and Tokyo contained much less stringent tariff reductions, for example on beef imports where Japan pledged to drop its tariffs from 38.5% to 19.5% on frozen beef and to 23.5% on fresh beef over 15 years (FT, 7 April 2014, web). The agreement was held up by Japanese negotiators as a sign of the kind of market access that might be feasible under the TPP. Unsatisfied with this level of liberalization, however, US trade negotiators and President Obama increased pressure on Japan for greater market access. In response, Prime Minister Abe quietly made advances in the Japan-US bilateral talks without fanfare. According to the Yomiuri Shimbun, Abe and Obama arrived at a "basic agreement" at their summit in April on how to proceed in the bilateral talks that would no longer interrupt the TPP negotiations. But Abe did not publicly discuss the details because of an April 27 by-election for a lower house seat in Kagoshima Prefecture where agricultural voters might have directed their support away from the LDP candidate (Nikkan Gendai, 13 April 2014, web; Chicago Tribune, 26 April 2014, web).

The Japan-US bilateral negotiations moved slowly from summer into fall facing the US midterm election and mounting US frustration about Japan's stance. Minister of State for Economic and Fiscal Policy Akira Amari, who was in charge of Japan's TPP negotiations, sought to reach a broad agreement on the TPP at the Beijing APEC Summit on November 10–11. During bilateral TPP meetings, Minister Amari allegedly put forward a significant compromise on tariff reduction on beef and pork. In addition, he offered a 50,000-ton special import quota for American rice beyond the existing 770,000-ton tariff-free access quota in place since 1993 (Mulgan, 2015). Curiously, Japanese newspapers failed to report these measures, and instead voiced concern for the TPP's future as Japan and the US could not reach any agreement at the APEC (Nikkei, 11 November 2014).

A few days after the APEC summit, Prime Minister Abe called for a snap election and dissolved the lower house. While the election was purportedly held on the issue of postponing the second phase of consumption tax increase that the previous Noda administration had slated for October 2015, Abe also sought a mandate on his overall economic policy. In 2014 Japan's economy did not grow as robustly as it did in 2013. Aggressive monetary policy with considerable yen depreciation did not allow Japan to achieve a significant export increase even though it did benefit some specific sectors. The first phase of the consumption tax increase in April 2014 prompted a fairly steep decline in consumption and caused the Japanese economy to reenter recession in the second half of 2014. Despite another round of massive bond-buying by the Bank of Japan in October, the economy did not rebound. At that point, it was crucial for the Abe administration to ensure Japan's economic recovery by postponing the second consumption tax increase. Moreover, Abe was allegedly looking to extend his tenure as the prime minister by calling a lower house election while he still enjoyed both relatively high popularity and the absence of opposing rivals within the LDP (See Endo and Pekkanen in this volume).

Hiding the TPP agenda in the 2014 election

Despite Japanese farmers' intense interest, the TPP did not constitute an important part of the electoral debate or party platforms for the 2014 election. There were three main reasons why the TPP was buried during the two weeks of fierce election campaigning in early December. First, the LDP was split among politicians who promoted Japan's joining the TPP and those who continued to oppose the agreement. The strongest opposition came from LDP members who were tied to agriculture. Prime Minister Abe was tactical in placing Koya Nishikawa, who was a prominent member of the agricultural policy tribe (*nougyou zoku*) in the LDP but who worked as Abe's key TPP coordinator within the party, as the MAFF Minister in September 2014. This move was seen as a way to subdue dissenting voices by enlisting a high-profile *nougyou zoku* member who had been supportive of the TPP (Mulgan, 2014). Despite consistent interest in and concerns over the TPP's future impact from prefectures with strong agricultural presence, most LDP politicians represented in these districts refrained from discussing the TPP.

The second reason related to the on-going agricultural reform implemented by the Abe administration since July 2014. The main organizer of TPP opposition in rural areas, where the TPP was widely portrayed as an enemy of the nation, was JA. In addition to the economic damage that the agricultural sector expected to experience through the lifting of high tariffs, the decrease in the price of rice was expected to immediately impact JA, whose funding base was tied to this price. The JA could not launch any attack on the LDP regarding the TPP during the December 2014 election, however, because the LDP was in the middle of reforming JA (See Maclachlan and Shimizu, this volume). One of the JA officials from Akita Prefecture was quoted as saying that "the LDP has been on the offensive against JA, and it is difficult to evaluate its policies regarding the important issues such as agricultural reform and TPP" (Asahi, 11 December 2014).

The third and final reason behind the lack of debate regarding the TPP during the election was that the LDP and the major opposition party, the DPJ, had similar stances toward the agreement. In its manifesto published in preparation for the 2014 election, the LDP asserted that it would "pursue the best avenue to meet Japan's national interest" as it engaged in TPP negotiations based on the LDP and Diet resolutions. Similarly, the DPJ's manifesto, though in support of the TPP, promised to leave the negotiations if they jeopardized the five sacred areas in agriculture or food safety in Japan. Minor parties that opposed TPP such as the Communist Party and the Social Democratic Party were not powerful enough to win large numbers of seats and change government policy. Hence, many voters felt that they had no alternative but to vote for the LDP.

Epilogue and conclusion

With the LDP's overwhelming victory in the December 2014 election, the prospect of the TPP negotiations' conclusion became brighter. At the round of Japan-US negotiations in early February 2015, Japanese and US negotiators' positions further converged. The US agreed to allow some level of tariffs on certain agricultural products, while Japan pledged to increase US market access in rice (by increasing the tariff-free import quota by 50,000 tons), beef (by reducing tariffs from 38.5% to 9% over the course of 15 years), and pork (by reducing tariffs on cheap port imports from 482 yen per kilo to below 20 yen) (Asahi, 3 February 2015).[7] All in all, both sides showed hope that the general contours of the TPP agreement would be decided in the first half of 2015.

At the same time, Prime Minister Abe also continued to advance the agricultural reform agenda. Since the LDP currently does not have to face more elections for a while (the next upper house election will be in summer 2016; the next Lower House election could be as late as December 2018), Abe can tackle "the largest agricultural reform" since 1955 (Asahi, 10 February 2015). Despite MAFF Minister Nishikawa's resignation due to a campaign finance rule violation, Abe appears to have the time and mandate to push his reform and TPP commitment forward. Hence, Abe's strategy of making the TPP a stealth agenda in the 2014 election made the TPP's prospect more auspicious on Japan's side.

Notes

1. The China-Japan-Korea FTA started its official negotiations in May 2012, and the RCEP began negotiations in November 2012. Japan's flirtation with the TPP in October 2010 became the trigger of these official negotiations (Solis and Katada 2015).

2. The US approved Japan's TPP participation on April 12. All TPP member countries confirmed Japan's inclusion at a meeting of APEC trade ministers on 20–21 April. However, US domestic law requires the executive branch to notify the legislative branch of impending trade negotiations with foreign countries 90 days before commencement, which at the time meant that Japan's earliest possible entry date to the negotiations would be in mid-July 2013.
3. Japan's entry coincidentally fell on the second-to-last day of the 18th round of TPP negotiations in Kota Kinabalu, Malaysia, so Japan could not take part in the discussions about tariff barriers that had been held earlier in the round.
4. Concerns over the future prospect of China's TPP participation were another reason for the petition from Congress (Chicago Tribune, 30 May 2013, web). Sixty of 100 US Senators also sent a similar letter to Obama on September 24, 2013. http://www.stabenow.senate.gov/?p=press_release&id=1171.
5. Though Koya Nishikawa, head of the LDP's TPP Affairs Committee, hinted at Bali that Japan might consider removing tariffs on some of the "sacred" goods, he was quickly criticized by anti-TPP LDP legislators and Japanese farmers, and the Abe administration denied that it planned to make any reductions.
6. Beijing proposed the FTAAP at an APEC trade minister meeting held in Beijing on 17–18 May 2014, which would subsume the TPP member countries into a larger regional agreement based on the APEC members.
7. On the other hand, the US will compromise on the reduction (or elimination) of its 2.5 percent import tariff on auto parts (*Asahi*, 3 February 2015).

References

Cabinet Secretariat (2011). EPA ni kan suru kakushu shisan [Assessments of EPA] http://www.cas.go.jp/jp/tpp/pdf/2012/1/siryou2.pdf. Accessed 2 March 2015.

Democratic Party of Japan (DPJ). (2012). Manifesto. http://www.dpj.or.jp/global/downloads/manifesto2012.pdf, accessed March 2, 2015.

Kan, Naoto (2010). Policy speech by prime minister Naoto Kan at the 176th Extraordinary Session of the Diet. http://japan.kantei.go.jp/kan/statement/201010/01syosin_e.html, accessed March 2, 2015.

Liberal Democratic Party (LDP) (2012). Manifesto. http://jimin.ncss.nifty.com/pdf/seisaku_ichiban24.pdf, accessed March 2, 2015.

Mulgan, Aurelia George (2013). Farmers, agricultural policies, and the election. In Robert Pekkanen, Steven R. Reed and Ethan Scheiner (eds) *Japan Decides 2012: The Japanese General Election*. pp. 213–224. New York, NY: Palgrave Macmillan.

Mulgan, Aurelia George (2014). Can Nishikawa Resolve Japan's TPP Agricultural Impasse? East Asia Forum. http://www.eastasiaforum.org/2014/09/09/can-nishikawa-resolve-japans-tpp-agricultural-impasse/, accessed March 2, 2015.

Mulgan, Aurelia George (2015). What the TPP portends for Japan–Australia agricultural trade. East Asia Forum. http://www.eastasiaforum.org/2015/02/12/what-the-tpp-portends-for-japan-australia-agricultural-trade/, accessed March 2, 2015.

Nippon Television Network Corporation (NTV) (2011–2014). Nippon Terebi Yoron Chousa [Nippon Television Public Opinion Survey] http://www.ntv.co.jp/yoron/, accessed March 2, 2015.

Schott, Jeffrey J., Barbara Kotschwar and Julia Muir (2013). *Understanding the trans-pacific partnership*. Washington, DC: Peterson Institute for International Economics.

Solís, Mireya and Saori N. Katada (2015). Unlikely pivotal states in competitive free trade agreement diffusion: The effect of Japan's Trans-Pacific Partnership participation on Asia-pacific regional integration. *New Political Economy* 20(2): 155–177.

TV Asahi (2012). Yoron Chousa [Public Opinion Poll]. http://www.tv-asahi.co.jp /hst/poll/201211/. Accessed 2 March 2015.

White House (2013). Joint statement by the united states and Japan. http://www. whitehouse.gov/the-press-office/2013/02/22/joint-statement-united-states -and-japan, accessed March 2, 2015.

Part V
Conclusion

21

Conclusion: Japan's Bait-and-Switch Election 2014

Robert J. Pekkanen, Steven R. Reed, and Ethan Scheiner

Abe's political brilliance won a smashing 2014 victory for an unpopular party with unpopular policies. Abe won because he succeeded in defining the alternatives – framing the election as a referendum on Abenomics, pursuing a consistent communications strategy, blurring policy differences on other issues – and timing the election brilliantly. The focus on Abenomics in the election has not prevented Abe from claiming a mandate on a broad range of policies, many of which are not popular with voters, and pursuing a bold, proactive agenda. This leads us to provide the election with its sobriquet, Japan's "bait-and-switch" election. This is not the first time a politician earning ambiguous support at the polls has enacted a sweeping agenda (we have in mind Margaret Thatcher in 1983, but readers may think of others). Despite their apathy in the campaign, Japanese voters might find that they have re-elected a prime minister who will transform their country.

A striking feature of the 2014 House of Representatives campaign was the lack of clear choices offered to voters. Indeed, it was an election with only one realistic option for voters. In large numbers of districts, the LDP offered the only viable candidate. At the national level, the opposition remained in disarray, thus making the LDP the only plausible government option. Moreover, this disarray left the opposition unable to challenge the LDP on policy grounds. As a result, when the LDP centered its policy campaign on Abenomics, no party offered a serious and coherent alternative, and no party took the LDP to task for ignoring other significant policy issues in the campaign. In this way, the LDP and its candidates could campaign as the only choice for those who held in contempt the DPJ's incompetent experience in government, as the only party with a plausible chance of victory, and as the only alternative to present coherent policy proposals. Because the LDP could present itself as the only alternative, it could avoid discussing any other issues that might drum up controversy and opposition.

With no clear choices available to them, it was not at all surprising that voters turned out in record low numbers with scarcely more than half of all eligible voters casting a ballot. It was as uninspiring a general election as any contested in the postwar era in Japan.

Though boring, predictable, and without drama, the 2014 race may well turn out to be the most important of any Japanese election in the past 20 years. Observers point with glee to the excitement of the 2005 race and the bold leadership of Prime Minister Koizumi who took on, and seemingly defeated, vested interests within the LDP. And anyone with even a passing interest in Japanese politics will note the significance of the 2009 House of Representatives poll, when, for the first time, a party other than the LDP – in this case, the DPJ – won a majority of seats. However, the long-term effects of the 2005 and 2009 races turned out to be limited, as traditional elements within the LDP made a comeback in 2006; and the unsuccessful DPJ government managed to change little and found itself out of power again in 2012. In contrast, the 2014 election may well produce lasting effects on the Japanese policy agenda.

The lack of choices available to voters may have been the most striking feature of the 2014 campaign, but Abe's "bait-and-switch" maneuver – in which the LDP campaigned on the "Abenomics" economic policy but then used the election results to claim a mandate for the prime minister's entire policy agenda – may be how observers of Japanese politics remember the 2014 election for years to come. As we explain below, Abe's snap election victory in 2014 may eventually remind political observers more of Margaret Thatcher in 1983 than Koizumi in 2005. Following the election, Abe used the LDP's victory to reinvigorate his efforts to move Japanese policy and politics in his preferred direction. Of course, Abe may fail or, more likely, his successors may return to traditional LDP models, but years from now we may look back on the post-2012 Abe administrations as having changed Japanese politics.

Abe learned

The difference between Abe's first term as LDP president and prime minister (2006–2007) and his second term (2012–) could not be more striking. Certainly, the 2012 election results provided Abe with the twin advantages of a divided opposition and a unified LDP, but Abe began his first term in 2006 in the afterglow of the LDP 2005 landslide and with the House of Councillors (HC) under LDP control. Incompetence, impotence, and policy immobility have been the hallmarks of recent Japanese prime ministers, including Abe's first administration. In his second administration, however, Abe displayed a proactive leadership and a deft handling of the media that moved a broad policy agenda steadily forward (Pekkanen and Pekkanen, 2015). We must look at Abe's leadership – and to the changes he has made to his leadership style – to explain his tremendous success in his current term. This time Abe has used his advantageous position to promote a bold and sweeping policy agenda.

A big part of this was that Abe's ability as prime minister to handle the media went from lamentable to masterful. He managed criticism of policies from Abenomics to restarting nuclear power plants with deft changes in his media messages. He faced down challenges from within the party, from the opposition parties, and even from foreign countries with calm persistence. His approach to politics and policy was proactive. The waffling that had characterized his first adminis-tration, indeed most LDP administrations, was nowhere to be seen. Abe stayed on message. As Kingston writes, there were "no improvis-ing, extemporaneous comments...that might lead to the gaffes that were the undoing of Abe I (2006–2007)" (Kingston, this volume). Instead, Abe's team focused on "the optics while cultivating favorable media coverage and keeping everyone, especially their boss, on mes-sage" (Kingston, this volume). This was the kind of leadership that Japanese voters had been waiting for, even if the content of Abe's poli-cies were not appealing in themselves. And, as Maeda (this volume) points out, Abe may have learned from his mistakes, but the Japanese public was also more forgiving than scholars had believed. After all, Abe is the first LDP prime minister to return to office in two discon-tinuous terms. In looking at the LDP, Endo and Pekkanen agree that Abe improved his communications strategy and point out that Abe also demonstrated improved personnel management strategies through his ministerial selection.

As impressive as Abe's learning in communications strategy was, probably the most important thing Abe learned was *when* to call an election – indeed, one might argue that no postwar Japanese prime minister has ever exploited the power of timing the election as effec-tively as Abe did in 2014.[1] Opposition to Abe's policies within the LDP had stalled his policy agenda and the opposition parties had begun to cooperate in attacking the LDP. By calling a snap election, Abe pre-served and reinforced his core advantages, thus allowing him to preempt his opponents (both inside and outside the LDP) and win a second consecutive election.

Abe won the 2014 election because he succeeded in defining the alternatives – framing the election as a referendum on Abenomics, and blurring policy differences on other issues – and timing the election brilliantly. In the 2012 volume, we argued that the 2012 LDP victory was a victory by default (Reed et al., *JD 2012*). In contrast, the LDP's 2014 victory was a victory by framing and timing.

Abe's political skills brought the LDP victory, despite only a moderate hand in personal popularity and a weak hand in policy approval. Though support for the Abe cabinet remained high (Maeda, this volume), there was nothing like the crowds that had greeted Koizumi, and sales of goods displaying the prime minister's picture did not rise under Abe as they did under Koizumi. Indeed, Abe's campaign trips had little net effect on the LDP vote (McElwain, this volume).

Abe's policies themselves were not particularly popular, and he faced some growing resistance within the LDP. Maeda shows those who cited Abenomics as a reason to support Abe did so because they felt hope that Abenomics would work in the future – which, as Maeda highlights, is very different from supporting Abe because of a belief that his policy had succeeded. This contradiction highlights what Kingston (this volume) dubs "the Abe conundrum": "the resilient popularity of the prime minister despite strong opposition to virtually all of his signature policies on security and energy, and very little enthusiasm for Abenomics, constitutional revision or his controversial views on history."[2]

However grateful the LDP might be for Abe's personal popularity, many of his policy initiatives faced opposition from within his own party. As numerous chapters in this volume make clear, calling the election enhanced Abe's strength, pending the result, as potential policy foes quelled their complaints. For example, Endo and Pekkanen identify the nascent opposition of the tax *zoku* within the LDP to the delay in the consumption tax hike. Similarly, Katada and Wilbur find that on Trans-Pacific Partnership (TPP) free-trade efforts "the primary obstacle to Japan's involvement lay in Abe's own party, the LDP, where Abe had to contend with many politicians whose rural district backgrounds and close relationships with agricultural associations . . . led them to strongly oppose Japan's participation." And Maclachan and Shimizu argue that the snap election strengthened Abe (through the Kantei) against rival LDP agriculture policymakers (most notably, *zoku*). These examples highlight the significance of the snap dissolution as a pre-emptive move aimed against intra-party rivals and toward strengthening Abe's position within the party after the election.

Certainly, Abe emerged from the election as more powerful within the LDP, not only because of the larger number of years before a new election would need to be called (which gave backbenchers breathing space), but also because of Abe's bait-and-switch maneuver with the results of the election: Despite repeatedly framing (baiting) the election as a referendum on Abenomics, after the election Abe, in a switch, appeared to claim that the election victory gave him a mandate on a broad range of policies (including many that were less than popular with the public).

Framing the Election: bait-and-switch

Second only to his timing of the election, Abe's bait-and-switch approach to policy in the 2014 election was a masterful strategic stroke. Abe centered the campaign around Abenomics, but his overwhelming victory enabled him to claim a mandate on his entire policy agenda – even though he had narrowly focused on Abenomics in the campaign. The contributors of this volume analyze policy in eight different areas: Abenomics, energy, agricultural reform, regional inequality, TPP, nationalism, foreign policy, and Okinawa. Outside of Abenomics (the "bait") and Okinawa (the exception) six of these issues fit the bait-and-switch model, as the chapters illustrate a striking parade of mandates claimed under the aegis of the election victory.

Many of our authors identify the bait-and-switch move as a deliberate strategy by Abe. Kingston argues the point most pungently in writing of "Team Abe" that "they know that nationalism and ideology are toxic to mainstream voters, but crucial to important rightwing organizations and thus position, segment and sell their man accordingly." Maeda offers an assessment in different language, suggesting that "it seems fair to say that Abe succeeded in framing the entire election campaign as a referendum on Abenomics. This communications strategy worked very effectively, not because Abenomics was widely applauded, but because it prevented the other issues from being a focus of debate before the election." The strategy appeared to work, as many seemingly significant policy areas received scant attention in the campaign: Hijino points out that major media outlets didn't even include "regional vitalization" as a policy for comparison in their charts highlighting differences on major policy issues among the parties. And, while a majority of articles at the outset of the election mentioned Abenomics, only 12%

mentioned nuclear plants or energy policy, 20% collective self-defense, and 3% "empowering women" (Maeda).

Although "bait-and-switch" has a pejorative ring, we do not mean to employ it moralistically, but rather analytically. A more positive phrase conveying the same information would be "framing and claiming" – framing the election on Abenomics and then claiming the overwhelming victory as a governing mandate. A central issue here is the interpretation of the breadth of Abe's mandate – whether it should be narrowly focused on Abenomics, somewhat broadly on Abenomics and closely related economic policies, or broadly on all policies Abe advocates. In the final section, we compare the 2014 LDP victory under Abe to the 1983 Conservative victory under Margaret Thatcher. Our purpose there is to show that if parties gain only tepid support of voters but win a huge majority of seats, they can embrace bold policy ideas and significantly affect the course of the nation. That's why the "switch" is so important to our understanding of the importance of this election. The rest of Abe's policy agenda is indeed bold. Under normal political circumstances, any of his policy proposals could have been very difficult to pass. Only the twin advantages of a divided opposition and a unified LDP allowed him to pursue such ambitious goals.

Each policy chapter (again, except for those on Abenomics and Okinawa) highlights the significant policy consequences of the election. Each author expressed a degree of surprise at this result because the policy under examination had not become an issue during the election – hence memorable terms such as Katada and Wilbur's "stealth election," Kingston's "Abe conundrum," Hijino's "tepid election," and Hughes' and Krauss's "dog that didn't bark." We see this disjuncture between the issues in the campaign and the policy consequences of the election as due to Abe using the victory to successfully claim a mandate for his whole policy agenda[3] (or act as if he had one, the effect of which on policy is pretty much the same). The mere fact of victory renewed Abe's claim to leadership inside the LDP and voices of dissent have been temporarily silenced. Abe is using the "second honeymoon" provided by the election victory to push all of his sweeping policy agenda.

If any issue should have received top billing, it would be energy policy. Japan had experienced the second worst nuclear disaster in human history and high-profile opinion leaders in Japan sought to halt LDP plans to continue with nuclear power as a major energy source. In 2013, former Prime Minister Junichiro Koizumi called for Japan to abandon nuclear power. In 2014, Koizumi would join forces with another former prime minister, Morihiro Hosokawa, to promote renewable energy and oppose nuclear power. In March, the pair took out a full page advertisement in the major newspapers stating their case (see, for example, Yomiuri June 25, 2014). Yet even the combination of two of Japan's most popular prime ministers was unable to make nuclear power an issue in the election. Hughes argues that prior to the election the Abe government strategically sought to keep energy from acting as a major point of debate in the election by avoiding differentiation between itself and the opposition on nuclear policy, shifting responsibility for nuclear restart safety decisions to the newly created Nuclear Regulation Authority (NRA), and using power market liberalization to distance itself from the utility companies. Yet, at no point did nuclear power become a major topic of debate in the election, despite the fairly popular efforts of the former prime ministers.

Here's another gob smacker – in an election featuring very little discussion of agriculture policy or TPP, Abe used the LDP victory to claim a mandate to reform agriculture and support TPP. Maclachlan and Shimizu show the value of the "second look" we urged in the Introduction. They argue that "at first glance agriculture reform was a non-issue in Japan's 2014 lower house election ....Upon closer scrutiny, however, it is clear that the 2014 election mattered deeply for agricultural reform. For no sooner were the ballots counted than the Abe government announced that it would press forward on shelved [agricultural reform] proposals." The proposed reforms are serious and promise to change Japanese agriculture significantly, despite not having featured prominently in the election (Maclachlan and Shimizu) and with the snapping shut of the poll boxes figuratively still ringing in the voters' ears.

Similarly, Katada and Wilbur note that by keeping attention away from TPP in the campaign, Abe avoided "significant controversy that might divide key party members and constituencies...[which] preserved support for the TPP at the highest levels of the Japanese government." Katada and Wilbur aptly call this "Japan's Stealth Decision". Consistent with the bait-and-switch pattern in other areas, after the election Abe was able to move forcefully on TPP and related agricultural policy: In February 2015, Japanese and US positions further converged in their TPP negotiations, with the United States agreeing to allow some level of tariffs on designated agricultural products and Japan offering to increase US market access in rice, beef, and pork. Strikingly, the success of the bait-and-switch on TPP was due in large part to the lack of choice in the election. Katada and Wilbur point out that the lack of debate over TPP was in part due to the fact that the LDP and DPJ held similar positions on the issue. It also helped that the principal opponents of TPP were minor parties such as the JCP and SDPJ, which were uncompetitive.

TPP obviously has implications for Japan's agricultural policy, but it is still usually seen as part of foreign policy. Looking more broadly over a range of foreign policy issues, however, Krauss finds a similar pattern of "no choice" and "bait-and-switch" at work. Krauss calls foreign policy the "dog that didn't bark" in the election, meaning that it was a surprising non-issue. The surprise stems from Abe's positions on security issues and the gap between and public opinion. In Kingston's memorable phrase, foreign policy is a classic "Abe conundrum." Abe wants to push Japan's foreign policy into a more assertive posture by adopting a plethora of "unprecedented initiatives," including collective self-defense and constitutional revision (Krauss). However, opinion polls show that the public generally does not support these measures, with the results being clear enough that, as Krauss explains, "even Abe himself admitted that 'Unfortunately, we cannot say that the public is fully supportive' when it came to reinterpreting collective self-defense." Krauss attributes the LDP's silence on the issue during the campaign to "Abe's shrewdly focusing on the issues where he is stronger," thus hiding his focus on defense and constitutional revision until after the election when he could safely engage in the "switch" half of the bait-and-switch maneuver. Moreover, Krauss argues that the LDP was successful in diverting attention in the campaign away from these policies because of "the failure of the main opposition party to craft a viable alternative policy on foreign and defense policy issues," which left voters with no choice whatsoever on the issue.

Writing on nationalism and the election, Jeff Kingston forcefully argues that Abe succeeded through a "bait-and-switch" tactic. Kingston's prose sparkles throughout, but perhaps never more so than in a vivid turn of phrase about the LDP: "although nationalism is the talismanic calling card of the [LDP], and would be inscribed on its coat of arms if it had one, in campaign 2014 it steered clear of nationalist issues like a minefield..." Kingston sees Abe as holding strong views, which he did not run on in the campaign: "he framed the election as a referendum on Abenomics and remained silent about the nationalist issues that he really cares about such as constitutional revision, collective self-defense and revisionist history." This was no accident, in Kingston's view, but "a deliberate strategy of downplaying Abe's nationalist passions because party loyalists will vote for him anyway and there is no reason to arouse opponents. Just as in 2012, Abe campaigned on economic policies and the promise of better days ahead, the so-called 'good Abe,' while giving the nationalist 'bad Abe' a campaign holiday." Kingston sees making the election into a referendum on Abenomics as "inspired engineering, shifting attention away from Abe's unpopular nationalist initiatives and gestures and putting pragmatic bread-and-butter issues center stage" as "campaigning on Abenomics diverted attention from unpopular nationalist policies." However, Kingston has a nuanced view of nationalism in the campaign, believing that Abe sent just enough signals to those who cared the most about his policies, while not emphasizing policies in ways that would lose him votes: "the nationalist pit bull didn't bark in campaign 2014 because this would scare off many voters, but its fur bristled and it growled just enough to convince loyalists that it would fight their fight." And then the switch: "Post-election polls showed little enthusiasm for the LDP or PM Shinzo Abe's plans for constitutional revision or security, but that did not stop him claiming a mandate for this nationalist agenda."

Regional revitalization represents the final bait-and-switch issue that our policy chapter authors discuss. Regional inequalities have been much in the news, and a lively topic among pundits and scholars alike. In his chapter, Hijino agrees that, "regional issues linking the major issues of economic recovery, depopulation and socio-economic inequality could have become a focal point of the 2014 election," but finds instead "the 2014 election was certainly not one focused on regional development or rural-urban cleavages" and "electoral attention on regional issues during the campaign remained tepid." Why so tepid? Besides voters not trusting party pledges on regional issues any longer, Hijino also indicts policy convergence: "no clear alternatives have emerged in terms of regional policy among the LDP and DPJ," with both parties gradually de-emphasizing decentralization over the past two elections and converging instead on a policy of providing support to struggling regions. The Third Force parties had provided a kick to aggressive decentralization policy proposals, but have since diluted their positions. This contributes to a diminishing of attention paid to regional issues by the media.

Writing on Okinawa, Kagotani explains that the base relocation issue took a backseat to Abenomics across the country but could not be ignored in Okinawa, the exception that proves the bait-and-switch rule. Elections in Okinawa are fought over defense issues and 2014 followed this pattern (Kagotani, this volume). Okinawa has long been a two-party system: a nearly equal number of voters favoring US bases as those opposed. Anti-base candidates won every SMD in Okinawa. The LDP candidate in each district won a PR seat illustrating the balance between the two forces.

There was no choice

We were struck by the number of times the phrase "no choice" or "no alternative" appeared in this volume. For example, Krauss argues, "voters were confronted with a choice, especially in the SSD tier, of no real alternatives at all on foreign and defense policy," while Maeda concludes that explaining the LDP landslide "is simple. People felt they had no effective alternative to choose." Indeed, at the district-level, the national-level, and at the level of policy, the 2014 election offered voters only one viable option.

First, fundamentally, campaigns are conducted at the district level – and in 2014 the opposition was unable to develop a full slate of district-level challenges to the LDP. As Smith (this volume) points out, the snap election gave the opposition little time to find candidates to run in many districts. In part, the small number of candidates helped the opposition avoid many of the coordination problems it faced in 2012, as there were many fewer districts in which the DPJ faced both the LDP and a Third Force party candidate in 2014 (Scheiner, Smith, and Thies, this volume). However, the snap election also made it more difficult for the DPJ to contest enough races to even pretend to challenge the ruling coalition's control of the government. As Scheiner, Smith, and Thies (this volume) show, in 2014 the DPJ failed to run a candidate in 117 of Japan's 295 single-member districts, and no major opposition party (including the DPJ) at all ran a candidate in 48 of those districts – thus, eliminating any chance whatsoever of defeating the coalition in many districts.

Not surprising, the lack of viable options in many districts led voters to an unenviable choice: Many voters chose to cast a hopeless vote for the JCP. Of the total vote gains made by the JCP in SMD balloting, almost 25% came from districts in which only a coalition candidate and JCP candidate competed, even though such districts counted for less than 9% of the districts in which the JCP fielded a candidate (authors' calculations). Moreover, the lack of opposition candidacies led to obvious voter frustration, and a decline in turnout (Scheiner, Smith, and Thies, this volume).

Voters had as little choice at the national level. From the moment that Abe called the election, there was little doubt that the LDP–Komeito coalition would remain in power after the votes were counted. The coalition would have had to lose 88 seats to its majority. Moreover, with the opposition still divided – especially between the DPJ and the JIP – there was no alternative government on the horizon. In the past, voters who sought to oust the LDP could focus their support on the DPJ, but in 2012 the JRP and in 2014 the JIP were nearly as attractive, but also nearly as futile, answers. There was not even a feasible coalition that seemed capable of unseating the LDP because the two largest opposition parties were highly unlikely to form a coalition. Consistent with this description, 72% of respondents to one survey described the opposition parties as having no appeal, and 78% expressed the view that there were no opposition bloc parties capable of taking the reins of government (Asahi English, December 18, 2014).

In this context, the opposition offered no challenge to the LDP's stated policy agenda, most notably Abenomics, and therefore led to no serious policy choices presented in the campaign. The 2014 election might have presented a choice for Japan's economic future that energized and deeply engaged voters, especially as Abenomics was the central issue in the campaign. But, ultimately, Abenomics was not even debated in the campaign, as opposition parties offered no distinctive or compelling alternatives (see Noble, this volume). Ironically, as Noble notes, the lack of serious debate over Abenomics meant that the election outcome had a few consequences for macroeconomic policy – even though much of the support that existed for Abenomics may have been based more on "hope" for the policies, rather than any belief that it was actually working (see Maeda, this volume). Even on Abenomics, the signature issue of Abe's premiership and the focus of his dissolution speech, voters were divided. Maeda cites poll results showing that 38% of respondents were willing to vote for a candidate who endorsed Abenomics, but 38% didn't care and 20% wanted an anti-Abenomics candidate. Only 26% saw Abenomics as a success.

With the opposition unable to contest the central issue of the campaign, it was even less capable of raising a coherent set of policy viewpoints on other major issues of the day. As a result, Abe and the LDP were never forced to raise potentially controversial issues in the campaign, and instead set the terms for framing the election.

LDP dominance?

At the same time, Abe's clever snap election strategy, the bait-and-switch policy gambit, and the lack of choice are in no way evidence that the LDP will dominate Japanese politics for many years to come.

Referencing T.J. Pempel's classic work, Endo and Pekkanen put a question mark at the end of "Uncommon Again?" in their LDP chapter, but the answer is definitely "no."

One of the striking features of the LDP's victories in 2012 and 2014 was that the party was not even remotely popular even as it won in landslides. In 2012 "the LDP was the beneficiary of a mammoth loss of support for the DPJ, which, rather than generating a wave of support for the LDP, prompted huge numbers of voters to abstain . . . " (Reed et al., *JD 2012*: 34). In 2014, the LDP won because Abe called the election at a time when there was no alternative to the LDP–Komeito coalition or Abe's policy agenda, and brilliantly framed the election through communications strategy. All that would be required to re-establish a two-party system is an alternative to the LDP. Strikingly, the LDP has lost votes in each HR election since 2005, in numbers that have been outpaced only by the growing number of abstentions.

As a result, it is highly likely that many current non-voters may find themselves back into the voting pool, especially if the opposition consolidates more thoroughly around a single alternative. Indeed, there is good reason to expect a return to bipolar competition to become the norm soon, especially at the district level – and probably starting with the next election unless some new Third Force party attempts to challenge all current parties. Smith (this volume) highlights the progress made by the opposition in running a single candidate per district, and Pekkanen and Reed (this volume) note the reduction of the Third Force parties from four to one, so the winnowing of parties has in fact already begun. Even if the opposition does not consolidate nationally around a single opposition force, an alliance of opposition parties that coordinate across electoral districts might provide an opportunity to challenge the ruling coalition. At the same time, even though political science theories give us good reason to believe that Japan's single-member district structure will encourage the opposition to consolidate around a small number of options, nothing about the structure guarantees that these alternatives will be met with popular support.

In sum, there is good reason to expect that Japanese voters will be offered an alternative to the LDP within the next two elections. Nevertheless, it is far more difficult to predict precisely when, and whether that alternative will prove more attractive to voters than the LDP.

Conclusion

Abe's political brilliance won a smashing 2014 victory for an unpopular party with unpopular policies. The 2012 election had given Abe the twin advantages of a divided opposition and a unified LDP. He skillfully used these advantages to promote a sweeping policy agenda, and, by calling a snap election and winning a landslide, he further reinforced his position of strength. The landslide allowed him to claim a mandate for his policy agenda even when those policies did not play a prominent role in the election campaign. The opposition failed to rouse public debate on a wide range of policy issues and flopped as alternatives to continued LDP-Komeito rule. After the votes were tallied, Abe was poised to press his agenda forward with little resistance from the opposition or from within his own party.

The circumstances that made all this possible may prove temporary. Perhaps the LDP members will not remain unified behind their leader for long, especially with the party's massive majority. Equally, the opposition should not remain divided for long. The 2014 election reduced the number of opposition parties and forced the larger parties to coordinate their nominations. After the election, the opposition parties had the incentive and the time to learn from their errors.

However, as of early 2015, Abe's window of opportunity remains open and provides him the chance to make significant changes in Japanese politics and policy. It is possible that he will implement significant changes to Japan's policies. Making massive policy changes after a debatable mandate is not unique to Abe's agricultural policy. Readers might recall (or look up on Wikipedia) that Margaret Thatcher did something similar in the UK in the 1980s. Indeed, Japan's 2014 election bears a striking resemblance to events in the U.K. in 1983. Thatcher's Conservative Party had defeated a discredited Labour Party government in 1979. In the 1983 British election, the Conservative vote total and turnout both fell, but Thatcher's party faced an opposition that was ill equipped to contest the race: The opposition was fragmented, as Labour had split and a "third force" had emerged in the Alliance between the Liberals and Social Democratic Party.[4] Thatcher's Conservative Party won fewer votes (42%) than the two opposition parties (53% overall, divided into 28% for Labour and 25% for the SDP-Liberal Alliance), but through the workings of the electoral system the Conservatives nonetheless secured a healthy parliamentary majority. On the basis of the Conservatives' 42% of the vote – which translated into 397 seats (61% of the total) versus only 209 (32%) for Labour and 23 (4.5%) for the Alliance – and even though many of her policies were not supported by voters and were opposed by many within her own party, Thatcher pursued a sweeping policy agenda and fundamentally altered UK politics. Recent history gives us caution in expecting Japanese prime ministers to successfully enact much significant policy, and some may feel we go too far in comparing Abe with the transformative Thatcher. However, following in the footsteps of Britain's "Iron Lady," Abe certainly found a way to flatfoot his opponents in their time of weakness and win a huge victory despite limited popular support for many policies. What remains to be seen is if he can similarly harness the power of that election's results to enact his own political agenda and then transform his country.

Notes

The authors thank Saadia M. Pekkanen for comments on an earlier version of this chapter.

1. There are a few other contenders – 1980, 1986, and 2005 – but we stick by our claim. In a few years, we might also be ready to claim Abe as the most successful LDP PM of all time.
2. Kingston further observes that, "An intriguing aspect of the Abe conundrum is how an ardent nationalist may well become Japan's longest serving postwar premier in a nation where nationalistic sentiments are relatively tepid."
3. Abe will be naturally inclined to view his election triumph as a mandate. Interestingly, Maeda presents post-election opinion poll results from Asahi and Yomiuri alike showing a majority of respondents wished the LDP had won fewer seats (Maeda). We consider Abe's acting as if he won a mandate on a specific policy to be de facto claiming a mandate. For example, agriculture was not a featured issue in the election but Abe proclaimed the LDP triumph at the polls as a mandate for Abenomics, and this included structural reforms in agriculture. The next day, Abe announced that he would take action on regulatory reform, which would include the agricultural sector, and the following day (December 16, if you're counting), MAFF Minister Koya Nishikawa discussed a planned bill to amend the Agricultural Cooperative Society Law to be submitted during the upcoming Diet session (Maclachlan and Shimizu). Similarly, Japanese TPP negotiating positions changed enough that Katada and Wilbur title a section "Hiding the TPP Agenda in the 2014 Election" (Katada and Wilbur). Supporters of these policy moves (or of PM Abe) will probably contend that they were an inevitable corollary of Abenomics that voters had just endorsed overwhelmingly. See discussion above on interpretation of a mandate.
4. And the main opposition Labour took policy positions so out of the mainstream that one analysis concluded that there was no real alternative to the Conservatives in the election (Miller, 1984).

Bibliography

Miller, W. L. (1984). There was no alternative: The British general election of 1983. *Parliamentary Affairs* 37: 4.

Pekkanen, Robert J. and Saadia M. Pekkanen. (2015). Japan in 2014: All about Abe. *Asian Survey* 55(1): 103–118.

Appendix: Table of Contents of Japan Decides 2012

Contents

Index

Note: The locators followed by 'n' refer to notes

CPSIA information can be obtained
at www.ICGtesting.com
Printed in the USA
LVOW04*1029081215
465927LV00012B/61/P